Amp Your MySpace Page

Essential Tools for Giving Your Profile an Extreme Makeover

Eric Butow

Michael Bellomo

New York   Chicago   San Francisco   Lisbon
London   Madrid   Mexico City   Milan   New Delhi
San Juan   Seoul   Singapore   Sydney   Toronto

The McGraw·Hill Companies

Cataloging-in-Publication Data is on file with the Library of Congress

McGraw-Hill books are available at special quantity discounts to use as premiums and sales promotions, or for use in corporate training programs. For more information, please write to the Director of Special Sales, Professional Publishing, McGraw-Hill, Two Penn Plaza, New York, NY 10121-2298. Or contact your local bookstore.

Amp Your MySpace Page: Essential Tools for Giving Your Profile an Extreme Makeover

1234567890 CUS CUS 01987

ISBN: 978-0-07-149072-6
MHID: 0-07-149072-8

Sponsoring Editor
Roger Stewart

Editorial Supervisor
Patty Mon

Project Manager
Vasundhara Sawhney,
International Typesetting
and Composition

Acquisitions Coordinator
Carly Stapleton

Technical Editor
Joel Elad

Copy Editor
Margaret Berson

Proofreader
Laura Bowman

Indexer
WordCo Indexing Services

Production Supervisor
Jean Bodeaux

Composition
International Typesetting
and Composition

Illustration
International Typesetting
and Composition

Art Director, Cover
Jeff Weeks

Cover Designer
Pattie Lee

This book is dedicated to my sister and brother-in-law, Lisa and Jay Scalzo, who have faced down tremendous challenges during the past year. They are an inspiration.

—Eric Butow

This book is dedicated to Florence Presnell, for her warmth and graciousness. May the sun always rise over your roof and the snow never block the driveway.

—Michael Bellomo

About the Authors

Eric Butow is the CEO of Butow Communications Group (BCG), a technical writing and web design firm based in Roseville, California. Eric has authored or coauthored ten books since 2000, the latest being *Special Editing Using Microsoft Windows Vista* and *User Interface Design for Mere Mortals*. Eric is also an online course developer and instructor for Ed2Go, Virtual Training Company, and California State University, Sacramento. When Eric isn't busy writing, teaching, or running his own business, you'll find him reading, hanging out with friends (usually at the nearest Starbucks or bookstore), or enjoying the company of his family at his parents' home in the Sierra foothills or the family vineyard in northern California.

Michael Bellomo holds a JD and an MBA and has worked as an e-commerce consultant in the Silicon Valley dotcom boom times, a think-tank researcher, corporate counsel, and aerospace risk manager. He has written 17 books in various nonfiction fields, including technology, business operations, and "mass market" science. Michael lives in Los Angeles, California. His weekends are split between surfing the fringes of the World Wide Web, hiking the wilds of Griffith Park, and finding the best Thai lunch in the city for under $8.

Contents

Acknowledgments

No book is successful without the help of strong editors, and I was fortunate to have the team of Roger Stewart, Carly Stapleton, and Joel Elad to work with. I'd also like to thank Karen Wells for letting me use her MySpace profile as an example. I would also thank my cat, Mewsette, for letting me use her picture for the book, but when I mentioned this to her she simply looked up at me and meowed in her "serve me *now, tofu head*" tone of voice. Unfortunately, Mewsette passed away during production of this book at the ripe old age of 19, but she left this world on her terms.

—Eric Butow

I'd like to acknowledge Roger Stewart and Carly Stapleton for making the book mellifluous, Joel Elad for ensuring that it's salubrious, and Michael Call and the band members of Drop 8 for kicking butt onstage and letting me hold them up as a shining example of how to "amp up" your MySpace page.

—Michael Bellomo

Introduction

This book is the only resource you'll need for using and getting the most out of MySpace. The book is divided into three parts.

Part I, "Customizing Your MySpace Pages," starts with the basics of creating your MySpace profile and then editing it using HTML and CSS, adding images and photos, and animating your profile with Flash and other animation tools. Even if you're brand new to MySpace you can get your profile up and running quickly.

Part II, "Expanding Your MySpace Presence," tells you how to polish your profile through the use of third-party templates and plug-ins (of which there are many), creating your own blog, and using many other ways to update your profile.

Part III, "Making Your MySpace Presence Extreme!," shows you how you can establish yourself in the MySpace community and create an online following. In this section you'll also learn how to unleash your inner artist and market your music on MySpace.

The Appendixes section contains helpful references to HTML commands and color and style tables.

Part I

Customizing Your MySpace Pages

Chapter 1

The Basics of Updating Your Profile

If you're brand new to MySpace, you need to start by signing up for an account. This is easy: Just go to http://www.myspace.com in your browser and then click the SignUp link at the upper right-hand corner of the blue MySpace bar at the top of the page. The signup process is on one page that asks you to fill out some basic information, as shown in Figure 1-1.

The first box is the Email Address box. You may want to consider adding a different e-mail address than you already use. MySpace is a free and open social networking site and sometimes you will get unwanted information, invitations, or other messages from MySpace that you may not want others to see or that will interfere with your other work.

TIP *Having a separate free e-mail address that you can get from portal web sites like Yahoo and Google will keep all your MySpace mail separate so you can view it online through the portal site later.*

The rest of the signup process goes quickly. After you type your information into the boxes and select the appropriate options from the lists, click the Sign Up button. You'll see the Verify Account page

FIGURE 1-1 The signup page

where you read a graphic and then type the letters represented in the graphic. After you type the letters, click the Create Account button. Then you'll have the opportunity to upload photos and invite friends to your space. You'll also receive a "Welcome to MySpace" message in your e-mailbox, so you can click the link in the message to confirm your MySpace account.

After you create your profile you're presented with a home page, as shown in Figure 1-2.

The information in the home page gives you the ability to make changes to your profile, or settings, add and edit photos and videos, and more. If you scroll down the home page you'll see in the My Friend Space section that you automatically have one friend: Tom. Tom is Tom Anderson, the president and cofounder of MySpace. If you want to delete Tom and add other friends, you'll learn how to do that in Chapter 10. For now, the first order of business is to update your profile so everyone knows what you want them to know about you.

The first step in updating your profile is to update information about you including your interests, your background, and who you would like to meet.

FIGURE 1-2 The standard profile page

Start updating your profile by clicking the Edit Profile link next to your picture in the Hello box. (The title of this box in Figure 1-2 is "Hello, Amp'd MySpace!") The Profile Edit-Interests & Personality page within the Personal tab appears, as shown in Figure 1-3.

Below the Profile Edit – Interests & Personality header at the top of the page is the Profile Edit menu, which is a horizontal list of links to other sections of your profile. The Interests & Personality page appears first by default.

The Interest & Personality page is the place where you can tell other MySpace friends and members all about you. When other MySpace users view your profile, the following information that you put in this page is what they'll see:

- Headline, which gives people a sense of what you're all about. The headline will appear in quotes to the right of your photo when people view your profile. If you don't want a headline, don't type anything in this box.

- About Me, which tells people all about you. You can be as informative as you want in this section.

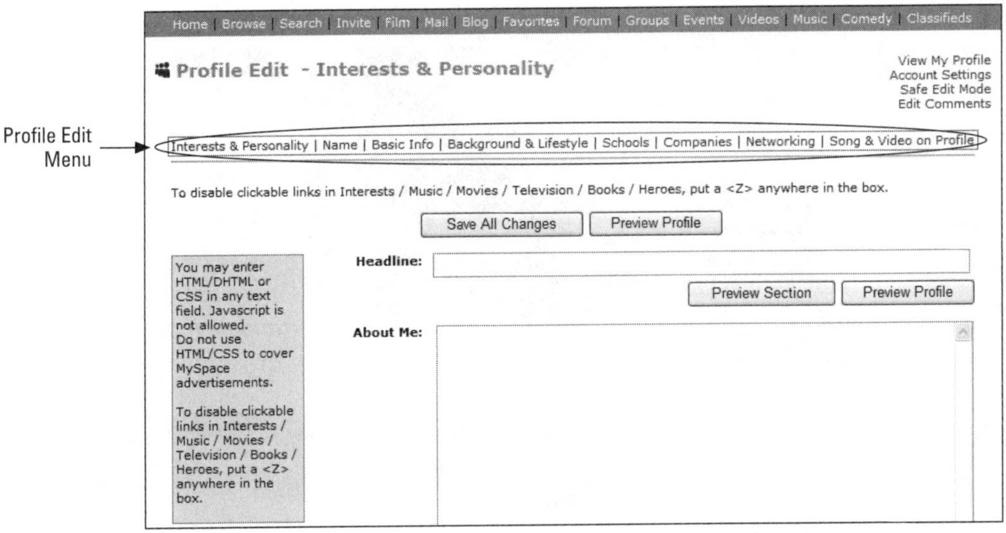

FIGURE 1-3 The Profile Edit – Interests & Personality page

- I'd Like to Meet, which tells people who you would like to meet (or not meet) on MySpace. You can be as specific or as general as you want. For example, you may want to meet other people who share your musical interests. Who you want to meet says a lot about you.

- Interests, which are your personal interests. Other MySpace users who have the same interests may look you up and make a connection so they can share with you.

- Music. You can specify different genres of music you like or be even more specific with the bands and/or artists you prefer, as well as songs and albums you prefer and why.

- Movies. See any good movies lately? Do you have any films that you feel are the best ever? Tell people what films get your thumbs up in this section.

- Television shows or series you like (whether you have DVDs of those television shows or not is not required).

- Books you've read recently or are on your all-time best seller list.

- Heroes, who are people you really look up to and are super in your eyes.

As you type information into each text box, you can click the Preview Section button to view how your text will appear in that section. As an example, shown in Figure 1-4, we are previewing the Headline section with the headline "Hello, world!"

NOTE   *This preview is how your text will look to other MySpace users. If you have any styles that apply to your entire page, for example if all your text appears in blue, then the preview won't show your text in blue.*

Click the Return to Edit Interests & Personality button to return to the Profile Edit page. If you want to preview how the entire profile will look after you type text into one of the boxes on the page, click the Preview Profile button. The profile preview appears, as shown in Figure 1-5. Click the Return to Edit Interests & Personality button to return to the Profile Edit – Interests & Personality page.

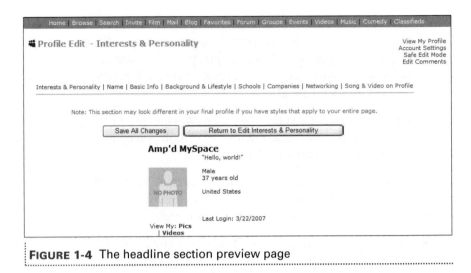

FIGURE 1-4 The headline section preview page

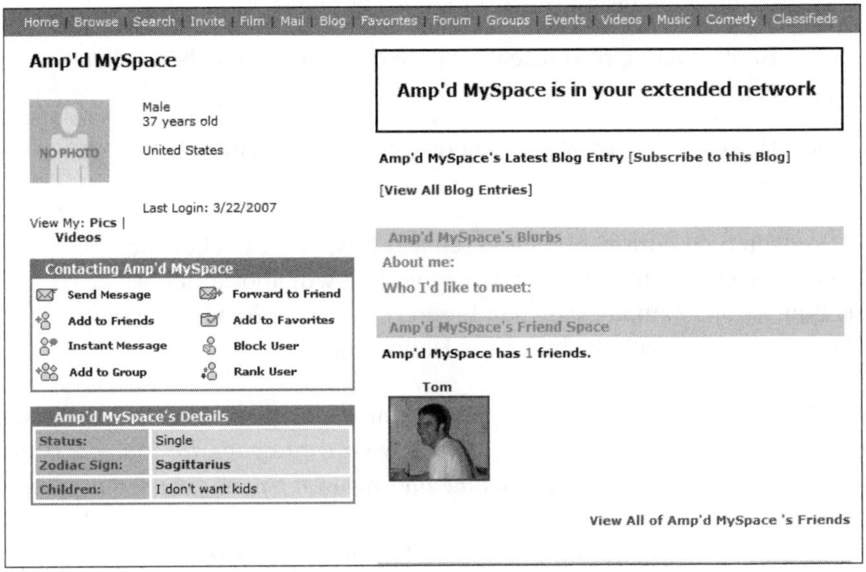

FIGURE 1-5 The profile preview page

As with previewing a section, the profile won't look this way if you have styles that apply to the entire profile. If you want to see your profile as it really looks, click the View My Profile link to the right of the Profile Edit – Interests & Personality title at the top of the page.

Don't feel compelled to answer all this information right away if you don't want to. You can take your time figuring out what you want to say, and if you don't like what you've added you can always change it. If you want other MySpace users to find you, be sure to give them easily identifiable keywords to let them know you have the same interests they do. For example, if you like the *Star Trek* television series, be sure to type the words **Star Trek** in the Television box.

When you're finished editing your interests and personality information, click the Save All Changes button at the bottom of the page. MySpace saves your information and displays "Profile Updated" at the top of the page.

CHANGE NAME INFORMATION

You can change your system name as well as the name you want other MySpace users to see by clicking the Name link. The Name page appears, as shown in Figure 1-6.

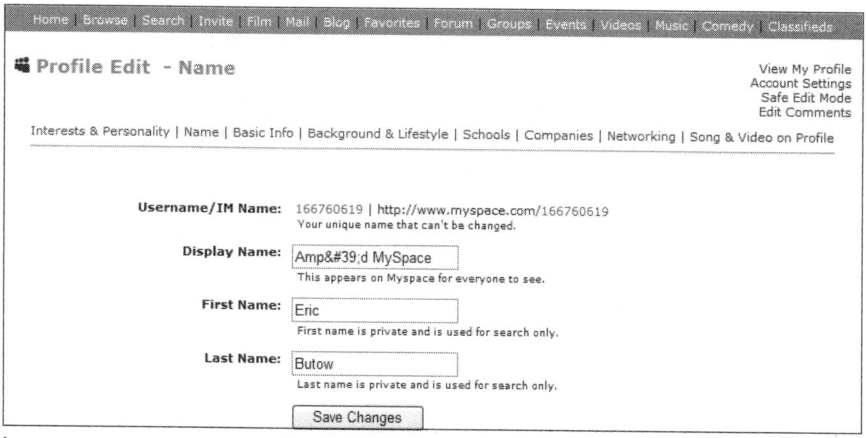

FIGURE 1-6 The Name page

This page displays your username and instant messaging (IM) name, which is your unique username that cannot be changed. You can change the display name that is shown to all other MySpace users, and your first name and last name. When you finish typing changes in the text boxes, click the Save Changes button. MySpace saves your information and displays "Profile Updated" at the top of the page.

Back in the days when I used bulletin board systems, or BBSs, most people (including me) used a "handle" that was a pseudonym that kept people anonymous. You can do the same with your display name, by leaving your first and last name fields blank, and keep yourself anonymous because no other MySpace user will see your real name. However, be certain that you don't give out clues as to your identity. For example, if you tell people where you live or information about your family and friends, you're going to be discovered sooner or later.

CHANGE BASIC INFORMATION

You can change basic information about yourself, such as your location and physical characteristics, by clicking the Basic Info link. The Basic Information page appears, as shown in Figure 1-7.

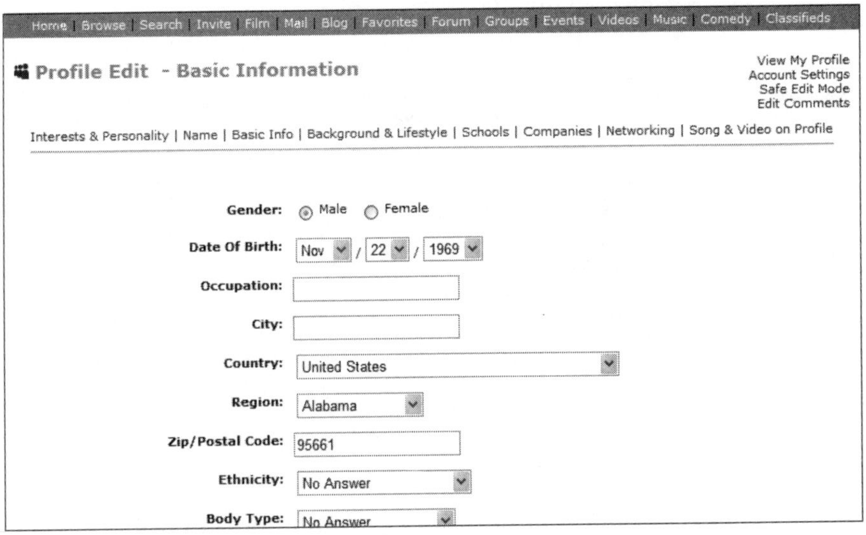

FIGURE 1-7 The Basic Information page

The only information in this page that appears is your gender, birth date, and zip code, which you added when you created your profile. You can add more specific information such as your ethnicity, body type, and height. You can also tell people the reason(s) why you're on MySpace so other users who are on MySpace for the same reason (for example, for dating) can find you more easily. You don't have to add this information if you don't feel it's necessary or don't feel comfortable letting others know this specific information about you.

When you finish making changes in the page, click the Save Changes button. MySpace saves your information and displays "Profile Updated" at the top of the page.

CHANGE BASIC LIFESTYLE INFORMATION

If you want to change information about your basic lifestyle, click the Background and Lifestyle link. The Background and Lifestyle page appears, as shown in Figure 1-8.

| Home | Browse | Search | Invite | Film | Mail | Blog | Favorites | Forum | Groups | Events | Videos | Music | Comedy | Classifieds |

Profile Edit - Background and Lifestyle

View My Profile
Account Settings
Safe Edit Mode
Edit Comments

Interests & Personality | Name | Basic Info | Background & Lifestyle | Schools | Companies | Networking | Song & Video on Profile

Marital Status:
- ◯ Swinger
- ◯ In a Relationship
- ◉ Single
- ◯ Divorced
- ◯ Married

Sexual Orientation:
- ◯ Bi
- ◯ Gay / Lesbian
- ◯ Straight
- ◯ Not Sure
- ◉ No Answer

Hometown: [   ]

FIGURE 1-8 The Background and Lifestyle page

You can change the following information in your Background and Lifestyle page:

- Marital status (the default is single)
- Sexual orientation
- Hometown
- Religion
- Smoker
- Drinker
- Children, meaning if you have, want, or don't want children
- Education, meaning the highest level of education you've completed
- Income, meaning your yearly income

With the exception of marital status, all questions have no answer by default. When you finish making changes in this page, click the Save Changes button. MySpace saves your information and displays "Profile Updated" at the top of the page.

ADD SCHOOL INFORMATION

If you want to tell people where you go or went to school to try to hook up with fellow students, professors, and/or alumni, you can add schools to your profile by clicking the Schools link. The Schools page appears, as shown in Figure 1-9.

Sharing school information can be a good way for you to connect with others at your school to share notes or even connect with your professor if he or she is on MySpace. There can be risks, however, such as the creepy guy from statistics class who may be inclined to e-mail you and/or chat you up in class because he read all about you on MySpace. If you have a concern about someone who may decide to be a little too friendly if he or she finds your profile on MySpace, you may want to first search for other students on your site to find out who is on MySpace. You'll learn more about searching for other users in Chapter 10.

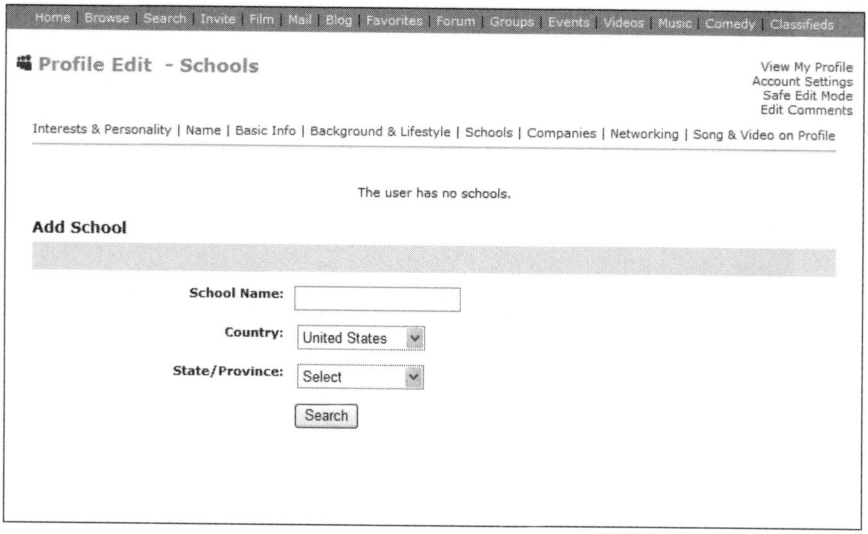

FIGURE 1-9 The Schools page

The first step is to search for the school. Type in the name of the school in the School Name box and then select the country and state or province where the school is located. Click the Search box. MySpace returns a list of schools, as shown in Figure 1-10. The figure shows that MySpace found my alma mater, Herbert Hoover High School in Fresno, and it's at the top of the list.

If you can't find your school, you can try searching again or use the link provided at the bottom of the School Finder box to submit your school to get it added into the MySpace school database. Since MySpace found my school, I clicked on the school to add more information about what I did during my time there. When you do this, a second Add School page appears, as shown in Figure 1-11, so you can add information.

You can specify if you're a current student or an alumnus; when you attended; the year you graduated; and your major, minor, and fraternity or sorority (if the school you're adding is a college or university), as well as any clubs or organizations you belong to.

When you finish making changes in the page, click the Submit button. MySpace saves your information and displays the school you

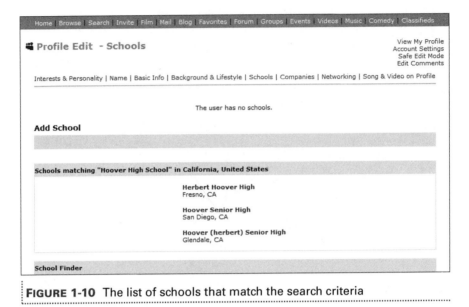

FIGURE 1-10 The list of schools that match the search criteria

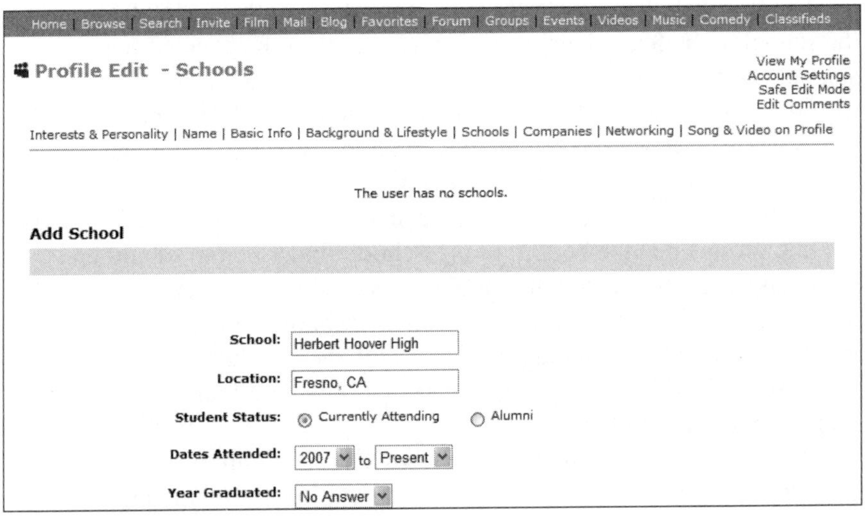

FIGURE 1-11 The Add School page

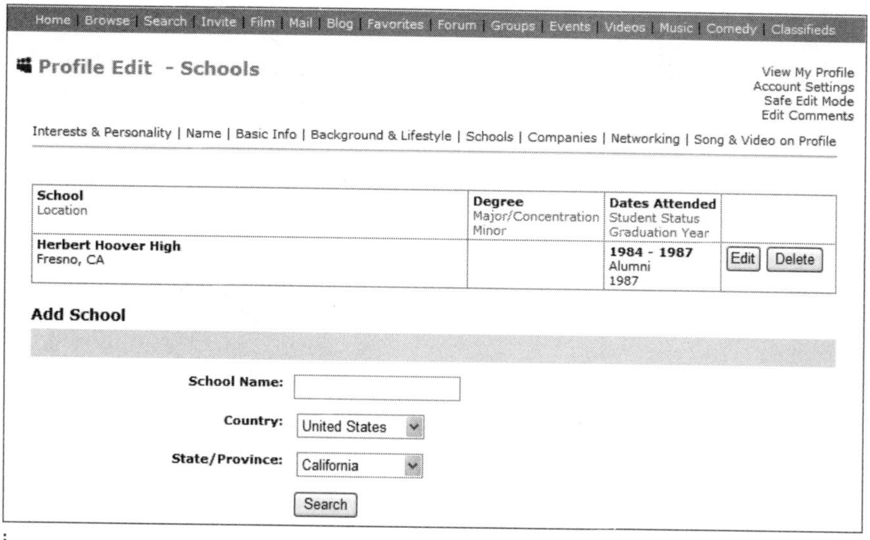

FIGURE 1-12 The Schools table

added in the Schools table, as shown in Figure 1-12. If you want to add another school, type another school name in the School Name text box and then click the Search button.

If you want to edit a school in the table, click the Edit button at the right side of the table within the row. You can also delete the school from the table by clicking the Delete button.

ADD COMPANY INFORMATION

If you're like me—you've worked for a number of companies over the years—you can add those companies to your MySpace profile in case you want to connect with other people who worked at the same company. For example, another MySpace user could search for profiles of users who worked at the same company you did so that MySpace user would contact you to catch up. When you search for MySpace users who work for the same company you work for, you can connect with those users.

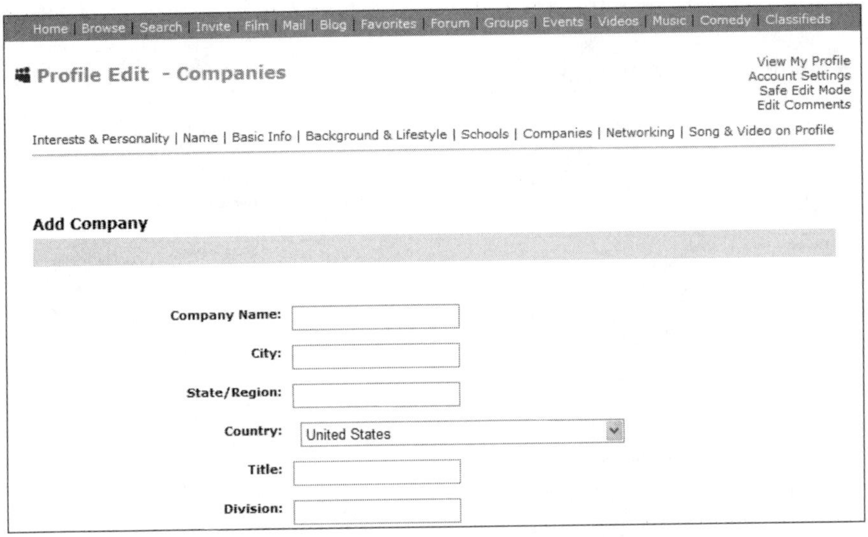

FIGURE 1-13 The Companies page

Add a company by clicking the Companies link. The Companies page appears, as shown in Figure 1-13.

Add a company by typing or selecting information in the following boxes:

- Company name
- City where the company was located when you worked there
- State/Region
- Country
- Title
- Division you worked in
- Dates employed

After you finish typing the information, click the Save Changes button. MySpace saves your information and displays the company you added in the Companies table, as shown in Figure 1-14.

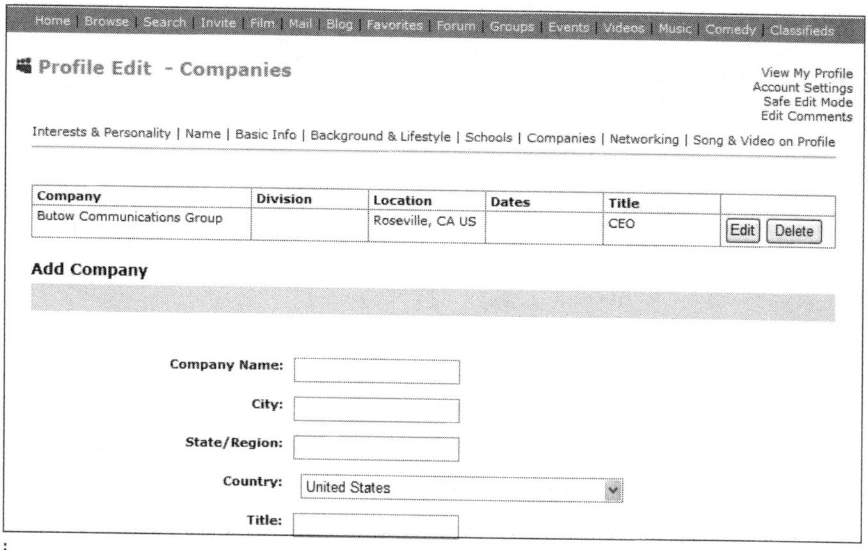

FIGURE 1-14 The Companies table

If you want to edit information about a company in the table, click the Edit button at the right side of the table within the row. You can also remove the company from the table by clicking the Delete button.

ADD NETWORKING PREFERENCES INFORMATION

If you want to network with other MySpace users who have similar interests, you have to let other MySpace users know about your interests. Set your networking preferences by clicking the Networking link. The Networking page appears, as shown in Figure 1-15.

Add a network category by selecting the field you're in, the subfield, and the role you play. You can also add a description of what you do and who you work for. When you're finished, click the Save Changes button. MySpace saves the information and displays the networking information you added in the Networking table, as shown in Figure 1-16.

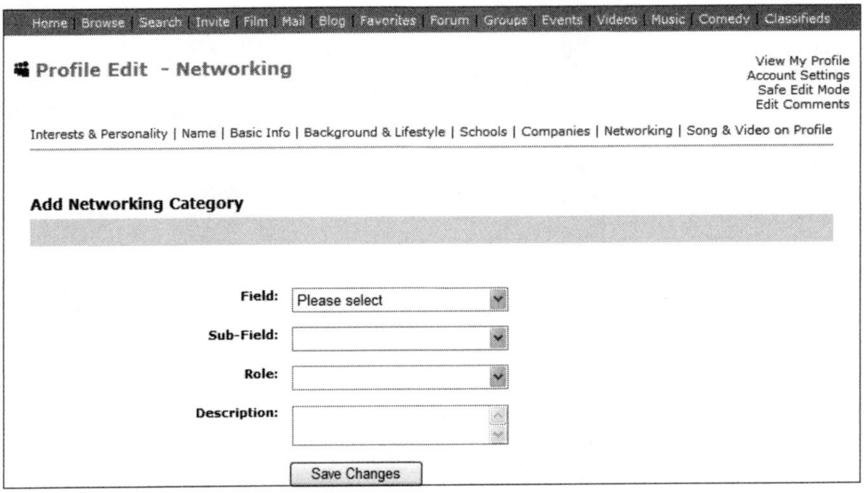

FIGURE 1-15 The Networking page

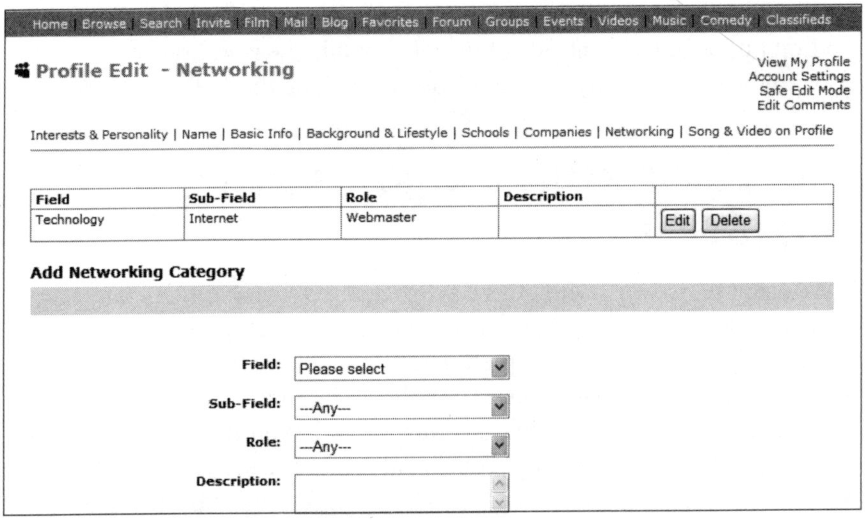

FIGURE 1-16 The Networking table

If you want to edit a category in the table, click the Edit button at the right side of the table within the row. You can also remove the network category from the table by clicking the Delete button.

Note that there is another link at the end of the Profile Edit menu: The Song & Video on Profile link. We'll cover that menu option in Chapter 6.

FAQS

How do I set my profile to private? MySpace is a public web site, and the World Wide Web isn't called that for nothing. If you only want a select group of people (or no one at all) to see your profile, here's how:

In the home page, click the Edit Settings link. The Profile Edit – Interests & Personality page appears.

To the right of the Profile Edit – Interests & Personality header, click the Account Settings link (like the one shown in Figure 1-16).

The Change Account Settings page appears. Click the Change Settings link in the Privacy Settings row within the My Account Settings table, as shown in Figure 1-17.

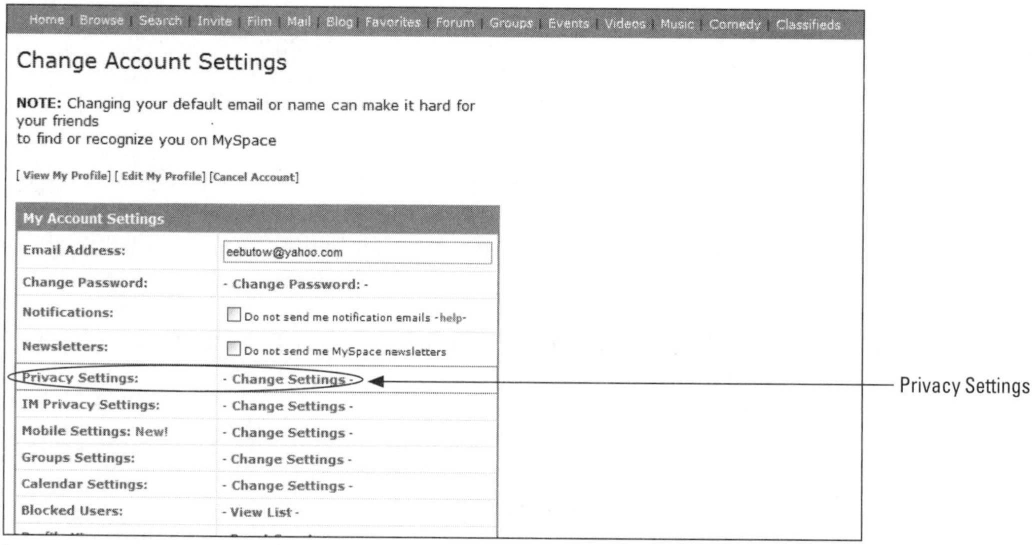

FIGURE 1-17 The Change Account Settings page

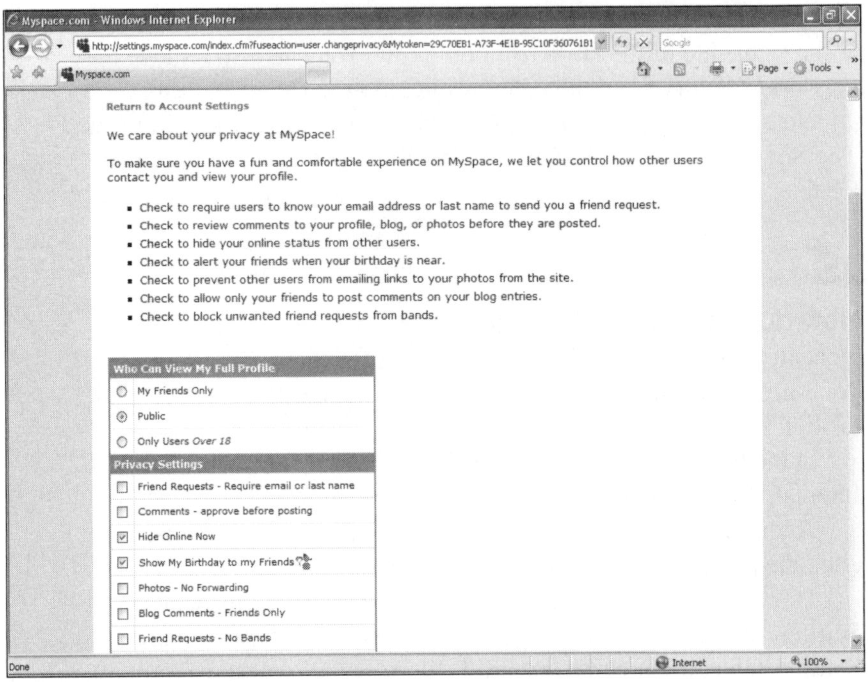

FIGURE 1-18 The Privacy Settings page

You should now see the Privacy Settings screen, as shown in Figure 1-18. You can hide your profile by selecting the Hide Online Now check box in the table.

Click the Change Settings button. MySpace updates your settings, and the sentence "Your Privacy Settings have been updated" appears above the table. Return to the Account Settings page by clicking the Return to Account Settings link at the top of the page.

How do I delete my profile or another profile, such as my child's profile?   If you want to delete your own profile, here's how:

In the home page, click the Edit Settings link. The Profile Edit – Interests & Personality page appears.

To the right of the Profile Edit – Interests & Personality header, click the Account Settings link.

The Change Account Settings page appears. Click the Cancel Account link shown in Figure 1-19.

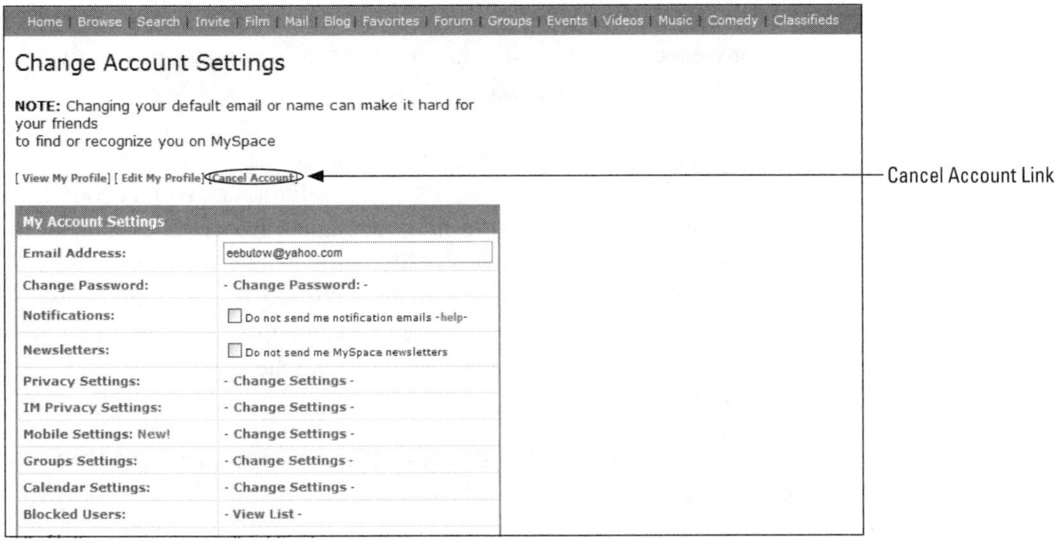

FIGURE 1-19 The Cancel Account Settings page

In the Cancel MySpace Account page that appears, shown in Figure 1-20, click the red Cancel My Account button. Remember that once your account is deleted, all the information in the profile is gone. If you change your mind, click the green Keep My Account button.

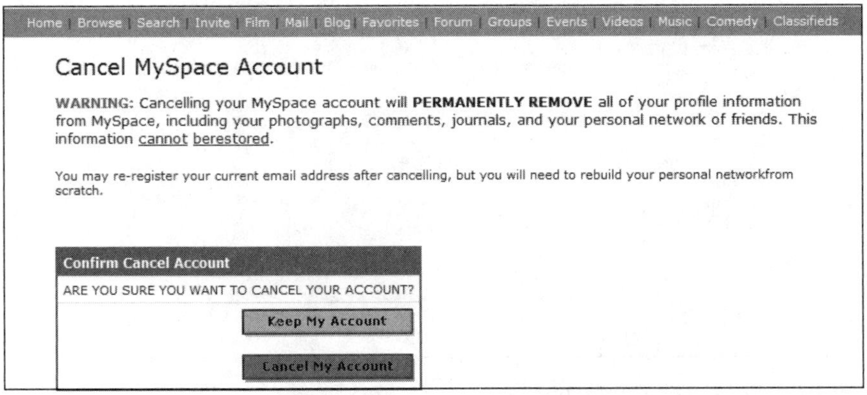

FIGURE 1-20 The Cancel MySpace Account page

A second Cancel MySpace Account screen appears that asks you for any cancellation comments and gives you another opportunity to keep or cancel your account. Click the red Cancel My Account button.

MySpace will send an e-mail message to the e-mail account on file that will tell you how to confirm cancellation of your account.

If you don't receive this e-mail message, remove all content from the profile and type **Remove Profile** in the About Me section of the profile you're deleting. Then contact MySpace and let them know the web address of the profile, and you can copy this from your browser's Address bar and then paste it into the e-mail you send to MySpace support.

Someone's profile pretends to be me. How do I get this profile off MySpace?   MySpace needs to verify your identity to ensure that you are who you say you are. Therefore, MySpace asks that you send a "salute"—an image of yourself that you or another person takes. In this image, you need to be holding a handwritten

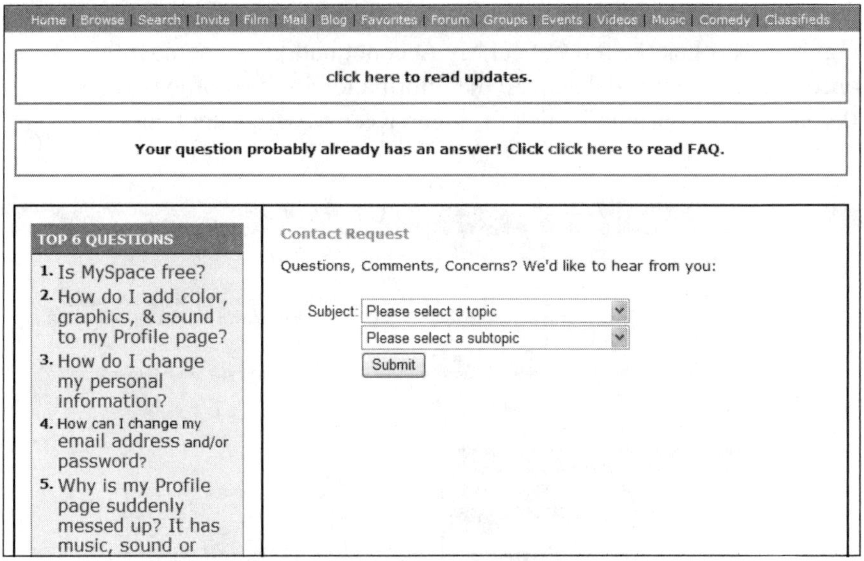

FIGURE 1-21 The Contact Request page

sign with the word "MySpace.com" and the friend ID, which appears in the web address after "friendID=" when you view your profile. When you contact MySpace support, be certain to send the offending profile, web address to MySpace support. You can copy this from your browser's Address bar and then paste it into the e-mail you send to MySpace support.

What happens if MySpace doesn't update my profile?   If the profile doesn't update, the problem may be a system error. Report system errors to MySpace immediately so they can look into the problem and fix it as soon as possible. To report a system error, scroll down to the bottom of the page and click the Contact MySpace link. A new browser window opens and displays the Contact Request page, as shown in Figure 1-21, so you can send information directly to the MySpace tech staff. If the techies need more information, they will contact you through the e-mail address you entered when you created your account.

Chapter 2

Using HTML to Enhance Your Page

In Chapter 1 you populated your profile with information, and now it's time to make that information look the way you want to other MySpace users. You can change the look of your profile page in the Profile Edit – Interests & Personality page. As you learned in Chapter 1, the rest of the options in the Profile Edit window let you set your personal information and add a song and/or video on your profile. You only need knowledge of HTML (HyperText Markup Language), which is the programming language used to create web pages, to make cosmetic changes to your web site, including changing colors, font styles and sizes, the appearance of boxes, and background colors.

Before you begin, MySpace has some rules that you need to be aware of:

- You can add HTML, Dynamic HTML (known as DHTML), or Cascading Style Sheets (known by its acronym CSS) into any profile section. These are all pretty scary-sounding acronyms, but don't fret. You don't need to worry about DHTML, and you'll learn a little bit about CSS in this chapter and much more in Chapter 3. For this chapter, however, we'll concentrate on HTML so you can get the basics of using HTML and CSS to change the look of your profile page.

- When you add HTML and CSS, you can add that information anywhere on the page. Be sure that none of your graphics overlaps an advertisement that appears on the page. MySpace is free because there are plenty of opportunities for advertisers to get their ads in front of many eyes. Advertisers and MySpace will not be happy with you if they find your graphics are hiding ads. The chances of advertisers finding out that your cosmetic changes have hidden their ads are pretty small. Chances are much better that other MySpace users who visit your site will alert MySpace that you're violating the rules.

- In the Interests, Music, Movies, Television, Books, and Heroes boxes, you may include text that includes links to outside sites. If you would rather not have people click outside your profile to see more about what you like,

type **<Z>** anywhere in these boxes and all links will be
disabled automatically. You can also type HTML code to
have the linked page open in a new browser window. You'll
learn how to do that in Chapter 3.

On top of all that, you should be aware of what you want your
profile to look like when it's finished and what message you want to
convey. If you have background colors or images combined with text
that is hard to read (or, worse, makes visitors avert their eyes), then
your profile won't be very popular. Figure 2-1 shows an example of
a bad-looking profile page.

If you're not sure about what your page should look like, look at
other MySpace profiles by clicking the Browse link and browsing
for people who have similar interests. For example, you can search
for people in your preferred age group who are on MySpace for
networking. (You'll learn more about browsing as you grow your
circle of friends, which we'll talk about in Chapter 10.)

FIGURE 2-1 A bad-looking profile page

MySpace recommends that if you don't know how to program in HTML or CSS, you should ask the MySpace users who created your favorite profiles how they put theirs together. That way, you'll make new friends and get information you can use to make your profile look the way you want.

Or not. If you would rather learn HTML on your own, let's start with a quick and dirty introduction to HTML.

ADDING HTML

The two primary building blocks of HTML are elements and tags.

Elements tell the browser how you want the web page to be presented. Elements consist of three parts: a start tag, content, and an end tag.

A *tag* tells the browser that the content of an element is placed inside that tag and its end tag. All tags start with the less than sign "<" and end with the greater than sign ">". The difference between the start tag and end tag is that the end tag starts with a forward slash that immediately includes the less-than sign (with a few exceptions). HTML includes many different tags for programming your web page. To learn HTML is to learn a large number of tags and how to apply them correctly.

The tags alert the browser that the content between the start and end tags must reflect the style referenced within the tag. For example, HTML has six built-in heading tags in hierarchical order from `<h1>` through `<h6>`. The `<h1>` heading is the heading with the largest font, `<h2>` is the next largest font, and so on until `<h6>` has the smallest font. Here's an example of a heading tag:

```
<h1>The Largest Heading</h1>
<h2>The Next-Largest Heading for a Subhead</h2>
```

The text in between the `<h1>` and `</h1>` tags will appear in the font size and style specified by the `<h1>` tag. Note that the tags appear in lowercase. Though your browser doesn't care how the tags appear, the standard convention is to write tags in lowercase.

You may want to emphasize certain words in your profile with colors or with boldface and italics. To give you a taste of what you can do, here's how you can use some basic HTML tags to create colored text as well as text in boldface and italics. You can add this text in any of the boxes within the Profile Edit – Interests & Personality page. When you finish typing this information into the box, click the Preview Section button to view how your changes look.

Apply Color to a Word or to the Entire Page

Now let's explore some other built-in tags. The following example changes the text of the following content from the default (black) to purple:

```
<font color="990099">
Hello, world!
</font>
```

In HTML, you use a tag nested within brackets (`<>`) and you place your text within the start tag `<font>` and the end tag `</font>`. These tags tell the browser to change the font style, size, and/or color. In the preceding example, the start `<font>` tag is followed by the argument `color`, which specifies the color of the font. The argument is followed by an equal sign and the value of the color, which in HTML is a six-digit hexadecimal number. MySpace translates the HTML six-digit number into the corresponding color, which is purple. Therefore, the tag `<font color="990099">` translated into plain English is, "Change the font of the text within this tag to the color that equals purple." When you preview this section you'll see that the text "Hello, world!" (the standard greeting for first-time programmers) is in purple.

Apply Boldface and Italics

If you want to make text bold or apply italics, use the `<b>` and `<i>` tags, respectively. For example:

```
<b>Hello, world!</b>
<i>Hello. How are you?</i>
```

When you preview the text, the text "Hello, world!" between the start `<b>` tag and the end `</b>` tag is in boldface, and the response between the start `<i>` tag and end `</i>` tag is in italics. Simple as that.

But what if you want to make text bold *and* italic? You can apply both tags at the same time. For example:

```
<b><i>Hello, world!</i></b>
```

HTML understands that if there are two tags next to each other, it should apply both of those tags to the content that follows those two tags. You need to be sure to include the end tags at the end and close the last start tag first. As you see in the preceding example, the `<i>` italic tag comes after the bold `<b>` tag. Therefore, the closing `</i>` tag must be listed before the closing `</b>` tag.

ADDING CSS

HTML requires a number of tags, and you have to apply the tags to all the content in your web page. That repetition can become annoying very quickly. What's more, HTML is fairly rigid and doesn't provide much design flexibility. The solution to these problems is Cascading Style Sheets, known popularly by the acronym CSS. CSS is like the style sheet in your word processing program. Once you add the CSS code into your profile, you can apply the style tags in that code to content in one or more web pages. You can add CSS code in any box within the Profile Edit – Interests & Personality page.

One way to use CSS is to create a background picture or color for your profile. Here's an example of adding a background picture to your profile:

```
<style>
body { background:url(http://www.butow.net/mewsette.jpg); }
</style>
```

The CSS style is set off by the `<style>` and `</style>` tags.

When I preview the code, Figure 2-2 shows the preview of the background that is a picture of my cat Mewsette. The picture automatically tiles across the screen. If you don't like the background, you can simply delete the code from the appropriate box in the Profile Edit – Interests & Personality page.

This is just a taste of what CSS can do. In Chapter 3 we'll delve into greater detail of how to program CSS and show you why CSS makes your life easier. As you learn about CSS and expand your design repertoire in the next chapter, you'll also learn about good and bad design techniques.

Want more information about HTML? One good place to start is Appendix A for a list of HTML commands from A to Z, including

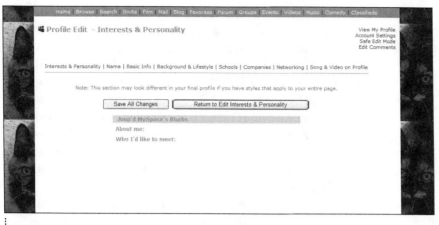

FIGURE 2-2 Mewsette abounds in the background.

CSS tags. You can also get a good start with HTML tutorials and information at the following web sites:

- http://www.html.net/

- http://www.w3.org/MarkUp/Guide/

- http://www.w3.org/MarkUp/Guide/Style

- http://www.w3schools.com/html/html_intro.asp

These sites go into much more detail about HTML and programming on the web. A couple of these sites are produced by the World Wide Web Consortium, which you'll learn more about in Chapter 3 as we delve into Cascading Style Sheets (CSS) in more detail.

WHAT HAPPENS IF...

It's very important to be persnickety about adding HTML code. For example, if you start a block of text with the <b> tag and you forget to add the end </b> tag at the end of the text you want to bold, you may become confused about why the rest of your text is boldface when you didn't want the text to appear that way.

Unfortunately, MySpace doesn't include any tools for checking your HTML code beyond the preview option. There are plenty of free web editors, though, if you want to develop your HTML code in one of these editors first, test the code for errors, and then copy the code from the editor and paste it into the appropriate box in MySpace. The Free Site (http://www.thefreesite.com/Free_Software/HTML_freeware/) has a list of free HTML editors you can download and try.

If your HTML code doesn't have any errors, the problem is likely a MySpace "feature": bad HTML code embedded in a comment that someone left on your web site. (This same "feature" also causes music to play in your profile if someone embeds a music file in the comment.) The best way to remove the problem is to remove the comment. Here's how:

Click the Edit Comments link to the right of the Profile Edit – Interests & Personality header.

The View Comments page displays the list of comments in newest to oldest order, as shown in Figure 2-3.

When you see the comment you want to delete, click the Delete My Comment link.

If you don't have or can't find any comments that could be causing the problem, you have two choices: Scrub all the HTML out of your page and see if that solves the problem, or contact MySpace support because there may be a serious issue. Don't delete your profile because that will remove all data within the profile and you'll have to rebuild your profile from scratch.

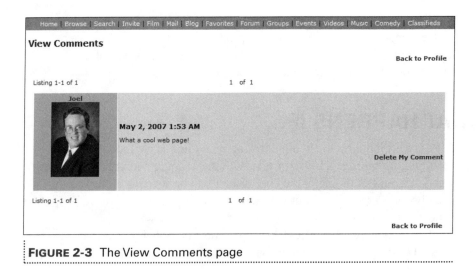

FIGURE 2-3 The View Comments page

Chapter 3

Using CSS to Change Your Profile

If you use a word processor, you're familiar with style sheets, which let you apply formatting styles like 12-point red text for a particular paragraph you want the reader to pay attention to. In the web world, Cascading Style Sheets, or CSS, works the same way.

WHAT IS CSS?

CSS is a style-sheet language that describes how a web page looks and where web objects (such as a block of text) should appear on the page.

As the web became more popular in the mid-1990s, the HTML (Hypertext Markup Language) code used to program web pages became larger with more capabilities for specifying styles in a web page. These new capabilities gave developers the ability to make their pages look better than ever, but it also meant they had to write more code.

What's more, the battle for web browser supremacy between Microsoft Internet Explorer, Netscape Navigator, and other competitors also made it hard for developers to display web sites that looked the same in all browsers.

Users helped take care of this problem by adopting Internet Explorer as their primary browser of choice (with assistance from Microsoft). The World Wide Web Consortium, popularly known by its acronym W3C, also took care of this problem by standardizing style sheets. The W3C was founded by web inventor Tim Berners-Lee, and as of this writing has 441 members including Apple, Google, and Microsoft. Style sheets have been around since the 1970s when markup languages were in their infancy, but the W3C focused the effort on creating one standard style-sheet language that became CSS.

CSS has a number of advantages:

■ One style-sheet document can be applied to a number of web pages, so all you have to do is link the web site to the style-sheet document and then apply the styles from the style sheet directly in your web page.

- You can have more than one style-sheet document for different audiences, such as a style sheet for a layout that you can view on your mobile phone or PDA.

- CSS uses a number of English keywords as the names of style properties, such as bold, italics, color, and font.

A CSS style sheet requires you to set up the style according to certain rules. You define the characteristics of a style by writing a "declaration block," which consists of text contained within curly braces (that is, { and }). Each declaration defines a value for some aspect of the style, as you'll see in the example. Each declaration is on its own line and is separated by a semicolon. The declaration includes a property, a colon, and then the value.

You can also embed CSS styles within your HTML file, and in MySpace you embed your CSS styles within the appropriate box when you edit your profile instead of creating a separate CSS file. To embed CSS styles in an HTML file, you must place the CSS styles within the `<style>` and `</style>` tags. For example:

```
<style type="text/css">
.note {
  background: yellow;
  font-color: red;
  font-weight: bold;
  font-size: 12px;
}
</style>
```

The preceding example defines a CSS class called `"note"` with the background color using the property called `background` and the value `yellow`, the font color (red), the font weight (bold), and the font size (12 pixels, with pixels abbreviated as px). Within the opening style tag, I have specified the type of style as a text/CSS file. You can then apply the class `"note"` to the text in your HTML code. For example:

```
<p class="note">This is a warning!</p>
```

The argument `class="note"` in the HTML code tells your web browser that the paragraph block "This is a warning!" must have the properties specified in the class `"note"` with a yellow background, and red bold text that is 12 pixels high.

Now that you know the basics, let's use CSS styles to change features in your MySpace page in the following sections. For all the examples in this chapter, we'll add the information in the About Me box. In the main MySpace page, click the Edit Profile link to open the Profile Edit – Interests & Personality page, so you can add your CSS and HTML code in the About Me box.

MySpace is a web application, so it contains a number of built-in CSS styles. When you know the names of the styles, you can use them to redefine the standard definitions in MySpace. For example, the `td` class is used for most of the text in your MySpace profile, but not all. You'll learn about those exceptions in the next section.

CHANGE YOUR DEFAULT FONT TYPE, SIZE, AND COLOR

Two style tags and one style class apply to text in your MySpace profile page:

- The `div` tag applies to text in your MySpace URL that appears in the Tell People About Your MySpace module, as shown in Figure 3-1.

- The `.text` class applies to text next to your profile photo.

- The `td` tag applies to most of the rest of the text in your profile. You'll learn more about other text tags in the rest of the sections in this chapter.

It's easy to make changes to your default font type, size, and color. Here's an example of how you can make changes to text tags and classes:

```
<style type="text/css">
td {
font-family: Georgia, Times New Roman, serif;
font-size: 10pt;
color: DarkBlue;
}
```

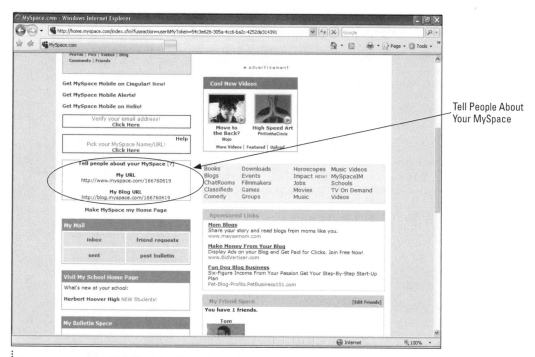

Tell People About Your MySpace

FIGURE 3-1 The Tell People About Your MySpace module

```
div {
font-family: Georgia, Times New Roman, serif;
font-weight: bold;
}
.text {
font-family: Georgia, Times New Roman, serif;
font-weight: bold;
}
</style>
```

When you preview the code in this section, you'll see the results of the changes you made in your code, as shown in Figure 3-2. If you don't want to change an attribute within the tag or class, don't add the attribute. For example, if you want to keep the text around your profile photo as the default blue color, don't specify the color in the .text class.

FIGURE 3-2 The changes you made appear in the profile preview.

CHANGE YOUR MODULE TITLES AND HEADINGS

When you view your profile there are a number of modules along the left side of the profile page, where you can include schools you attend or have attended, networking information, company information, and more. These modules appear in different boxes that have a blue title bar at the top, as shown in Figure 3-3.

To the right of the modules are sections with light orange heading bars that contain orange text. For example, you see Amp'd MySpace's Friend Space to the right of the Contacting Amp'd MySpace module.

MySpace contains built-in CSS styles for the module titles, headings, and other links. You'll learn how to change the format of

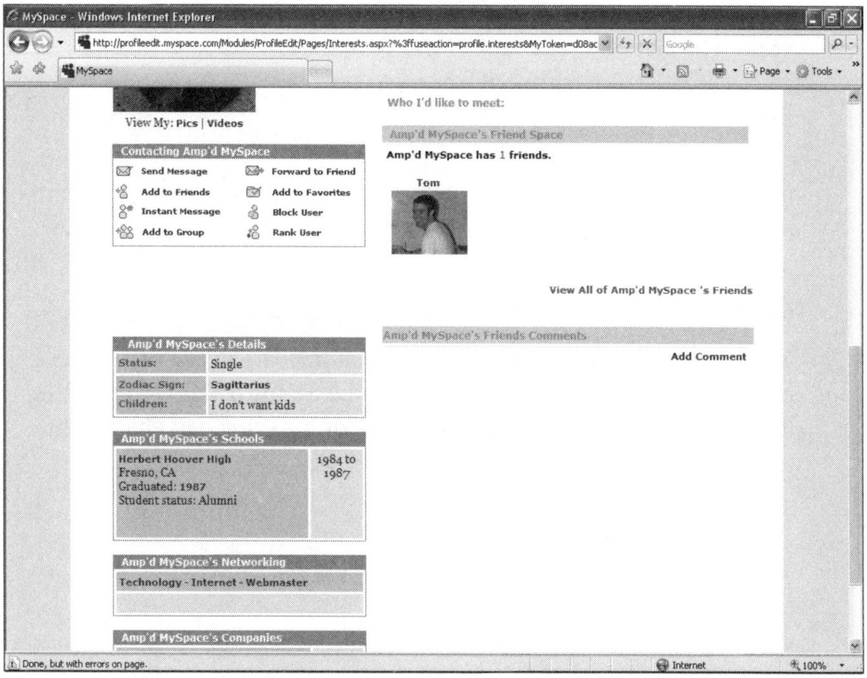

FIGURE 3-3 The modules along the left side of your profile page

links in the next section. For this section, we'll focus on changing module titles and headings that have the following styles:

- `whitetext12` for the module title text
- `lightbluetext8` for module heading text
- `orangetext15` for section title text

Change Module Title Text

Here's an example of how you can change the style for the module title text:

```
<style type="text/css">
.whitetext12 {
font-family: Georgia, Times New Roman; serif;
```

```
color: yellow;
text-align: center;
}
</style>
```

Preview the profile by clicking the Preview Profile button below the About Me box. The yellow text appears in the title bars of all the modules.

Change Module Heading Text

Module heading text is the blue text that appears in the light blue bars within the module. For example, the Status heading appears in the Details module. Here's an example of how you can change the style for the module heading text:

```
<style type="text/css">
.lightbluetext8 {
font-family: Georgia, Times New Roman; serif;
color: DarkGreen;
text-align: center;
}
</style>
```

Preview the profile by clicking the Preview Profile button below the About Me box. The dark green text appears in the headings of all the modules.

Change Section Title Text

Here's an example of how you can change the style for section title text:

```
<style type="text/css">
.orangetext15 {
font-family: Verdana, Helvetica, Arial, sans-serif;
font-size: 14pt;
color: blue;
}
</style>
```

Preview the profile by clicking the Preview Profile button below the About Me box. The blue, 14-point Verdana heading text appears in the title bars of all the sections.

CHANGE THE TEXT FOR LINKS AND INTERESTS

Styles for the links text and the text in the interests section are different from other text styles, so you have to be sure to apply the correct style tag to change the look of the interests section and your links.

Change the Interests Text

Here's an example of how you can change the style for the interests text:

```
<style type="text/css">
a.searchlinkSmall {
font-family: Verdana, Helvetica, Arial, sans-serif;
font-size: 12pt;
color: DarkBlue;
}
</style>
```

The interests text uses the `a.searchlinkSmall` tag. Preview the profile by clicking the Preview Profile button below the About Me box. The interests text appears in 12-point, dark blue, Verdana font in the Interests module.

Change Links Text

There are four different styles for the appearance of links and you can change the color of each one:

- ■ `a:link` is the default link color.

- ■ `a:hover` is the link color when you place (or "hover") the mouse pointer over the link.

- ■ `a:active` is the color of the currently active link.

- ■ `a:visited` is the color of a link you previously visited.

Here's an example of how you can change the style for the links text:

```
<style type="text/css">
a: link {
font-family: Verdana, Helvetica, Arial, sans-serif;
font-size: 12pt;
color: blue;
}
a.hover {
font-family: Verdana, Helvetica, Arial, sans-serif;
font-size: 12pt;
color: red;
}
a.active {
font-family: Verdana, Helvetica, Arial, sans-serif;
font-size: 12pt;
color: green;
}
a.visited {
font-family: Verdana, Helvetica, Arial, sans-serif;
font-size: 12pt;
color: yellow;
}
</style>
```

Preview the Profile by clicking the Preview Profile button below the About Me box. This code will make all links blue. When you move the mouse pointer over the link, the color of the link turns red. If you click the link, the linked page appears and the link turns green. If you have visited another link previously, that link color will be yellow.

MATCH THE MYSPACE LINKS TO YOUR PROFILE LOOK

You should color your links so that they match your profile look. In other words, the link colors should complement what you have on the rest of the site. For example, if you have blue links on your profile page as the default MySpace profile does, you should have a color for the hover links that should complement the links.

For example, the hover link in the default MySpace profile is red so it stands out.

You may also want to consider changing the link colors to colors that match other parts of your profile look. For example, if the module heading text is teal, you may want to change the link color to teal.

ADD A BANNER ON TOP

Do you want to announce your profile title for everyone to see? You can add a banner and place it in a specific location on the profile page. Here's an example where I place a banner for my business on the profile:

```
<style>
body {
margin-top: 200px;
}
</style>

<style>
banner {
position: absolute;
top: 0%;
left: 50%;
width: 900px;
margin-left: -450px;
height: 193px;
}
</style>
<div class="banner">
<img src="http://www.butow.net/bcglogo2005_banner0.jpg">
</div>
```

In the preceding example I use a `div` tag, which defines a division or section in an HTML document. The `div` tag also defines the styles for certain sections of your HTML document. The `div` tag is a section with the class `"banner"` into which I can place the banner graphic. After I add the code in the About Me box and click the Preview Section button below the box, the banner appears in the About Me section, as shown in Figure 3-4.

FIGURE 3-4 The banner in the About Me section

REDESIGN YOUR CONTACT TABLE

The Contact table is the place where visitors can contact you and add your profile to their circle of friends. (You'll learn more about adding to your circle of friends in Chapter 10.) The Contact table has eight links:

- **Send Message**   A user can send you a note.

- **Add to Friends**   Visitors can add your profile to your circle of friends.

- **Instant Message**   Users can send you an instant message.

- **Add to Group**   A visitor can add your profile to one of their groups.

- **Forward to Friend**   A user can forward your profile to one of their friends.

- **Add to Favorites**   A visitor can add your profile to their favorites list.

- **Block User**   A visitor can block your profile from their searches.

- **Rank User**   A visitor can rank one or more photos you have posted on your web site.

The Contact table isn't very attractive, but you can make changes to the table background to make it look the way you want. The Contact table is only 300 pixels wide by 150 pixels in height, so you need to design your background to fit within those constraints.

This is because the Contact table links are in the foreground, so when you create your background, you have to make sure that the link text in the background is close to the links in the foreground. You may have to experiment a bit with the positioning by designing your first draft of the background and then previewing the profile to see if the link areas match up with the text in the background.

If you try to make the Contact table background image larger than 300 by 150, MySpace will crop the background image to 300 by 150. This can result in both your background images and text being cut off and/or in the wrong places.

To design your Contact table background, the first thing you must do is add the new contact table information. Then you must hide the old contact table so it doesn't show up on top of your new contact table. Here's the code, which includes some comments so you can see what it does:

```
<style type="text/css">
/* place the new background image in the Contact table*/
.contactTable {
width:300px;
height:150px;
background-image:url("http://www.butow.net/
contact_table.jpg");
background-repeat:no-repeat;
background-color:transparent;
background-attachment:scroll;
background-position:center center; padding:0px;
}
/* make the old Contact table background transparent */
.contactTable table, table.contactTable td {
background-color:transparent;
background-image:none; padding:0px;
}
```

```
/* set up the contact button table block */
.contactTable a {
display:block;
height:28px;
width:115px;
}
/* hide the old contact buttons */
.contactTable a img {
visibility:hidden;
border:0px;
}
.contactTable .text {
font-size:1px;
}
</style>
```

Preview the profile by clicking the Preview Profile button below the About Me box. You'll see the new background in the Contact table, as shown in Figure 3-5. The background also includes somewhat different link names to give your Contact table a little more of an edge.

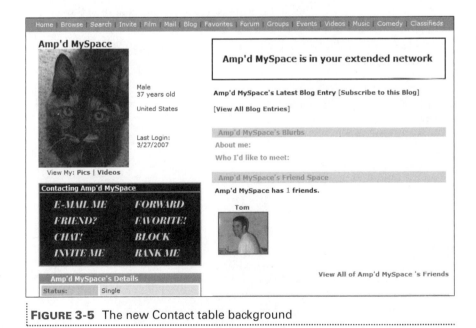

FIGURE 3-5 The new Contact table background

*If you don't want to create your own Contact table background, there are plenty of MySpace Contact table image sites to choose from. Type **MySpace contact tables** into your favorite search engine and you'll see plenty of sites from which to choose.*

ADD BORDERS AND LINES

The default MySpace profile template includes borders around the modules on the left side of the profile but none around the sections on the right side. What's more, the modules and sections don't have lines that separate the titles from the rest of the text. If you want to have borders and lines, type the following code. I've included comments so you know what the following code block does.

```
<style type="text/css">
/* third-level tables have borders around them */
table table table {
border-width: 5px;
border-style: thin;
border-color: blue;
margin: 0px;
background-color: orange;
width: 100%;
/* Change the profile name style to include a bottom border */
.nametext {
padding-bottom: 5px;
border-bottom-width: 3px;
border-bottom-style: solid;
border-bottom-color: red;
/* Change the module heading style to include a bottom border */
.whitetext12 {
width: 320px;
padding-bottom: 5px;
border-bottom-width: 3px;
border-bottom-style: solid;
border-bottom-color: red;
}
</style>
```

View your new table borders and lines by clicking the Preview Profile button below the About Me box. You'll see the solid red lines that separate the title bar from the rest of the text in the module, and you'll also see the blue box around each module and section. We'll talk about table levels and how to create a consistent look with your tables and sections in the next... well, section.

CREATE A CONSISTENT LOOK WITH YOUR TABLES AND SECTIONS

A MySpace profile page is made up of a number of nested tables within HTML. A nested table is like the Russian doll toy where there is a large doll that you open up to reveal a smaller doll, and when you open the smaller doll there is an even smaller doll. Eventually you open all the dolls as they get smaller in size until you find the smallest doll. In nested tables, there is one large table, and you can place a smaller secondary table inside that large table, and then place an even smaller table within that secondary table.

When you apply the same styles to these tables, you can create a uniform look that looks much cleaner than the default MySpace profile. There are a number of table style codes that you need to change:

- `table, tr, td`
- `table table`
- `table table td`
- `table table table`
- `table table table td`
- `table table table table`
- `table table table table td`
- `.whitetext12` (the module headings style)
- `.nametext` (the profile name style)
- `table tr td table tr td table tr td div` (the URL box style)

You can tell what the table hierarchy is by the number of table tags. For example, the tag with only one table tag (`table, tr, td`) is the first-level table. The `table table` tag is the second-level table, `table table table` is the third-level table, and so on.

Add the following code to change the look of all the tables. As with previous examples, I've added comments that tell you what this block of code does.

```
<style type="text/css">
/* change the primary and secondary table width and background */
table, tr, td, table table, table table td {
border-width: 0px;
background-color: transparent;
}
/* change the third level table characteristics */
table table table td {
background color: transparent;
margin: 0px;
padding: 10px;
}
/* change the fourth level table characteristics */
table table table table {
border-width: 0px;
background-color: transparent;
padding: 0px;
margin: 0px;
}
/* change the fourth level table margin and padding */
table table table table td {
padding: 0px;
margin: 0px;
}
/* change the tables' background color to sky blue */
table table table {
margin: 0px;
background-color: 00CCFF;
width: 100%
}
/* set the table module heading max width */
.whitetext12 {
width: 320px;
}
```

```
/* set the profile name heading max width */
.nametext {
width: 320px;
}
/* set the URL box max width */
table tr td table tr td table tr td div {
width: 320px;
}
</style>
```

After you add this code, you won't be able to see the code in the preview page. View the code by clicking the Save Changes button above the Headline box. Then click the View My Profile link to the right of the Profile Edit – Interests & Personality header at the top of the page. You'll see your new profile page with well-ordered tables and sections that look spiffy in sky blue.

Now that you can see your changes, you can tweak the sections to make them look the way you want. For example, you can change the color, or if you don't want any color, you can set the background-color style to transparent. You can also change the border widths and/or add lines as you did in the previous section.

There are also plenty of sites on the web that offer free MySpace profile layouts if you want to use a premade layout or if you want to get ideas. Type **myspace layouts** in your favorite search engine and you can browse the many sites that appear in the results page.

FAQS

I have a CSS style that has several colors in it. I want all the colors to appear in the text, but only the last color I added appears. How do I fix this? Cascading Style Sheets have "cascading" in the title because you can use multiple styles at once. If the styles conflict with one another, then the last one you added is the one the HTML document uses because the styles "cascaded" down to the last color style you specified.

If you want to fix this, the solution is to create several different styles and then apply the style with the color to the text you want. For example, create two styles named "green" and "purple" and then apply the green style to the text you want green and apply the purple style to the text you want purple.

After I preview my CSS handiwork and go back to the Profile Edit – Interests & Personality page, all the less-than (<) and greater-than (>) brackets turn to < and >. And all the comments disappear too! What's going on? MySpace automatically converts brackets to their HTML code equivalents and deletes all comments when it processes your HTML code. These changes don't affect the quality of the code, though in the case of the changed less-than and greater-than signs, the HTML code equivalents can be harder to read at first.

Are the profile style tags in this chapter the only styles I can change? No. This chapter only gets you started with the basic style tags you can change in MySpace. You can view a complete view of style tags in Appendix B.

Do you have any other suggestions for making my profile look the best it can be? Chapter 2 contains a figure with a bad-looking MySpace profile. A bad-looking MySpace profile has several telltale characteristics. The web site MySpace Please has an excellent article with five tips for creating a good MySpace profile layout (http://www.myspaceplease.com/badmyspacelayout.php) that you should adhere to:

1. Don't use glittering text. No one likes to read text that is, at best, barely readable.

2. Don't use animated backgrounds. They make your profile hard to read or make people avert their eyes.

3. Don't place lots of movies or videos on your profile. They can take a long time to load and you can easily tax your visitors' patience.

4. Don't place songs on your web site, especially two songs at once that overlap each other. Repeating songs get old quickly, and two songs competing with each other could mean your profile only emits noise.

5. Use correct grammar and spelling. If you don't, then you come across as being uneducated—and your text can be hard to read.

We'll talk about other layout do's and don'ts in other chapters, such as Chapter 5 when we discuss how much is too much when it comes to Flash animation.

Chapter 4

Images and Photos

MySpace is not just a place to transmit text that describes who you are, what you do, and what you like (or dislike). MySpace is a visual medium that allows you to share photos and other images with other MySpace users who visit your profile. We'll start by adding a background image to your profile.

For all the examples in this chapter, we'll add the information in the About Me box. In the main MySpace page, click the Edit Profile link to open the Profile Edit – Interests & Personality page so you can add your CSS and HTML code in the About Me box.

ADD A TRANSPARENT BACKGROUND IMAGE

In Chapter 2 you learned how to add a background image to your page. However, the default MySpace profile template has a white background. That's clean enough, but it may not reflect you. After all, your background helps your profile visitors understand who you are. It's easy to add a background image to your profile by typing the following code. In this code, you must add your new background image first and then make the existing background color transparent so the image will show through.

```
<style type="text/css">

body {
background-image: url("http://www.butow.net/mewsette.jpg")
}

</style>
```

In this example I added my cat Mewsette as the background image. The main profile box with the white background is not affected. If you want this box to be transparent, add the following code to the previous code example:

```
table, td {
background-color: transparent;
}
```

Now the background will show through the main profile box. Click the Save All Changes button and then click the View My Profile link

FIGURE 4-1 Mewsette is everywhere in the background.

that appears to the right of the Profile Edit – Interests & Personality header. Mewsette appears everywhere, as shown in Figure 4-1.

If you would prefer to have a color in the background instead, replace the background-image style with the following style:

```
Background-color: 990099
```

The background color sets the background color to the six-digit hexadecimal color, which is purple.

CHANGE YOUR PROFILE
NAME TO AN IMAGE

A trite saying is, "A picture is worth a thousand words." And sometimes your profile name just doesn't describe you as well as an image does. MySpace lets you customize your profile name so it displays an image instead.

You will need to add CSS code as shown in the following example. In the code, you will change the `.nametext` class, which specifies the profile name style.

```
<style type="text/css">
.nametext {
width: 135px;
height: 54px;
display: block;
background-image: url("http://www.butow.net/bcglogo2005_banner1.jpg");
background-position: top;
background-repeat: no-repeat;
font-size: 0px;
color: CC9900;
}
</style>
```

The width and height are the same as the size of the image I want to import. In the code I also specify that the image should not repeat, and the font size is 0 so the profile name text does not appear. Click the Preview Profile button to look at your new profile name image, as shown in Figure 4-2.

The font color is the same as the bar around my company logo: gold.

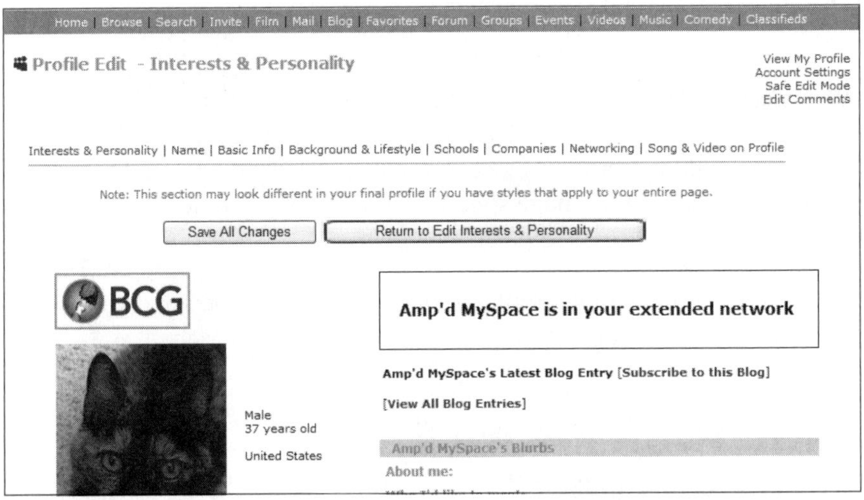

FIGURE 4-2 The new profile name image

If you don't set the text color to the same color as the background of your image, you'll see a very small line across the top of your logo, which is your text in a very tiny font.

CHANGE YOUR EXTENDED NETWORK TO AN IMAGE

The extended network box appears in the upper right area of the page that states in large type, "[User name] is in your extended network." This information isn't terribly important and you can make better use of the space by changing the Extended Network box to an image.

MySpace has reserved the CSS style `.blacktext12` for changing your text or image styles in the Extended Network box. The box itself can accommodate an image that is 435 pixels wide by 75 pixels high. Here's the code to change your Extended Network box into an image:

```
<style type="text/css">
table table table td
span.blacktext12 {
color:transparent;
visibility:visible;
background-color:transparent;
background-image:url ("http://www.butow.net/extended.jpg");
background-repeat:no-repeat;
background-position:center center;
font-size:0px;
color: blue;
letter-spacing:-0.5px;
width:435px;
height:75px;
display:block
}
span.blacktext12 img {
display:none;
}
</style>
```

Click the Preview Profile button to look at your new profile name image.

ADD LOTS OF PHOTOS
TO YOUR PROFILE

It's easy to add a photo to your profile. Here's how you do it:

1. On the MySpace home page, click the Add/Edit Photos link to the right of your profile photo. The Photos page appears, as shown in Figure 4-3.

2. Read the photo policy by clicking the photo policy link so you are aware of what you can and cannot upload.

3. In the Upload Photo area, click the Browse button to find your photo on your computer. The Select File(s) to Upload dialog box appears.

4. In the dialog box, navigate to the folder that contains the file you want to upload and then click the Open button. The uploaded filename and path information appear in the file box.

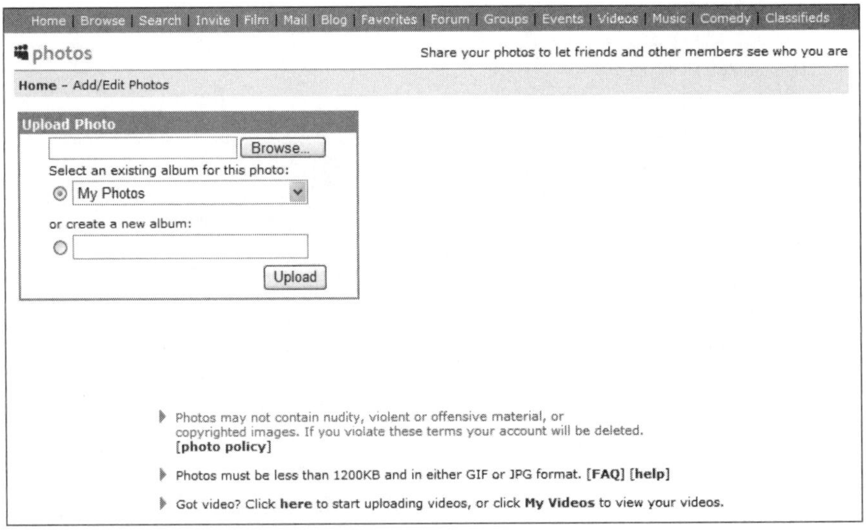

FIGURE 4-3 The Photos page

5. Click the Next button. Select the album to which you want to add the photo. The My Photos album is the default selection, but you can create a new album by clicking the button to the left, or you can create a new album box and then type the new album name in the box.

6. Click the Upload button. MySpace uploads the photos.

7. Scroll down to the bottom of the screen. Under the Your Current Albums header you'll see that there is one photo and this notification appears under your album name, as shown in Figure 4-4.

8. If you want all photos in the album to be viewed only by you, click the You button. If you only want your friends to see the photo, click Friends Only. The default selection is to let everyone see your photos.

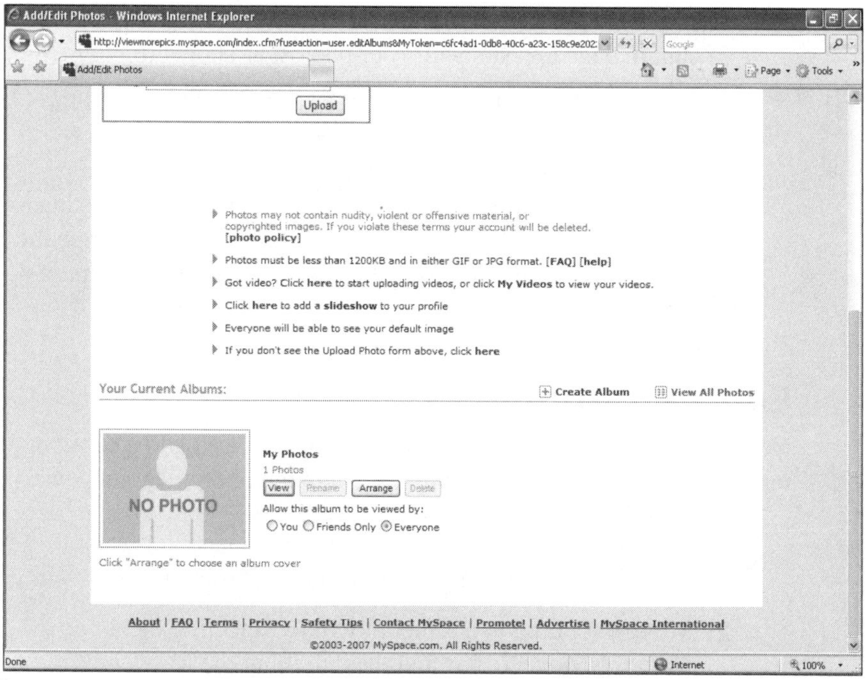

FIGURE 4-4 The number of photos appears under the My Photos album head.

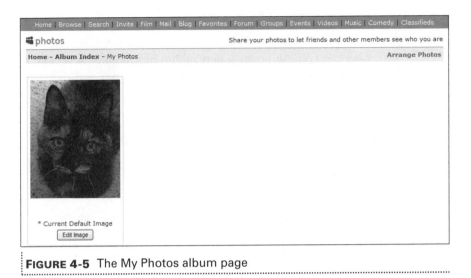

FIGURE 4-5 The My Photos album page

9. View the photo by clicking the View button. The My Photos album page appears with your photos, as shown in Figure 4-5.

10. The text "Current Default Image" appears underneath the default photo—the one that appears on the profile page, which is the first picture you add to My Photos. Make another photo in your album the default photo by clicking the Set as Default button under the photo. If you change the default photo, it may take up to 24 hours for the new photo to appear to visitors.

Edit Your Photos

Now that you have opened your album page you can add a caption, move the photo to another album, or delete the photo. Here's how:

1. Click the Edit Image button under the image you want to edit. The Edit Image page appears, as shown in Figure 4-6.

2. Move the photo to another album by selecting the album from the Move To list and then clicking the Move button.

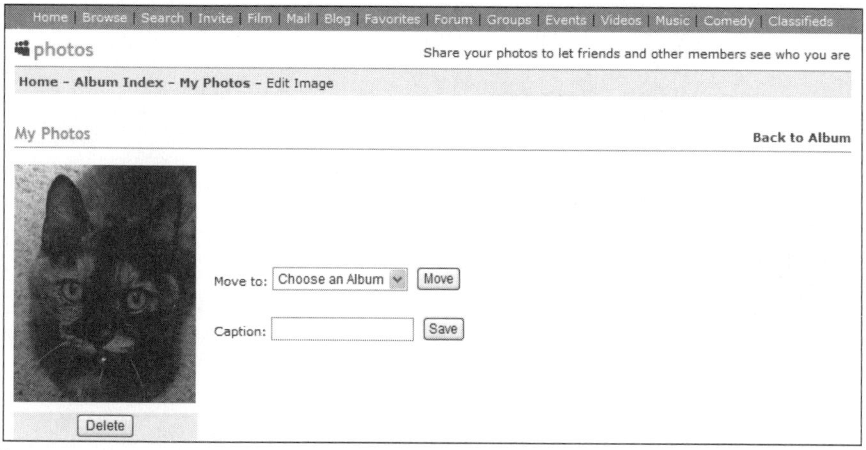

FIGURE 4-6 The Edit Image page

3. If you want to add a photo caption, type the caption in the Caption box and then click the Save button.

4. If you decide you no longer want your photo on your site, you can always delete the photo by clicking the Add/Edit Photos link, scrolling to the bottom of the page, and then clicking the Delete button that appears underneath your photo.

Arrange Your Photos

For some reason, MySpace uses the Arrange button in the Add/Edit Photos page to select an album cover. Here's how you select an album cover:

1. On the MySpace home page, click the Add/Edit Photos link to the right of your profile photo.

2. Scroll down to the bottom of the screen. Under the Your Current Albums section, click the Arrange button. The Order Manager page appears and displays the album cover and your other pictures.

3. Click the Save button. The Edit Album Cover page appears, as shown in Figure 4-7.

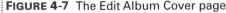

FIGURE 4-7 The Edit Album Cover page

4. Resize the box with the handles around it within the editing area at the bottom to select the area of the photo you'd like as your album cover. As you move the box around, the preview box above and to the right of the editing area shows what your album cover will look like.

5. Click the Save Album Cover button. The new album cover appears next to your album name in the Add/Edit Photos page.

Note that if you would rather use another picture in your album as the album cover, click the "or pick another image from your album" link below the Save Album Cover button.

CREATE SLIDE SHOWS OF YOUR PHOTOS

MySpace not only makes it easy to upload a photo but also to create a slideshow out of the photos you've uploaded. Here's how to create a slideshow:

1. On the MySpace home page, click the Add/Edit Photos link to the right of your profile photo.

2. Under the Add a Slideshow to Your Profile! section, click the here link as shown in Figure 4-8.

3. Copy the code under the slideshow you choose by selecting the entire code in the window underneath the slideshow style you want and then pressing CTRL+C.

4. In the light blue menu bar at the top of the page, click the Home link.

5. Click the Edit Profile link next to your profile photo. The Profile Edit – Interests & Personality page appears.

6. In the About Me box, paste the selection by clicking in the box and then pressing CTRL+V.

7. Click the Save All Changes button above the Headline box near the top of the screen.

8. Click the View My Profile link to the right of the Profile Edit – Interests & Personality page to view the slideshow that appears in the About Me section.

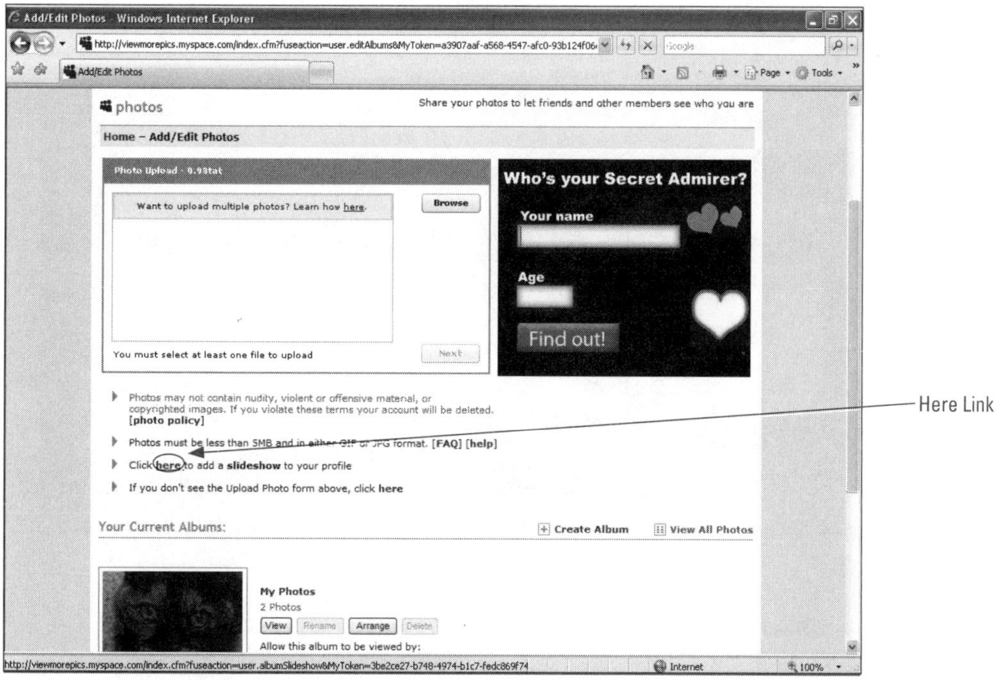

FIGURE 4-8 The here link

NOTE *Since you need to place your slideshow within the confines of the boxes, be sure the slideshow is within the box dimensions. If you have a slideshow with large dimensions, you may throw off the look of your profile. You may want to experiment to find out what the right dimensions should be for your slideshow.*

USE THIRD-PARTY SITES TO HOST EVEN MORE PICTURES

MySpace can upload a few photos at a time. However, it's tedious to upload a large number of photos to MySpace using the MySpace photo editor. Other companies have rushed in to fill the gap. One popular third-party site is Photobucket (http://www.photobucket.com). Figure 4-9 shows their home page.

You can share photos and videos on the Photobucket web site for free. However, you do have to sign up by clicking the Join Now button.

FIGURE 4-9 The Photobucket home page

Photobucket also has tools to let you link from your MySpace page to the Photobucket site.

If you want to see other alternatives, go to your favorite search engine site and search for "photo sharing." You'll find plenty of sites that let you upload and share images with others and integrate with your MySpace profile.

FAQS

How do I change my default picture? On the MySpace home page, click the Add/Edit Photos link next to your profile photo. Underneath the photo you want to be your default picture, click the Set to Default button. This will change your default picture to the one you want.

I'm trying to upload an image, and I am getting an error message. Why? Use this checklist to find out why MySpace is rejecting the image you've uploaded:

- The file must be in GIF or JPEG format with the file extensions .gif or .jpg, respectively.

- The filename must be short and include letters or numbers only—there must be no spaces or other characters.

- MySpace does not accept files that are larger than 1.2 megabytes (MB), or 1,200 kilobytes (KB).

- Ensure that the file is not corrupted. If you can open the file in your image editing program but you can't upload it to MySpace, try saving the file with a new name from within the image editing program and then try to upload the file again.

MySpace recommends that you download the free image editing program IrfanView from the Download.com Web site (http://www .download.com) to open, edit, and save image files if you don't have image editing software already installed on your computer. You can also find recommendations for free image editing programs on the About.com Web site for Windows (http://graphicssoft.about.com/cs/ imageediting/tp/freephotoedw.htm) and for the Mac (http://graphicssoft .about.com/cs/imageediting/tp/beginphotoedm.htm).

Chapter 5

Animate Your Profile with Flash and More!

Flash is the de facto standard for creating simple or sophisticated animated graphics on the web. Adobe coveted Flash so much that they bought Macromedia, who developed and owned Flash, just to get the product. Other image creation programs now let you create animated graphics in their programs and export them into Flash format.

MySpace understands that its users want to create animated graphics and text in their profiles. Therefore, MySpace includes built-in support for creating scrolling text marquees as well as support for animated GIF format graphic files that are also popular on the web. Though it's exciting to create all these animations, it's easy to get carried away. At the end of this chapter we'll talk about how much is too much when it comes to adding animations on your profile.

START SIMPLE: SCROLLING MARQUEES

A scrolling marquee is simply text that scrolls across the screen when a MySpace user visits your profile. MySpace includes the built-in `marquee` style tag so you can quickly add a marquee. This tag also allows you to add modifiers including a limit on how often the marquee should scroll, the scrolling behavior, and the scrolling direction.

Here's how you can create a scrolling marquee:

1. On the MySpace home page, click the Edit Profile link to the right of your profile photo. The Profile Edit – Interests & Personality page appears.

2. In the About Me box, type the following code:

```
<marquee>
There are three things you need to know about me: I work
hard. I play hard. I sleep hard.
</marquee>
```

3. Click the Save All Changes button above the Headline box.

4. Click the View Your Profile link to the right of the Profile Edit – Interests & Personality title. The marquee appears in the About Me section, as shown in Figure 5-1.

FIGURE 5-1 The marquee in the About Me section

Your marquee will continue to scroll unless you tell it to stop using the marquee style loop modifier. The marquee scrolls by default. Using the behavior modifier, you can have the marquee slide to the edge of the screen and then stop by adding the slide value, or have the marquee scroll from left to right and back again with the alternate value. By default, the marquee scrolls from right to left. If you want the marquee to scroll from left to right, add the direction argument.

So what does all this mean? Let me give you an example:

```
<marquee loop="5" behavior="alternate" scroll="right">
There are three things you need to know about me: I work
hard. I play hard. I sleep hard.
</marquee>
```

In this example, the text scrolls from left to right based on the modifier scroll="right". Once the text reaches the right side of the screen, it will scroll back to the left based on the modifier `behavior="alternate"`. The marquee will go from left to right and back again five times before the marquee stops based on the modifier `loop="5"`.

INSERT ANIMATED GIFS INTO YOUR PROFILE

The GIF format allows you to save multiple images in one GIF file and include control data in the file so you can have the GIF file show multiple graphics in sequence to give the file the appearance that it's animated. (If you're curious, GIF stands for Graphic Interchange Format, which is a standard image file format, and the G in GIF is soft, so it's pronounced like Jif, the peanut butter brand.) You can create animated GIF files in any image creation and editing program that supports the creation of animated GIF files.

Before you insert an animated GIF file, you need to upload the GIF file to a web server so MySpace can access the file all the time. You can put the file on your web server or, if you don't have one, you can post the site on free photo- and video-sharing web sites like Photobucket, as we talked about in Chapter 4. There are plenty of web sites that have animated GIF files, so you can link to them as well by typing the code into the appropriate box in the Profile Edit – Interests & Personality page when you edit your profile.

In the following example, I'm going to add a link to an animated GIF file of a globe on my company's Web site. This isn't just a static globe—it spins so you can see all the continents of our little blue planet. I downloaded this globe for free from the Animations Galore Web site (http://www.animations-galore.com). Type the following in the Profile Edit – Interests & Personality page:

```
<a href="http://www.butow.net">
<img src="http://www.butow.net/spinning.gif" border="0">
</a>
```

Click the Preview Section button to see the globe in action, as shown in Figure 5-2!

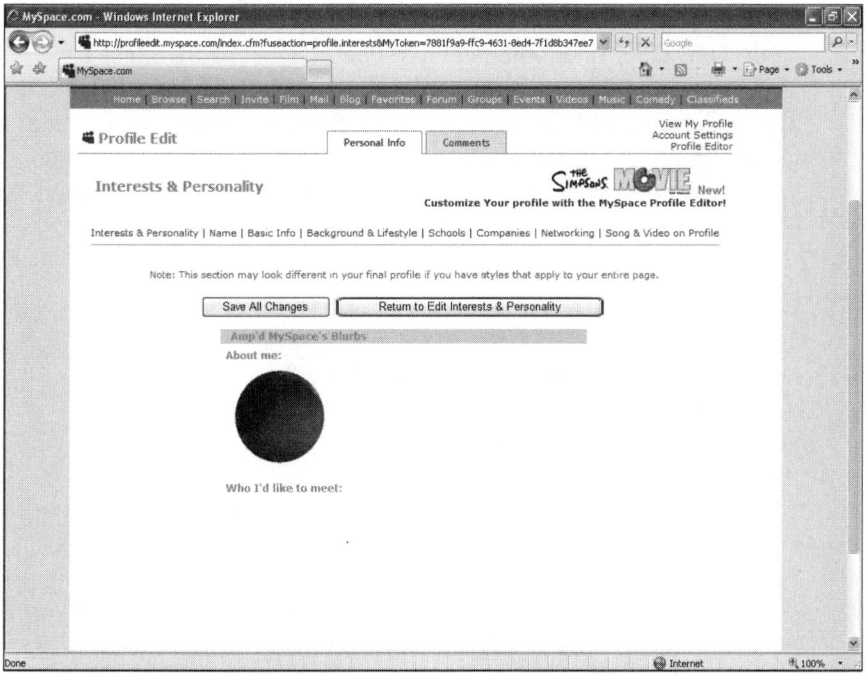

FIGURE 5-2 Globe in action

> TIP
>
> *There are plenty of free animated GIF creation programs available on the web. Just type **create animated GIF** into your favorite search engine site and you'll see a list of programs you can download and try.*

ADD FLASH MOVIES AND GRAPHICS TO YOUR PROFILE

Animated GIF files only provide rudimentary animated graphics. If you really want to get involved with animation, you need to purchase Adobe's Flash software. Flash lets you create a number of different animations either in sequence or simultaneously along a timeline. You can also open a different animation in response to an event (such as clicking on a button). And if you really want to get control over what Flash does, you can program in ActionScript, the Flash programming language.

Before you add a Flash movie, you need to upload the file to your web server or another site like Photobucket so MySpace can access the movie all the time. After you have uploaded the Flash file, open the Profile Edit – Interests & Personality page. You'll add the information about the Flash file (which is in .swf format) by typing the following code into the About Me box in the Profile Edit – Interests & Personality page:

```
<embed allowScriptAccess="never" src="http://
www.yourserver.com/flashmovie.swf" quality=high
pluginspage="http://www.macromedia.com/shockwave/
download/index.cgi?P1_Prod_Version=ShockwaveFlash"
type="application/x-shockwave-flash" width="200"
height="200">
</embed>
```

Replace the text *http://www.yourserver.com/flashmovie.swf* with the server path and the Flash filename.

TIP

So where do you find software to create your own Flash movies if you don't want to spend hundreds of dollars on Flash? You can view a list of downloadable Flash tools on the Download.com web site at http:// www.download.com/Flash-Design-Tools/3150-6676_4-0.html.

HOW MUCH IS TOO MUCH?

There are plenty of examples of bad MySpace layouts on the web. Go to the following MySpace profile: http://www.myspace.com/ jimmbay1. Don't worry. I'll wait.

Did your eyes cross at some point from all the animations as you scrolled down the profile page? This page was shown as an example of bad MySpace design on the Worst of MySpace site (http://www .worstofmyspace.com), and it is a good example of someone going overboard because they really like animations. Of course, you probably didn't like all the distractions and didn't know what to look at first.

Also take into account that animations and glitter on a MySpace site are trendy, and that may not be what you want if you want to stand out from the crowd. If you look like everyone else, you may not look interesting to others and they may not visit your site again, let alone be your friend.

FAQS

So what are the good points to create a good-looking profile? There are three features you should always keep in mind:

- Content is the jewel in the crown that is your profile. Make sure that your text is easy to read. If your text is too dark and you make your visitors highlight text to read it, your visitors won't come back.

- Be sure you have colors that contrast well. If you use colors that don't work well together, such as green text on a red background, people won't come back to your profile.

- If you want to use a customized layout you find on one of many MySpace layout web sites, be choosy. Don't accept the first flashy layout you find. Take your time and find a layout that reflects your interests and your style instead of the latest trends. After all, your profile is all about you.

Part II
Expanding Your MySpace Presence

Chapter 6

Make Your Profile Multimedia Ready!

In the last chapter you learned how to create animated graphics. Now it's time to learn how to add multimedia files. After all, the World Wide Web is a multimedia environment, and MySpace provides easy ways to show off videos of yourself or a favorite video clip you want to share. You can also add your own audio files if there's a particular song you think captures who you are especially well.

In this chapter you'll learn how to add audio files, songs, and video clips using MySpace's built-in tools. Then you'll learn how to configure your profile for automatic audio or video playback so your audio or video file will open immediately when another MySpace user visits your profile.

ADD AUDIO FILES TO YOUR PROFILE

You may want to add an audio file of your favorite song or even an audio recording of yourself and/or others. There are many types of audio file formats available. If you are creating your audio file, you will have to select the format that is best for you when you create your audio file and then save it in a specific format. If you find an audio file you like, you may be asked to select a format. Which format do you need? The three most popular formats include:

- WAV, which is Microsoft's audio file format. This format is widely used with the Windows operating system and the audio quality is quite good, but the audio files themselves can be quite large.

- MP3, which has decent sound quality and is easier to transmit on the web because the MP3 file size is far smaller than WAV format.

- WMA, which is the Windows Media Audio format, also has decent sound quality and is meant to be the successor to the WAV format and a competitor to the MP3 format, but this format has been slow to catch on. The size of a WMA file is even smaller than an MP3 file.

It's easy to embed an audio file in your profile: Just add a little code when you edit your profile. Here's how:

1. Upload the audio file you want to use onto your own web server or another file-sharing site such as LimeWire (http://www.limewire.com).

2. In the MySpace home page, click the Edit Profile link to the right of your profile photo. The Profile Edit – Interests & Personality page appears.

3. In the About Me box, type the following code to embed your audio file:

```
<embed allowScriptAccess="never" src="http://www.
example.com/sample.wav" height="60" width="145"
autostart="true" loop="false">
<noembed>
<bgsound src="http://www.example.com/sample.wav"
loop="false"> </noembed>
</embed>
```

4. Replace the http://www.example.com/sample.wav link with the web site, path information, and filename for your audio file.

5. Listen to the audio file in preview mode by clicking the Preview Profile button.

A small control area appears in your profile so you can control the audio playback.

NOTE *You may want to add the HTML tag <p> after this code to separate your audio file control area from the rest of the content in your About Me section.*

ADD SONGS TO YOUR PROFILE

MySpace is a great place to hear songs that you may not find in your local music store (or the music section of a store that sells more than

FIGURE 6-1 The Music page

just music). MySpace also makes it easy for you to upload songs stored on MySpace into your profile.

1. In the MySpace home page, click the Music link in the menu bar. The Music page appears, as shown in Figure 6-1.

2. Search for artists from the many different sections on the page. You'll have to scroll down the page to see all the search options available. If you know the band or artist you're looking for, type the band or artist name (or even part of the name if you're not sure what the full name is) in the Keyword box within the Search Artists area.

3. In the artist's page, click the Add link under the title of the song you want to add, as shown in Figure 6-2.

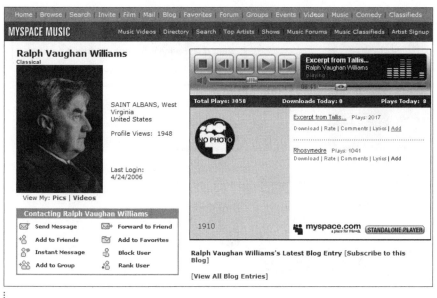

FIGURE 6-2 Click the Add link.

4. MySpace asks you if you want to add this song to your profile, as shown in Figure 6-3. Click the Add Song To Profile button. MySpace reports that the song has been added to your profile.

5. In the menu bar, click the Home link. The MySpace home page appears.

6. Under your profile picture, click the Profile link. You can view your profile and view the audio playback module underneath the Contact module, as shown in Figure 6-4.

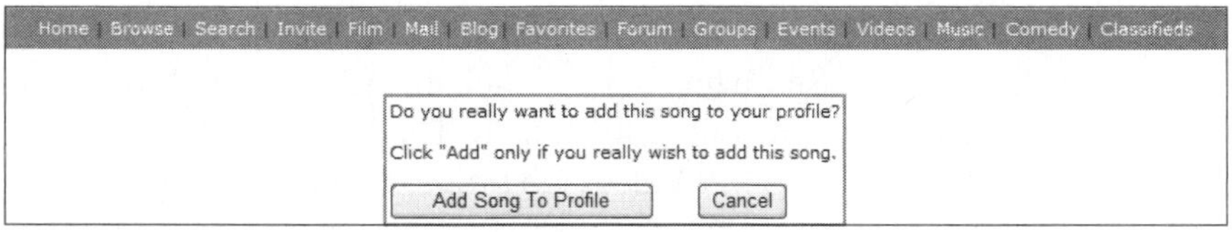

FIGURE 6-3 Click the Add Song To Profile button.

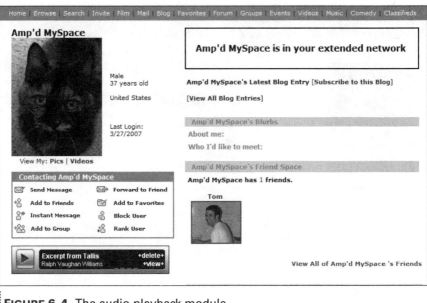

FIGURE 6-4 The audio playback module

UPLOAD VIDEO CLIPS TO YOUR PROFILE TO SHARE

Have you come across a video clip from MySpace or another source on the Internet? Or perhaps you want to record a video of you or your friends that you think helps visitors understand you and who you are (hopefully you don't act too goofy). It's easy to upload video clips to MySpace and then put a copy of the video code into your profile so all your visitors can see the video clip you're so proud of. Here's how:

1. In the MySpace home page, click the Add/Change Videos link to the right of your profile photo. The MySpacetv page appears with the My Videos tab active, as shown in Figure 6-5.

2. Click the Upload Videos link. The Upload Video page appears, as shown in Figure 6-6.

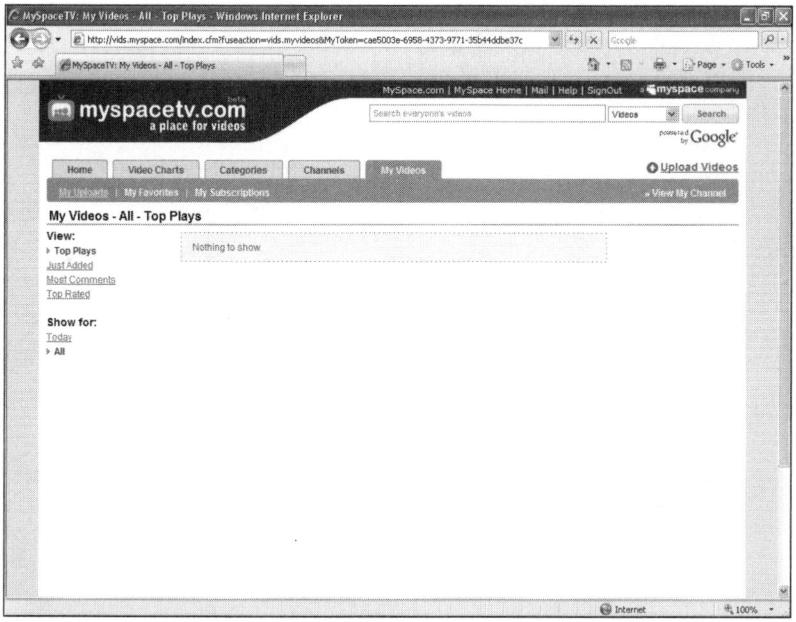

FIGURE 6-5 The My Videos page

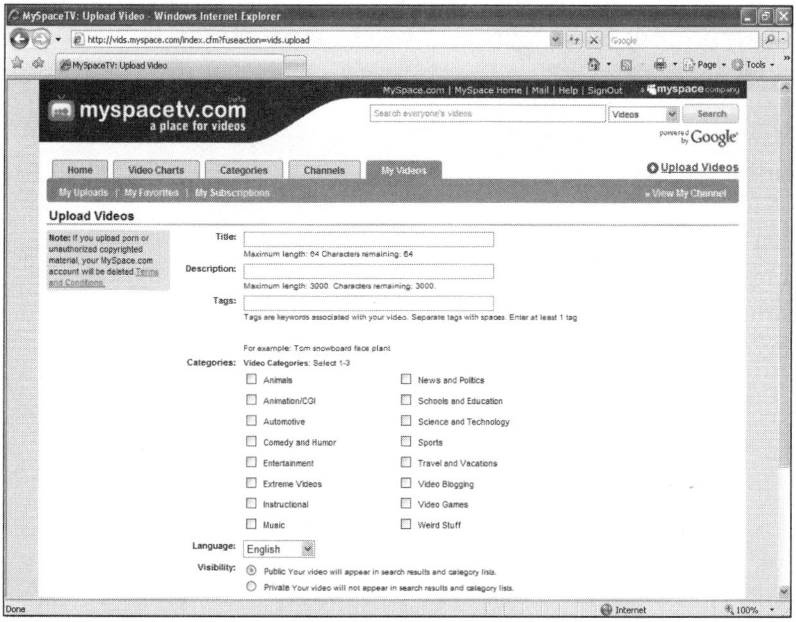

FIGURE 6-6 The Upload Videos page

3. Type the video title, description, and tags in the Title, Description, and Tags boxes, respectively. You have to type something in each of these three boxes if you want to upload your video.

4. Select one to three check boxes in the Categories section that describe your video. You must select at least one check box.

5. If you want to set the visibility of your video to private, click the Private radio button. Otherwise, leave the default Public radio button selected so everyone can see your video.

6. Select the I Agree to the MySpace Terms and Conditions check box. You can't upload your video without selecting this check box. If you want to read the conditions, click the Terms and Conditions link.

7. Click the Continue button. The Step 2 page appears, as shown in Figure 6-7.

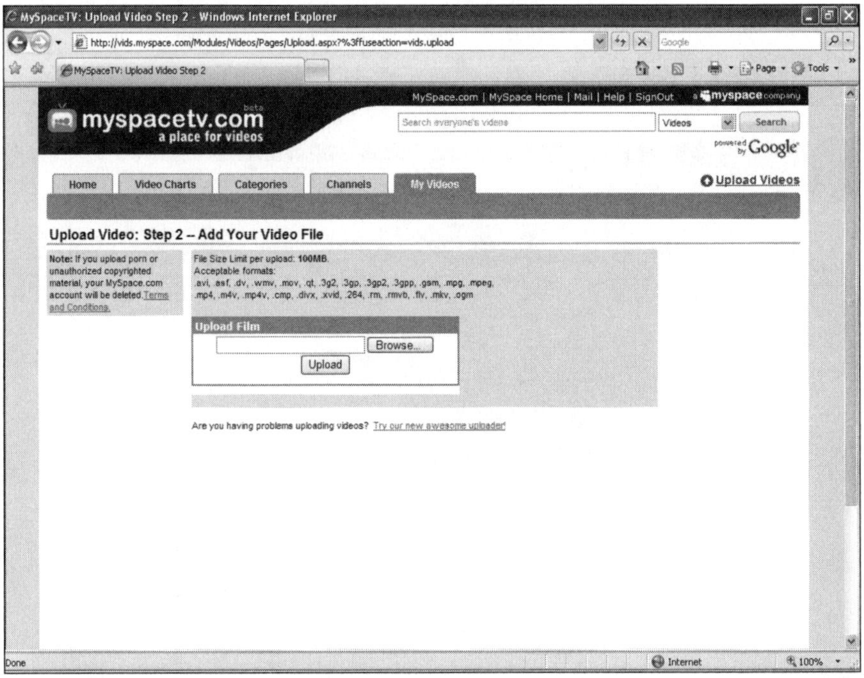

FIGURE 6-7 The Step 2 page

8. In the Upload Film area, click the Browse button to find the video. The Choose File dialog box appears so you can navigate to the folder that contains the video file.

9. When you navigate to the selected file, click the Open button. The file path and name appear in the Upload Film box.

10. Click the Upload button. MySpace uploads the video and displays your uploaded video in the My Videos tab.

NOTE *There may be a delay after uploading the video while MySpace processes the file.*

11. Click the video to play it. The video playback page appears, as shown in Figure 6-8.

12. Scroll down the page to view the Video Code box, as shown in Figure 6-9.

FIGURE 6-8 The video playback page

FIGURE 6-9 The Video Code box

13. Double-click on the Video Code box to select all the code in the box.

14. Press CTRL+C to copy the code.

15. In the menu bar, click the Home link.

16. In the MySpace home page, click the Edit Profile link to the right of the profile picture.

17. In the Profile Edit – Interests & Personality page, click on the box for the module in which you want to display the video. I'll choose the About Me box.

18. Press CTRL+V to paste the video code into the About Me box.

19. Click the Save All Changes button.

20. Click the Preview Profile button below the About Me box to view your video in your profile, as shown in Figure 6-10.

FIGURE 6-10 The video in your profile

CONFIGURE YOUR PROFILE FOR AUTOMATIC AUDIO PLAYBACK

When you embed the MySpace audio player on your site, it's easy to configure your profile to play automatically when the visitor accesses your site. Here's how you configure audio playback in your profile:

1. In the MySpace home page, click Edit Profile.

2. Click the Account Settings link to the right of the Profile Edit – Interests & Personality heading. The Change Account Settings page appears, as shown in Figure 6-11.

3. In the My Account Settings table, click the Change Settings link in the Music Settings row. The Music Settings page appears, as shown in Figure 6-12.

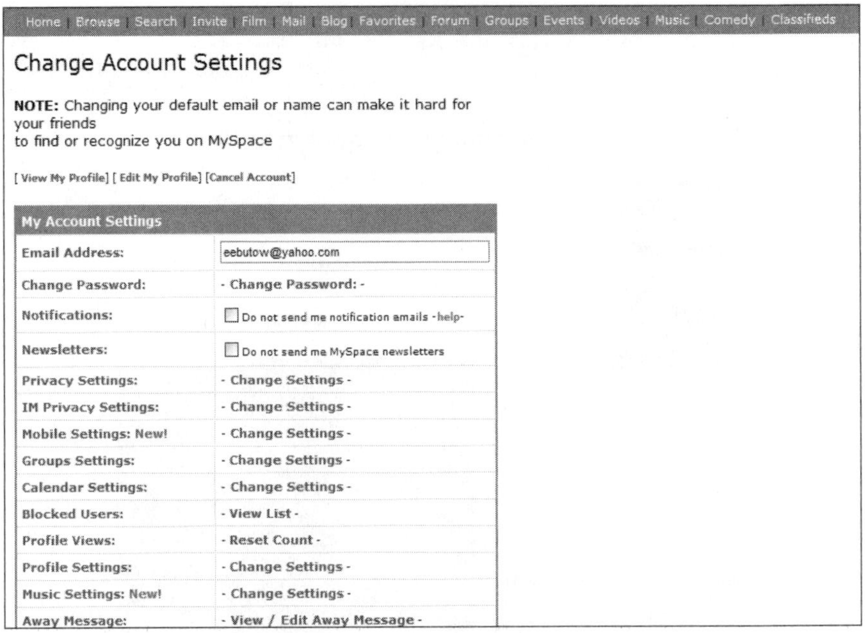

FIGURE 6-11 The Change Account Settings page

FIGURE 6-12 The Music Settings page

4. Clear the Disable My Player from Automatically Starting check box.

5. Click the Change Settings button. The screen displays the message "Your Music Settings have been updated," and you can click either the Home link or the Return to Account Settings link.

Now your audio will start automatically when another MySpace user visits your profile.

FAQS

How big can my videos be and what formats are supported? When you open the Step 2 page, there is information at the top of the page that tells you the maximum file size limit (100MB) and the video file extensions MySpace supports. Of course, if you're hosting the video on another site, you don't need to worry about the file size limit because you're not hosting your video on MySpace.

So if I have my video stored on a web server, can I open the file on that web server when I upload a video? Yes. In the Upload Film area, type the web address and then the name of the file in the box. For example, type **http://www.myserver.com/ filename.avi**. Replace this dummy web site address and video name with the actual address and filename.

How big an audio file can I upload to MySpace? You should not have an audio file that is larger than 10MB.

Chapter 7

Finding Third-Party Templates and Plug-Ins

MySpace has become such a popular place for people to get together online that Business Week magazine in its July 25, 2006 issue referred to third-party companies and web sites that have sprouted to serve the needs of MySpace users as the "MySpace ecosystem." There are many different sites available for finding third-party templates and plug-ins—all you have to do is type **MySpace templates** or **MySpace plug-ins** into a search engine to get hundreds of thousands of sites.

Two of the most popular types of plug-ins and web sites are profile editors and portfolios so you can share items like photos. The information you share could also mean that other MySpace users will add your profile to their favorites list, and you may add profiles you like to your favorites list. So we'll talk about all three in this chapter.

NOTE *Just before this book went to press, MySpace debuted the beta version of the MySpace Profile Editor, which you can access from your home page. The Profile Editor interface allows you to customize your profile by applying one of the MySpace themes, or you can customize your profile background, modules, images, text, and/or links.*

WHAT ARE PROFILE EDITORS?

MySpace profile editors are available on various web sites. These editors allow you to customize the look and feel of your MySpace profile through an interface that makes it easier to add features to your profile page. You learned how to edit your own profile starting with Chapter 2, but if you're not looking to show off your HTML and CSS programming skills in your profile, you may want to use a profile editor instead.

Most profile editors have differences in their approaches to the interface they use. Some editors are more text oriented—you type in or select information (like a color) in several fields, and then you can copy and paste the text directly into your MySpace profile page. Others have premade profile layouts that you can customize.

SOME OF THE MORE POPULAR EDITORS

Here are some of the more popular editors based on a Google search of the best MySpace editing sites. These three sites also show the differences in the approaches of different editors.

FIGURE 7-1 The MySpace Toolbox page

MySpace Toolbox

The MySpace Editor on the MySpace Toolbox page is pretty straightforward (see Figure 7-1). You'll find the editor at http://www.myspacetoolbox.com/myspace-editor.php. You can type the information into the Text, Table, and Scrollbar areas, or you can also select from different colors and styles by clicking various buttons and selecting options from drop-down lists. After you make your changes, click the Update Code! button at the bottom of the screen. The updated code appears below the button so you can copy it and paste the code into your MySpace profile.

Killerkiwi.Net

The killerkiwi.net page at http://www.killerkiwi.net/ (see Figure 7-2) contains a number of tools for creating your profile from scratch, including layout generators and the Kiwi Profile Editor.

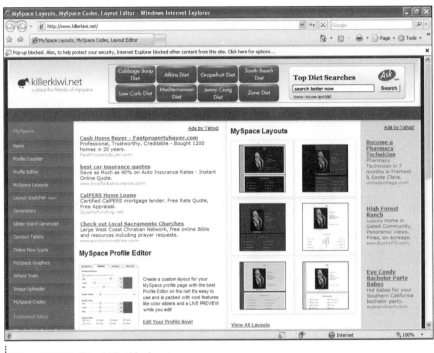

FIGURE 7-2 The killerkiwi.net page

When you click the View All Layouts link underneath the six sample layouts, a new browser window (or tab if you're using a browser that has tabbed windows) shows you the various MySpace layout samples, as shown in Figure 7-3.

You can click the layout sample you like and then copy the code on the page so you can paste the code directly into your MySpace profile. If you prefer to change your own profile, you can switch to the killerkiwi.net site and click the Edit Your Profile Now! link. The Kiwi Profile Editor window appears, as shown in Figure 7-4.

In this window you can click the tabs at the top of the profile to make changes to your profile. Kiwi Profile Editor makes it much easier to create a profile by using buttons and slider bars for selecting options, colors, and more. When you're finished changing your profile, you can click the Generate Layout button at the bottom right-hand corner of the sample profile. After you click the button, the Kiwi Profile Editor displays the code so you can copy and paste it into your MySpace profile.

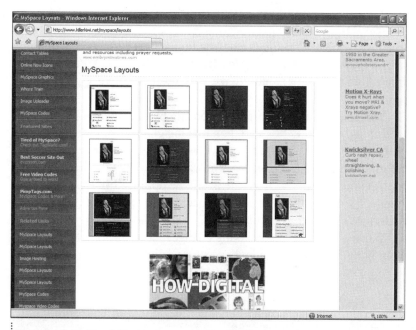

FIGURE 7-3 The killerkiwi.net sample MySpace layouts

FIGURE 7-4 The Kiwi Profile Editor

EasyMySpace

The EasyMySpace Profile Editor (see Figure 7-5) is something of a hybrid between what you find in MySpace Toolbox and killerkiwi.net. You'll find this editor at http://www.easymyspace.com/myspace_editor. html.

You can make changes to your profile by clicking the light blue tabs above the white box and then making changes to the appropriate parts of the profile. If you want to make changes, you can type the information into the box and/or click a gray box with the arrow next to it so you can choose from the available options. For example, Figure 7-6 shows the Text Styles tab and the available text fonts underneath the text font button.

When you're finished making changes, you can click the Preview Your New Profile link, and when you're satisfied with the changes,

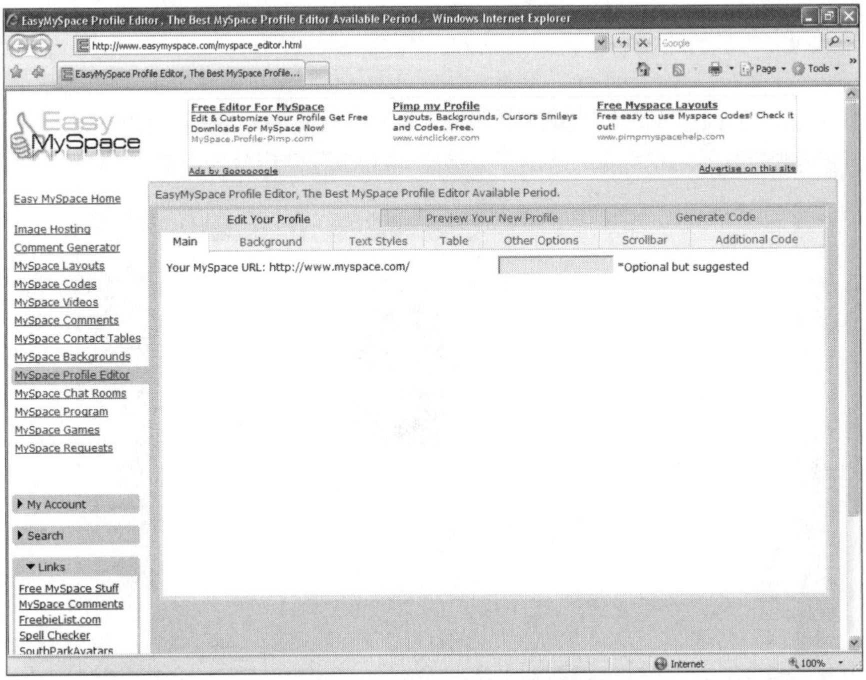

FIGURE 7-5 The EasyMySpace Profile Editor page

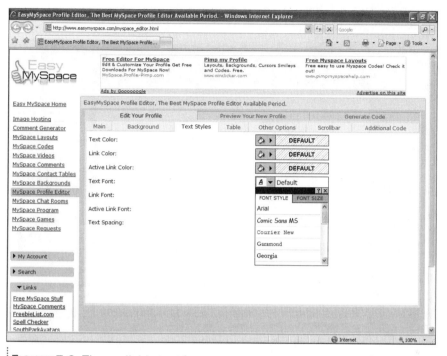

FIGURE 7-6 The available text fonts

you can click the Generate Code link to copy and paste the generated code into your MySpace profile.

SWAP PORTFOLIOS AND SHARE ITEMS

If you have a number of photos you want to share and you want to do so in a slideshow format, there are many options available. There are shareware programs with free portfolio programs based on Flash that you can post onto your MySpace page, or you can use outside sites as well. Here are some suggestions to get you started.

Flash Photo Portfolio Sites

The Shareware Connection site at http://www.sharewareconnection .com/titles/flash-photo-portfolio.htm (see Figure 7-7) is a good place

FIGURE 7-7 The Shareware Connection site

to start looking for free and shareware photo portfolio programs based on Flash. Once you create a Flash photo portfolio, you can place the Flash photo in your web site just as we talked about in Chapter 5.

Flash Slide Show Maker

The top program on the Shareware Connection site for creating Flash slideshows (and it gets five stars, so it doesn't get better than that) is AnvSoft's Flash Slide Show Maker, which you'll find at http://flash.dvd-photo-slideshow.com/flash_photo_gallary/create_portfolio_flash.php. AnvSoft offers a number of options, as you'll see when you scroll down the page shown in Figure 7-8, including the ability to export the slideshow to the Flash movie format. The only downside is that a message stating that the slideshow was produced by Flash Slide Show Maker will appear at the end of your slideshow.

FIGURE 7-8 The AnvSoft Flash Slide Show Maker web site

If you want this message to go away, you need to pay $29.95 for the professional version.

Slideroll

If you prefer to have a slideshow hosted on a web site, a popular site is Slideroll (http://www.slideroll.com/index.php). This site creates different slideshows in Flash format, but you don't have to know Flash to create your photos—Slideroll makes it easy for you to drag and drop photos into the system, create your slideshow, and then make it publicly available for viewing so you can link to your slideshow from your MySpace profile. Figure 7-9 shows the Slideroll home page. You can join Slideroll for free, but there are limits to what you can do, such as the number of photos you can upload. If you want more capabilities, you can upgrade to Slideroll's monthly payment plan of $3.75 per month.

FIGURE 7-9 The Slideroll web site

CHECK OUT MYSPACE FAVORITES

As you browse other MySpace profiles, which you may have already done, you can bookmark other MySpace profiles on your Favorites list if you really like them so you can visit those profiles often. If other MySpace users like your profile they'll bookmark you in their Favorites list, too.

For now, though, let's see how you add another profile to your Favorites list. Start by browsing for the profile you want to find. Click the Browse link in the menu bar. The Browse Users page appears, as shown in Figure 7-10.

Your default browse criteria appear at the top of the page. As you scroll down, you'll see the first page of MySpace profiles that match your criteria. Click on one of the profiles.

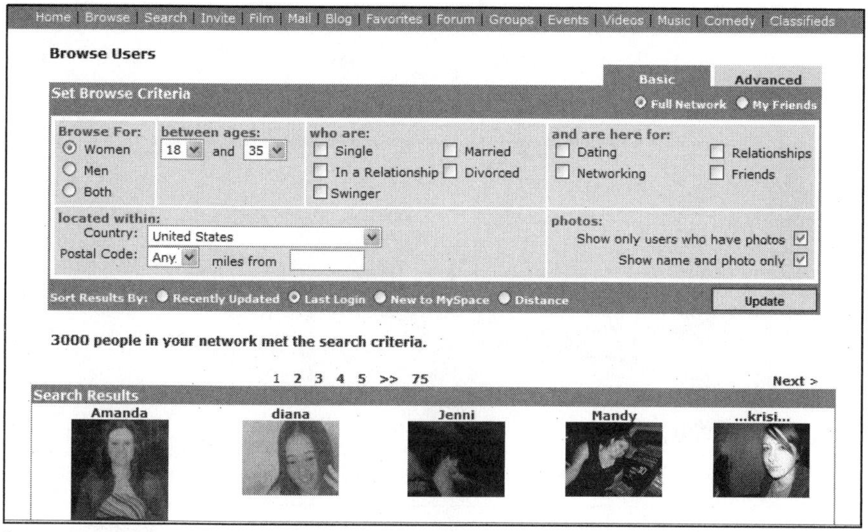

FIGURE 7-10 The Browse Users page

In the profile's Contacting area, click the Add to Favorites link. Note that if the user has customized their MySpace profiles, this link may say something like "Add me to your favorites" or something similar. After you click the link, a screen appears asking you if you want to add the favorite, as shown in Figure 7-11. Click the Add to Favorites button.

After you add the favorite, the Favorites page appears so you can view your latest favorite as well as other favorites in the list, as shown in Figure 7-12.

FIGURE 7-11 Click the Add to Favorite button.

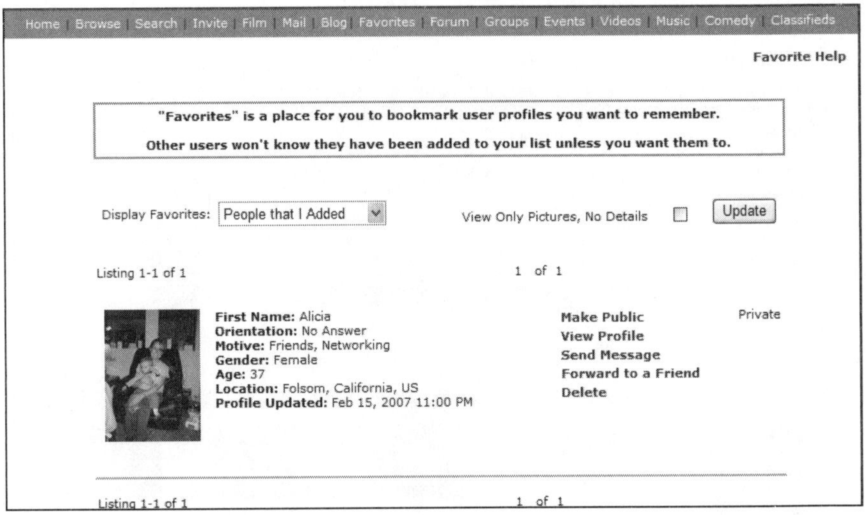

FIGURE 7-12 Your list of favorites

Other MySpace users won't know they have been added to your list unless you want them to know. You can send the favorite a message by clicking the Send Message link. You'll learn more about sending messages in Chapter 10.

Chapter 8

Blogging

Blogging is fun. A blog, which is short for "web log," is an online journal that allows other MySpace members to read more about what's going on in your life, hones your writing skills, and makes you and your profile more interesting. And the more interesting you are, the more popular you become on MySpace.

It's easy to create a blog in MySpace, but how do you know what to talk about? And if you'd rather not write, but instead add podcasts and video to your blog, you can do that, too. You may also want to link to other MySpace user blogs that you enjoy, and perhaps get those users to return the favor. How do you do all this? Read on....

LEARN BY SUBSCRIBING TO OTHER BLOGS

Unless you have previous experience with blogging, you should learn about what's interesting about other blogs before you write one of your own. People want to read interesting things in your blog, and if it's not interesting (such as what you had for dinner tonight), very few people will read it and you'll be wasting your time.

You'll also waste time if you keep going to different profiles to read the same blogs because MySpace includes a nice feature for subscribing to a blog once you find it. After you subscribe, MySpace will send you the latest posts from your favorite blogs so you don't miss anything. Here's how to subscribe to a blog:

1. In your MySpace home page (after you log in), click the Blogs link in the menu bar. The Blog Control Center page appears, as shown in Figure 8-1.

2. Click the View Most Popular Blogs link. The Most Popular Blog Posts page appears, as shown in Figure 8-2.

3. Click the blog picture or the posting title in the list. The blog appears in a new page, as shown in Figure 8-3. Note that if the blog is set to private, then the user must add you as a friend so you can see his or her blog.

4. Click the Subscribe link above the latest blog entry at the upper-right area of the page. The Confirm Subscribe to Blog page appears, as shown in Figure 8-4. Click the Subscribe button to subscribe to the blog.

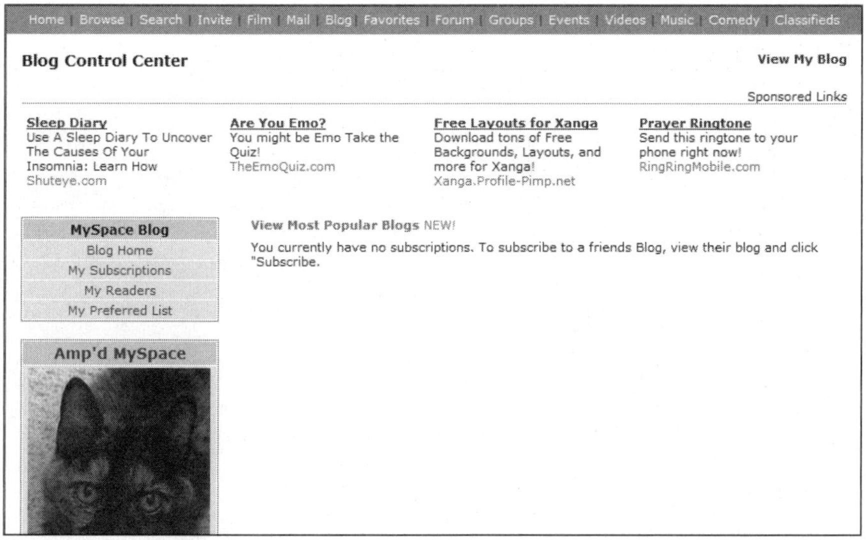

Home | Browse | Search | Invite | Film | Mail | Blog | Favorites | Forum | Groups | Events | Videos | Music | Comedy | Classifieds

Blog Control Center

View My Blog

Sponsored Links

Sleep Diary
Use A Sleep Diary To Uncover The Causes Of Your Insomnia: Learn How
Shuteye.com

Are You Emo?
You might be Emo Take the Quiz!
TheEmoQuiz.com

Free Layouts for Xanga
Download tons of Free Backgrounds, Layouts, and more for Xanga!
Xanga.Profile-Pimp.net

Prayer Ringtone
Send this ringtone to your phone right now!
RingRingMobile.com

MySpace Blog
Blog Home
My Subscriptions
My Readers
My Preferred List

View Most Popular Blogs NEW!

You currently have no subscriptions. To subscribe to a friends Blog, view their blog and click "Subscribe."

Amp'd MySpace

FIGURE 8-1 The Blog Control Center page

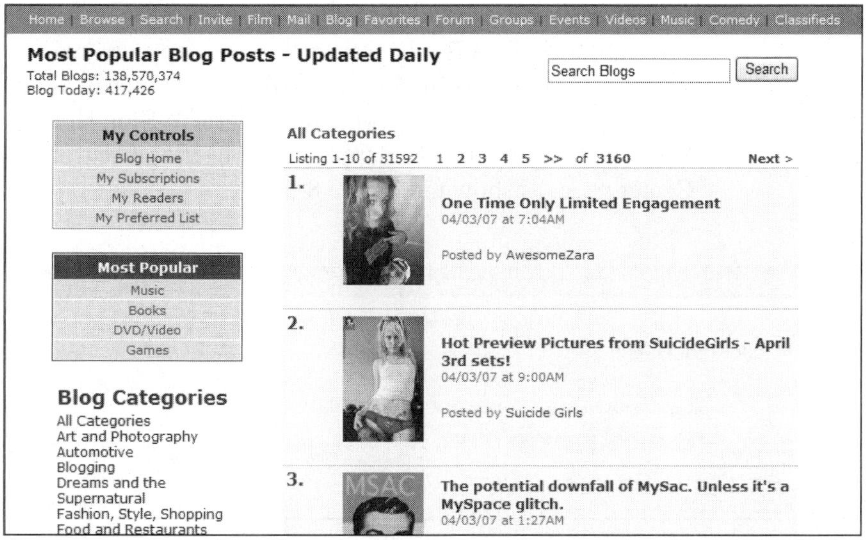

Home | Browse | Search | Invite | Film | Mail | Blog | Favorites | Forum | Groups | Events | Videos | Music | Comedy | Classifieds

Most Popular Blog Posts - Updated Daily
Total Blogs: 138,570,374
Blog Today: 417,426

Search Blogs   [Search]

My Controls
Blog Home
My Subscriptions
My Readers
My Preferred List

Most Popular
Music
Books
DVD/Video
Games

Blog Categories
All Categories
Art and Photography
Automotive
Blogging
Dreams and the Supernatural
Fashion, Style, Shopping
Food and Restaurants

All Categories

Listing 1-10 of 31592   1 2 3 4 5 >> of 3160   Next >

1.
One Time Only Limited Engagement
04/03/07 at 7:04AM

Posted by AwesomeZara

2.
Hot Preview Pictures from SuicideGirls - April 3rd sets!
04/03/07 at 9:00AM

Posted by Suicide Girls

3.
The potential downfall of MySac. Unless it's a MySpace glitch.
04/03/07 at 1:27AM

FIGURE 8-2 The Most Popular Blog Posts page

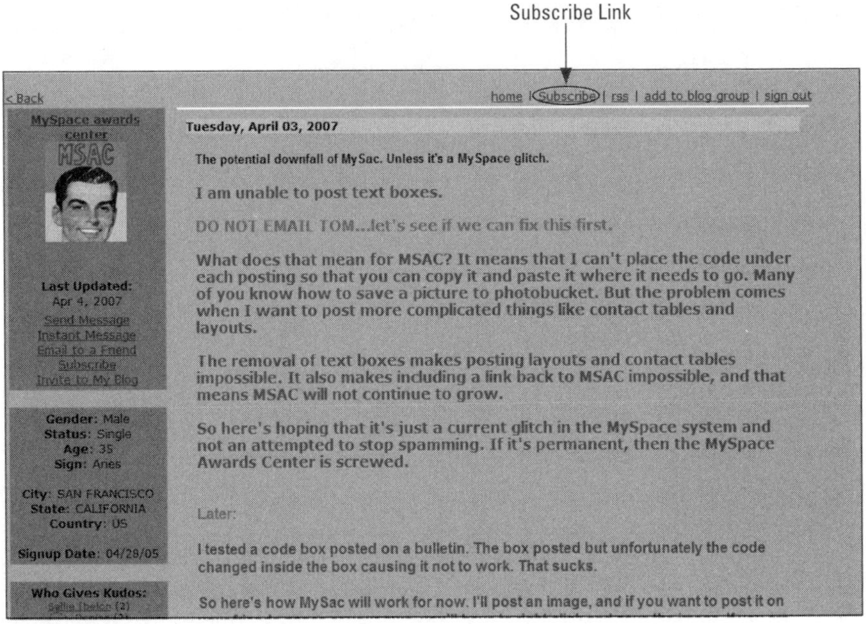

Subscribe Link

FIGURE 8-3 The blog posting

5. The Subscribe To A Blog confirmation page appears and informs you that you are now subscribed, and you can view the blog information by clicking the Return To Blog Home link. The latest blog entries appear on your Blog Control Center page, as shown in Figure 8-5.

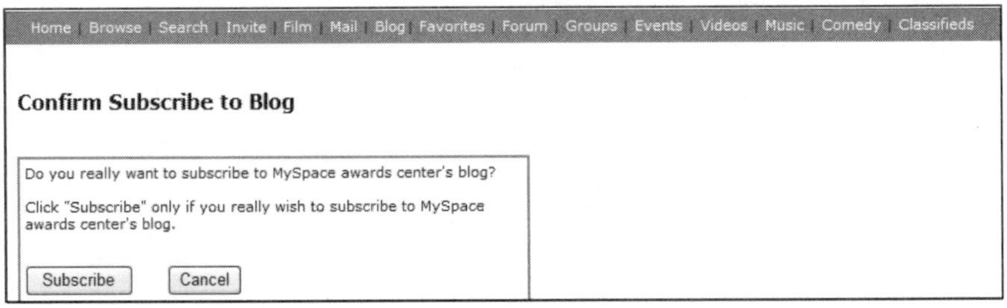

FIGURE 8-4 Click the Subscribe button.

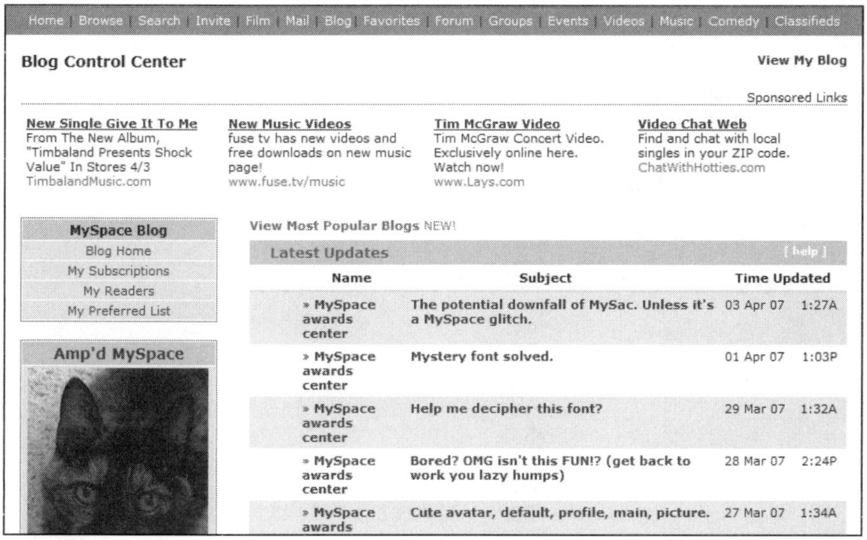

FIGURE 8-5 The Blog Control Center page with your subscribed blog entries

Whenever you want to see if there are any new blog posts, you can simply click Blog in the menu bar and view the new posts in the Blog Control Center. MySpace will also send you an e-mail every time a new posting appears on the blog.

CUSTOMIZE AND FORMAT YOUR BLOG

Now that you've had a chance to see what blogs others find interesting, MySpace makes it easy for you to customize your blog so it looks the way you want. Here's how you do it:

1. Click the Blog link in the menubar. You can also click the Manage Blog link to the right of your profile picture. The Blog Control Center page appears.

2. Scroll down the page until you see the Customize Blog link in the My Controls area, as shown in Figure 8-6.

3. Click the Customize Blog link. The Customize My Blog page appears, as shown in Figure 8-7.

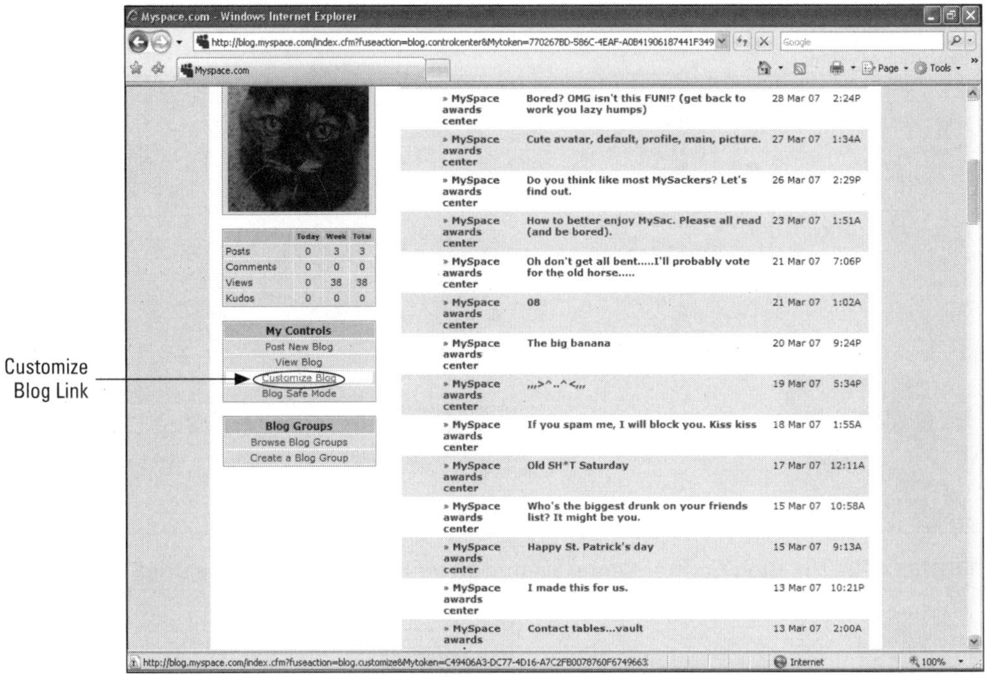

Customize
Blog Link

FIGURE 8-6 The Customize Blog link

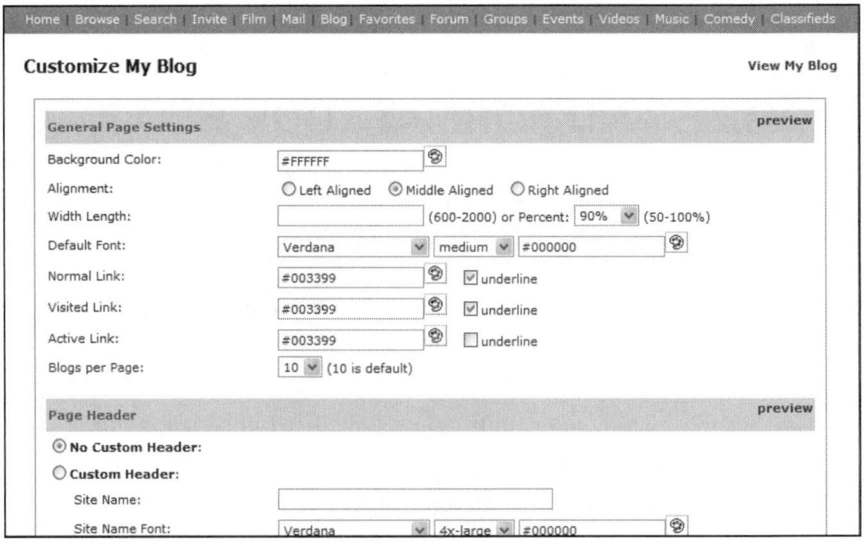

FIGURE 8-7 The Customize My Blog page

As you scroll down the page you'll see that there is a lot you can change—you can add information in seven different sections, from general page settings to adding CSS code. There's a lot here, so take a deep breath and we'll talk about how to lay out your blog to your specifications.

LAY OUT YOUR BLOG

We'll start with the section at the top: the general blog page settings, including fonts, colors, and the appearance of links.

1. Change the background color by typing the hexadecimal representation of the background color in the Background Color box, which is preceded by a pound sign (#). If you're not sure about the hexadecimal color to type in, you can refer to Appendix B or you can click the palette button to the right of the Background Color box, click on one of the colors in the palette window, shown in Figure 8-8, and then click the OK button.

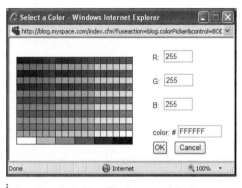

FIGURE 8-8 The Background Color palette window

2. For Alignment, click the button to tell MySpace how you want the blog aligned on the web page. The default is to have the blog aligned in the middle, or "centered."

3. Type the width of the blog box in pixels in the Width Length box. The range is from 600 pixels to 2000 pixels. If you'd rather not set a size but instead tell MySpace to resize the blog box to a percentage of the browser window's width, select the percentage from the Percent drop-down list. The default value is 90 percent of the browser window's width.

4. For the Default Font, select the font name and size from the left and right drop-down lists, respectively (that is, the lists that say "Verdana" and "medium"). Then you can type the six-digit hexadecimal font color in the box or select the font color by clicking the palette button to the right of the box.

5. Type the six-digit hexadecimal colors for the normal link, the visited link, and the active link in the Normal Link, Visited Link, and Active Link boxes. With each box you can click the palette button to the right of the box to select the color just as you did with the font and background colors. If you want the links to be underlined, select the Underline check box (or keep the box selected).

6. Select the number of blog entries that will appear on your blog page in the Blogs per Page drop-down list. The default number is 10, but you can have as few as 1 or as many as 15 blog entries on your page.

7. Preview your changes by clicking the preview link at the right side of the General Page Settings bar.

Now that you've changed the general page settings, it's time to change the rest of the settings in your blogs. Here we go.

Page Header

Your blog header appears at the top of your blog page and helps establish your blog's identity. By default, MySpace doesn't add a blog header. Here's how you add the page header:

1. Click the Custom Header radio button in the Page Header area, as shown in Figure 8-9.

2. Type the site name (which is the title of your blog) in the Site Name box.

3. For the Site Name Font, select the font name and size from the left and right drop-down lists, respectively (that is, the lists that say "Verdana" and "4x-large"). Then you can type the six-digit hexadecimal font color in the box or select the font color by clicking the palette button to the right of the box.

4. Type the blog tagline in the Tagline box. The tagline appears in a light blue box at the top of the blog page and should give your readers some idea of what your blog is all about.

5. For the Tagline Font, select the font name and size from the left and right drop-down lists, respectively (that is, the lists

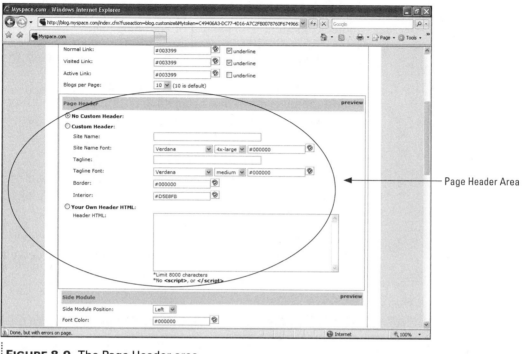

Page Header Area

FIGURE 8-9 The Page Header area

that say "Verdana" and "4x-large"). Then you can type the six-digit hexadecimal font color in the box or select the font color by clicking the palette button to the right of the box.

6. Type the six-digit hexadecimal colors for the border and the interior of the blog page in the Border and Interior boxes. In each case you can click the palette button to the right of the box to select the color.

7. Preview your changes by clicking the preview link at the right side of the Page Header bar.

Side Module

The section that typically appears to the left of the blog post area is called the Side Module. The side module contains information about your profile name and picture, online information, and links. Here's how to customize the Side Module so you can make the look of the Side Module consistent with the rest of your blog page:

1. Scroll down to the Side Module area, as shown in Figure 8-10.

2. Select the side module position from the Side Module Position drop-down list. The default position is to the left of the blog post area, but you can also choose to put the side module to the right of the blog post area.

3. Change the font color by typing the hexadecimal representation of the background color in the Font Color box or clicking the palette button to the right of the font Color box and choosing one of the colors in the palette.

4. For Alignment, select the radio button to tell MySpace how you want the text aligned within the side module. The default is to have the text "centered," or aligned in the middle.

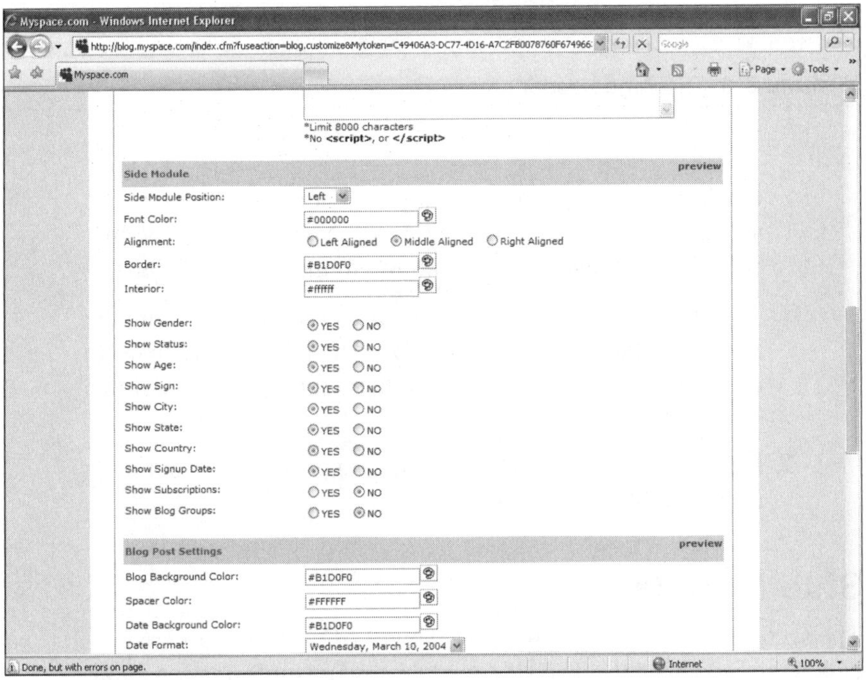

FIGURE 8-10 The Side Module area

5. Type the six-digit hexadecimal colors for the border and the interior of the side module in the Border and Interior boxes. In each case you can click the palette button to the right of the box to select the color.

6. The next ten radio buttons let you display (or hide) information about you in the Side Module, from your gender to the blog groups you belong to. The default selection for all ten buttons is Yes, but you can click the No button for each piece of information you don't want displayed within the side module.

7. Preview your changes by clicking the preview link at the right side of the Side Module bar.

Blog Post Settings

Your blog posts are what people come to your blog to read, and you can customize your blog posts so that they're consistent with the rest of your design. However, make sure the posts are easy to read by selecting a good color scheme for your text, background, and border colors. Dark blue text on a black background isn't readable, and a dark blue border won't show up well around a black box, but black text on a light blue background is readable. If you don't select a good color scheme, don't be surprised if you get few people reading your blog (or unfriendly comments from other users about what they think of your blog's readability). Here's how to change the look of your blog post settings:

1. Scroll down to the Blog Post Settings area, as shown in Figure 8-11.

2. Change the blog background, spacer, and date background colors by typing the hexadecimal representation of the background color in the Blog Background Color, Spacer Color, and Date Background Color boxes, respectively. If you would rather choose your color from a palette, click the palette button to the right of each box and choose one of the colors in the palette.

3. Select the format for the date you posted the blog from the Date Format drop-down list.

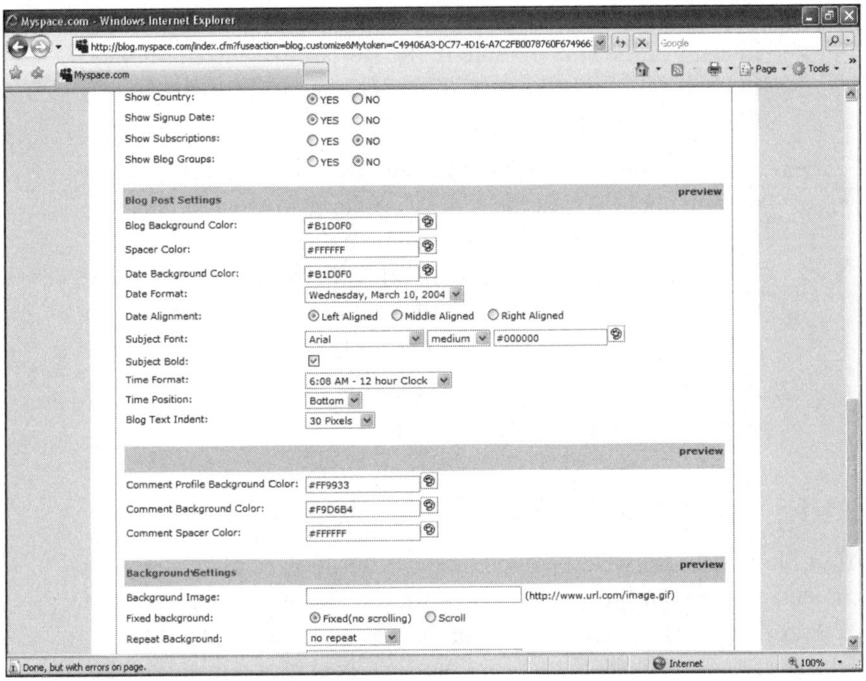

FIGURE 8-11 The Blog Post Settings area

4. For Date Alignment, click the radio button to tell MySpace how you want the date aligned on the page. The default is to have the date aligned to the left.

5. For the Subject Font, select the font name and size from the left and right drop-down lists, respectively (that is, the lists that say "Arial" and "medium"). Then you can type the six-digit hexadecimal font color in the box or select the font color by clicking the palette button to the right of the box.

6. If you want the subject line to be in bold text, leave the Subject Bold check box selected. If you would rather keep the subject font in regular text, clear the check box.

7. Select the format and position of the time stamp that indicates when you posted your blog by selecting the format and position from the Time Format and Time Position drop-down lists.

8. The text indent from the left side of the blog post box is, by default, 30 pixels. If you want to change this amount to any setting from 0 to 50 pixels, select the indent amount from the Blog Text Indent drop-down list.

9. Preview your changes by clicking the preview link at the right side of the Blog Post Settings bar.

Comments

You may get comments from other users who read your blog, so be sure to format your comments area appropriately not only so this section is consistent with the look of the rest of your blog, but also so you and others can see what text is part of your comment and what text is part of your blog. Here's how to update the look of your comments area:

1. Scroll down to the Comments area, as shown in Figure 8-12. You'll notice that for some reason the Comments area gray header bar doesn't have a title.

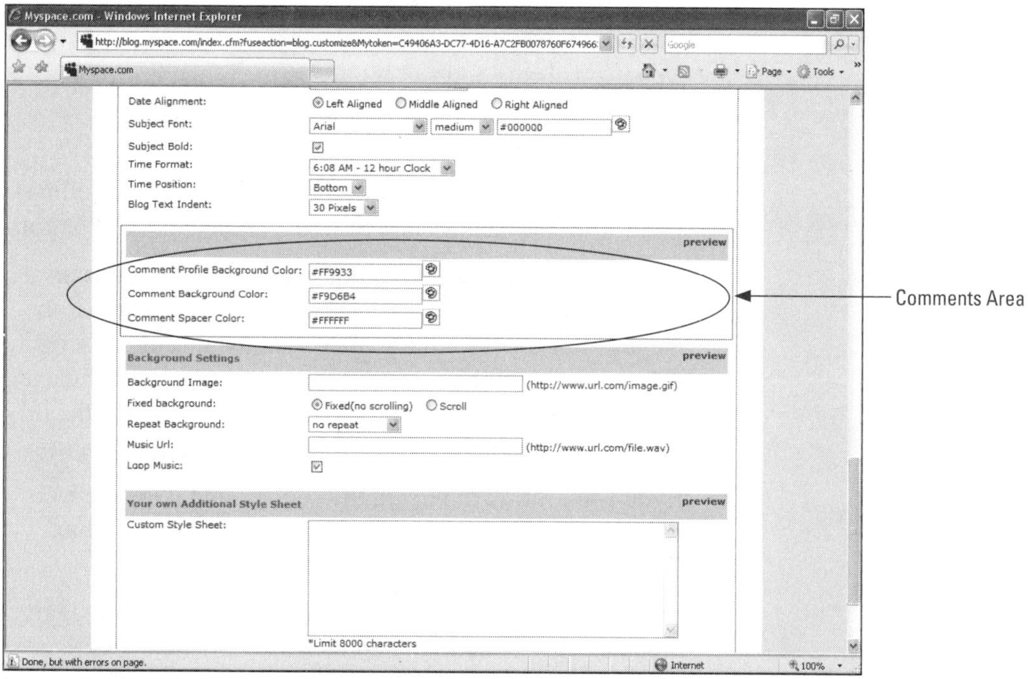

FIGURE 8-12 The Comments area

2. Type the six-digit hexadecimal colors for the comment profile background color, comment background color, and comment spacer color in the Comment Profile Background Color, Comment Background Color, and Comment Spacer Color boxes. With each box you can click the palette button to the right of the box to select the color just as you did with the font and background colors.

3. Preview your changes by clicking the preview link at the right side of the Comments area.

Background Settings

Now that you have your blog posting area, Side Module, and Comments areas modified, you may want to add a background image and music to your blog so people can enjoy your favorite images and songs as they read your blog. Here's how to change your blog page background:

1. Scroll down to the Background Settings area, as shown in Figure 8-13.

2. Type the web site address and the name of the image file in the Background Image box. The image must reside on another web site, like Photobucket.

3. The default fixed background setting is Fixed (no scrolling). If you want the background to scroll, click the Scroll button.

4. The background image does not repeat by default, meaning that the image only appears once on the page and if the image is too small for the screen, then the rest of the screen will be the default background color. If you want the image to repeat throughout the page, choose how you want the image to repeat from the Repeat Background drop-down list.

5. If you want music to play in the background, type the web site address and the audio filename in the Music Url box. The audio file must reside on another web site.

6. If you want the music to loop—that is, start playing again after the song is over—keep the Loop Music check

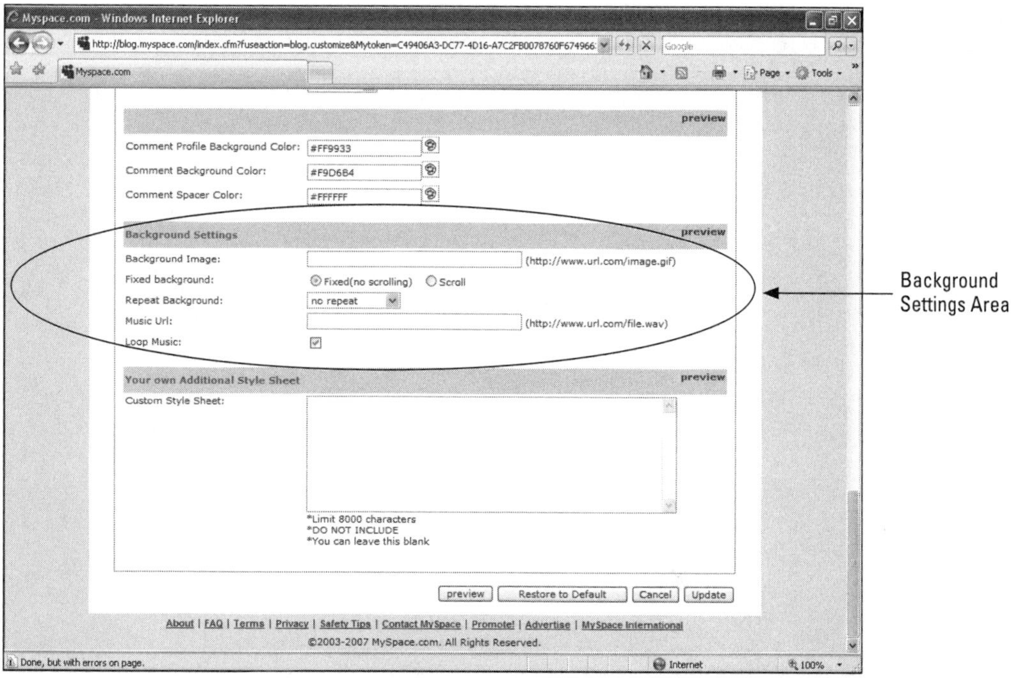

FIGURE 8-13 The Background Settings area

box selected. If you want the music to play only once, clear the check box.

7. Preview your changes by clicking the preview link at the right side of the Background Settings bar.

Your Own Additional Style Sheet

If you don't want to go through all the trouble of changing your blog through the sections described so far in this chapter, but would rather add your own style sheet for your blog instead (either your own or from another source), you can add the style-sheet information in the Your Own Additional Style Sheet area at the bottom of the Customize My Blog page. Here's how you add a style sheet to your blog page:

1. Scroll down to the Your Own Additional Style Sheet area, as shown in Figure 8-14.

Your Own
Additional Style
Sheet Area

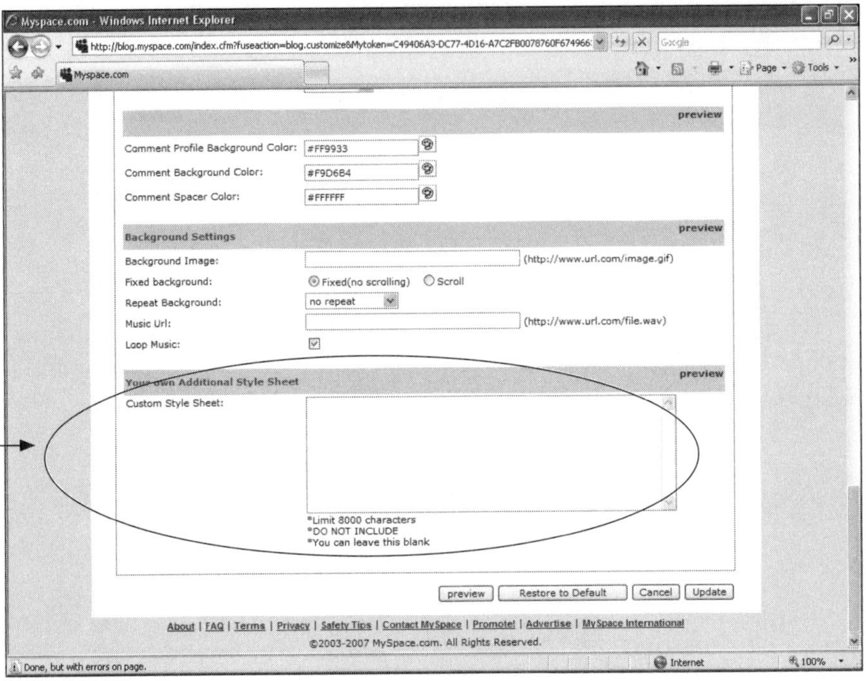

FIGURE 8-14 The Your Own Additional Style Sheet area

2. Type the CSS code you want to customize. You can apply styles to the following built-in MySpace blog classes:

- Background: `td.BlogCommentsProfile`
- Date: `p.blogTimeStamp`
- Subject: `p.blogSubject`
- Posted blog text: `table.blog`
- Time (text): `p.blogContentInfo`
- Time (links): `p.blogContentInfo a`
- Spacer: `tr.spacer`
- Comments background: `td.blogComments`
- Comments text: `p.blogCommentsContent`
- Spacer: `tr.commentSpacer`

For example, you can add the code to set your posted blog text alignment and font size and color:

```
table.blog {text-align: left; font-size:
10pt; color: blue;}
```

3. Preview your changes by clicking the preview link at the right side of the Your Own Additional Style Sheet bar.

The Last Thing to Do...

When you're finished updating your blog settings, click the Update button. MySpace will update your blog with the changes you made. If you decide that you don't like any of the changes you made and you want to return to the default selections, click the Restore to Default button.

ADD BLOG POSTS

Now that we've finished customizing your blog, it's time for the most important discussion of all in this chapter: How do you add a post to your blog? It's simple. Here's how:

1. In your profile home page, click the Blog link in the menu bar. The Blog Control Center page appears.

2. Scroll down the page until you see the My Controls section, as shown in Figure 8-15. Then click the Post New Blog link.

3. In the Post a New Blog Entry page that appears, the default post date and time are the current date and time in the Posted Date and Posted Time drop-down lists, as shown in Figure 8-16. If you want to change the date and/or time, select the date and/or time in the appropriate drop-down list.

4. Type the subject of the blog post in the Subject box.

5. Select the category from the Category drop-down list if you want this post to fall within a specific category. If you don't want to assign a category, leave the selection as "none."

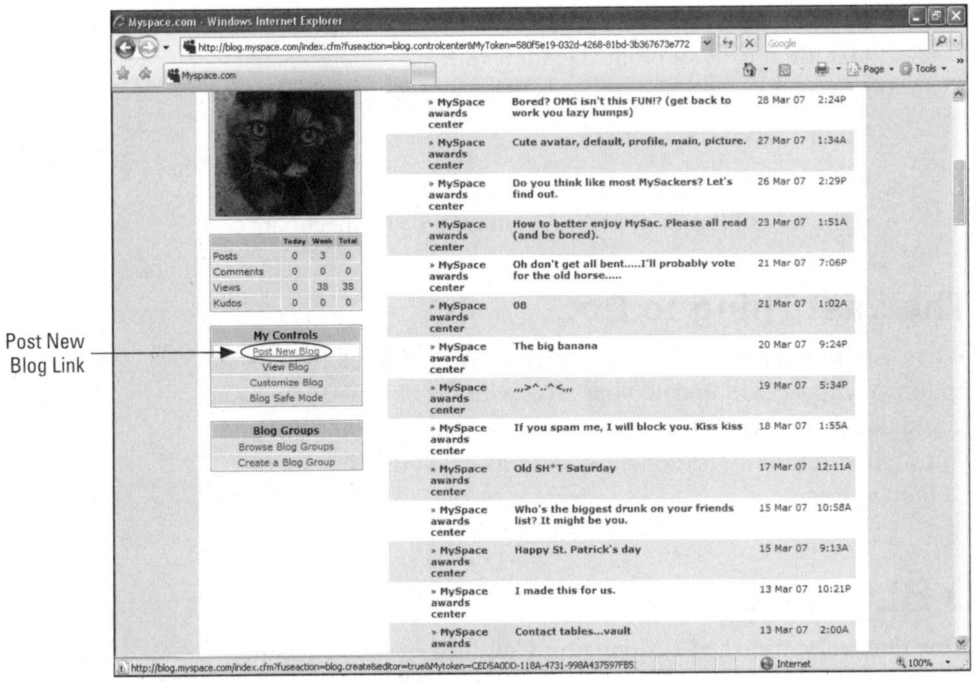

Post New Blog Link

FIGURE 8-15 The My Controls section

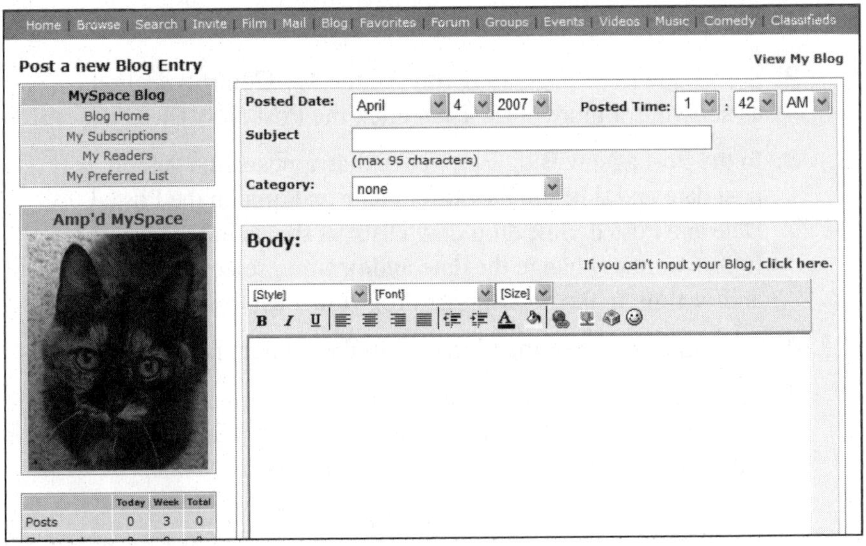

FIGURE 8-16 The Posted Date and Posted Time drop-down lists

6. Type the post in the Body box, as shown in Figure 8-17. You can use the formatting tools above the box to edit your text. For example, you can change the font, style, and text size.

7. If you want to control the look of your blog post using HTML and/or CSS code, select the View Source check box. Otherwise leave this check box blank. You can go back to Chapter 2 (for HTML) or Chapter 3 (for CSS) if you want a refresher.

8. Scroll down the page to view the section about your mood and other blog post options, as shown in Figure 8-18.

9. You can tell your readers what you're reading, viewing, or listening to by selecting the option in the drop-down list. The default is Playing (Music). If you want to get more specific, click the Search button and search for the music, book, DVD/video, or video game you're currently reviewing.

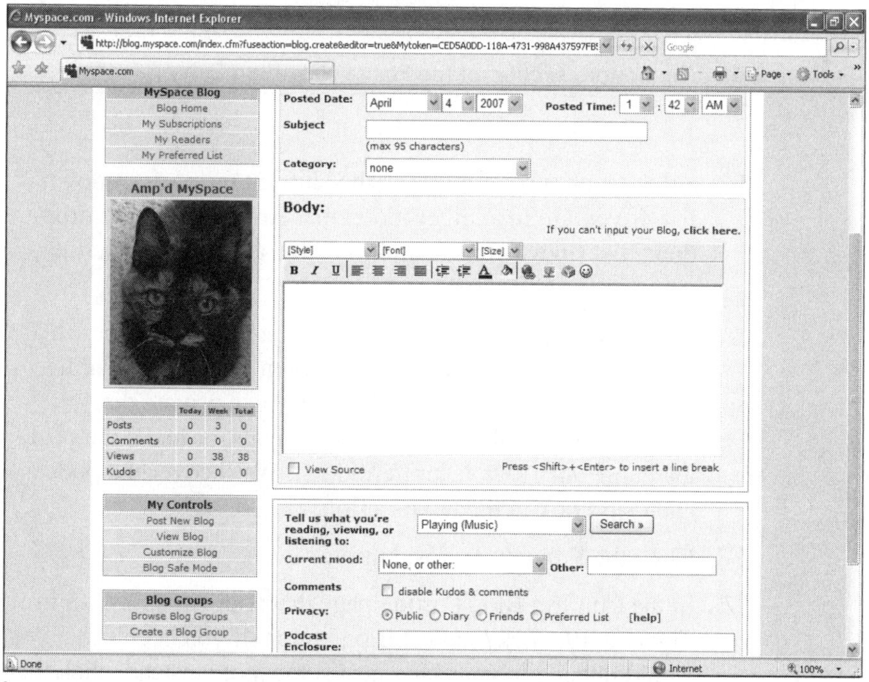

FIGURE 8-17 The Body box

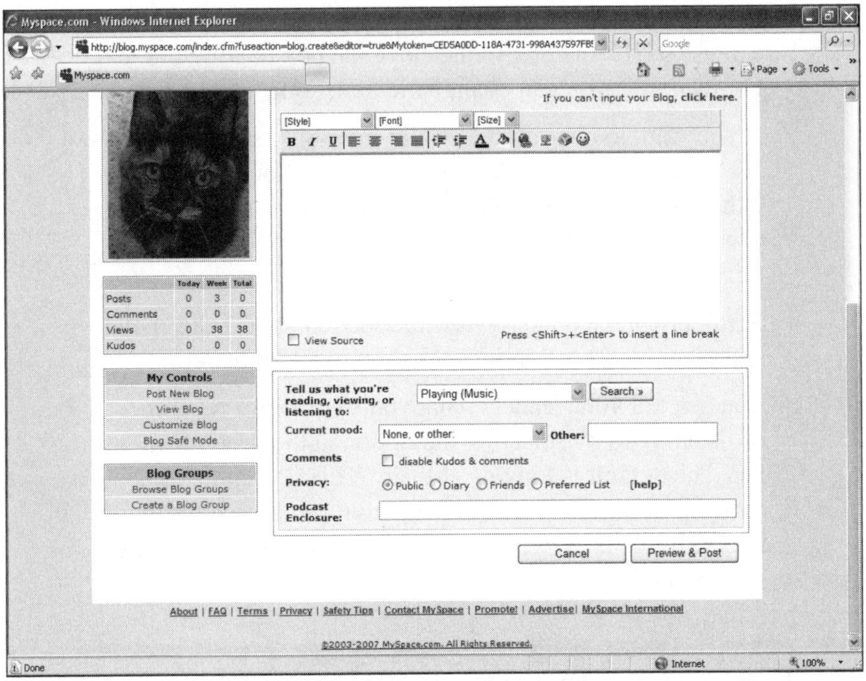

FIGURE 8-18 The bottom section of the Post a New Blog Entry page

10. Select your current mood in the Current mood drop-down list. If you are in another mood that isn't listed in the drop-down list (like a combination of several moods), type the mood in the Other box.

11. For Privacy, click the radio button that tells MySpace who you want to see your blog. The default selection is Public, but you can also make the blog your own private diary, have the post visible only to your friends, or make the post available only to your preferred list. We'll cover the podcast enclosure box in the next section.

12. Click the Preview & Post button.

13. In the Confirm Blog Posting page that appears, as shown in Figure 8-19, click the Post Blog button. If you decide that you would rather edit your blog post some more instead, click the Edit button to return to the Post a New Blog Entry page.

FIGURE 8-19 The Confirm Blog Posting page

After you publish your blog post, your blog with the new post appears in your blog page, as shown in Figure 8-20. If you decide that you want to tweak your post a bit more after reading it, click the Edit link below the blog post. Don't like the post at all? Just click the Remove link below the blog post, and then click the OK button in the dialog box that appears and asks if you really want to remove the post. Simple as that.

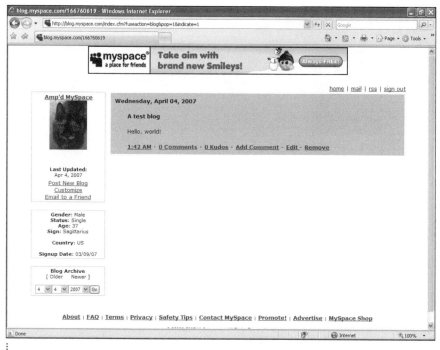

FIGURE 8-20 The blog post with the Edit and Remove links

ADD PODCASTS AND VIDEO TO YOUR BLOG

A podcast and/or video can be a replacement for a written blog, or it can augment what you've already written. For example, if you want your readers to see a video that you refer to in your blog post, you can embed the video in the blog instead of forcing your readers to go elsewhere. Adding a podcast to your blog is easy, and adding a video is a little harder.

Add a Podcast

Let's start by adding a podcast. Type a new blog post as you did in the "Add Blog Posts" section earlier in this chapter. Now follow these steps:

1. Scroll down the page to view the section about your mood and other blog post options, as shown in Figure 8-21.

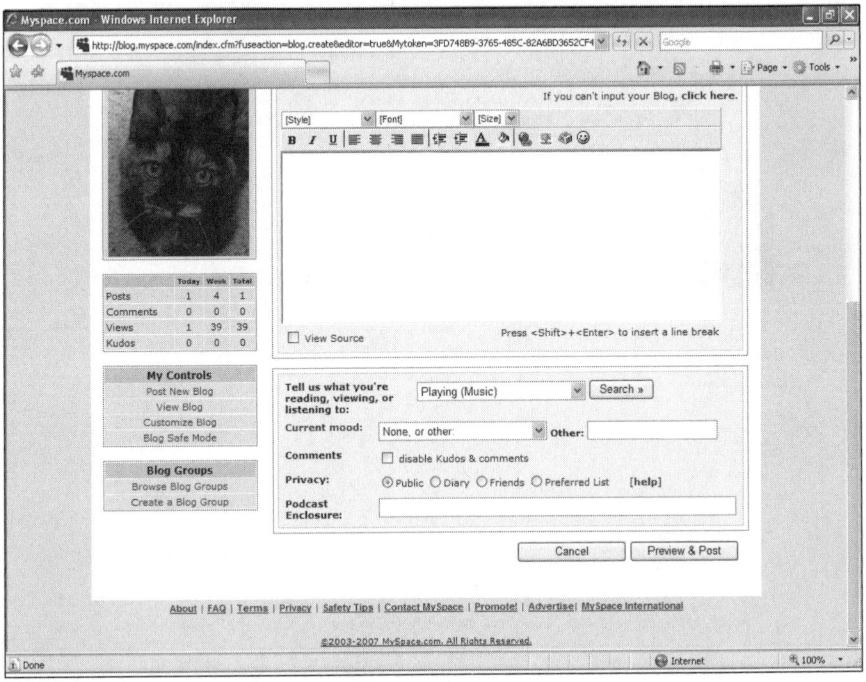

FIGURE 8-21 The bottom section of the Post a New Blog Entry page

2. The podcast has to be stored on another web server for MySpace to access it. In the Podcast Enclosure box, type the web address and filename of your podcast audio file in the format http://www.myurl.com/mypodcast.mp3 where you replace *www.myurl.com* with the name of your web site and replace *mypodcast.mp3* with the name of your audio file.

3. Click the Preview & Post button. You'll see the podcast controls in the blog post preview page so you can play the podcast and verify that it works.

4. In the Confirm Blog Posting page that appears, click the Post Blog button.

MySpace publishes your blog post and shows you the new post in your blog page complete with your embedded podcast.

Add Video to Your Blog

As I said before, adding video to your blog is a little harder because it requires you to copy and paste video from your Videos page to your Blog page. Here's how to add a video file from MySpace to your blog:

1. Click the Videos link in the menu bar. The Videos page appears.

2. Click the Featured, Videos, or My Videos tab, depending on where the video resides in MySpace.

3. Click the video you want to open. The featured video page appears and plays the video.

4. Scroll down the page until you see the Video Code box, as shown in Figure 8-22.

5. Click the code in the Video Code box and then press CTRL+C.

6. Click the Blog link in the menu bar.

7. Open the Post a New Blog Entry page as you did in the "Add Blog Posts" section earlier in this chapter.

Video Code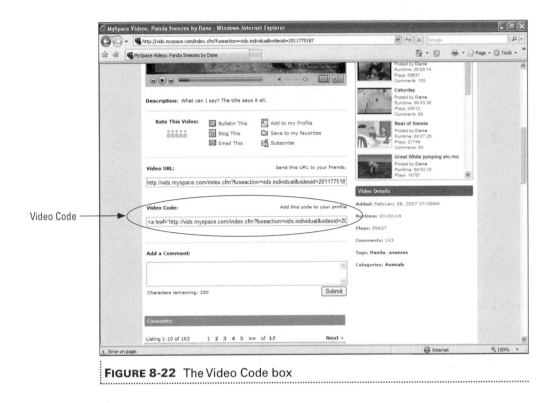

FIGURE 8-22 The Video Code box

8. In the Body area, you'll see a sentence in the upper-right corner that says "If you can't input your Blog, click here." Click the Click Here link, as shown in Figure 8-23.

9. Click in the Body box and then press CTRL+V to paste the video code into the box.

10. Click the Preview & Post button. You'll see the video controls in the blog post preview page so you can play the video and verify that it works.

11. In the Confirm Blog Posting page that appears, click the Post Blog button.

MySpace publishes your blog post and shows you the new post in your blog page complete with your embedded video. That wasn't hard at all.

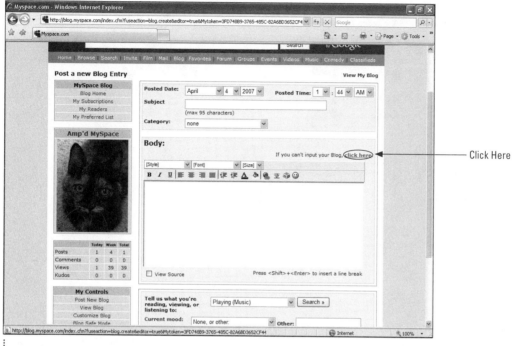

Click Here

FIGURE 8-23 The Click Here link

ALLOW COMMENTS TO YOUR BLOG

If you don't want to allow comments for a blog post, MySpace
makes it easy for you to disable comments for the post. Here's how:

1. Type a new blog post as you did in the "Add Blog Posts"
   section earlier in this chapter.

2. In the bottom section of the Post a New Blog Entry page,
   select the Disable Kudos & Comments check box, as shown
   in Figure 8-24.

3. Click the Preview & Post button. You'll see the video
   controls in the blog post, preview page so you can play the
   video and verify that it works.

4. In the Confirm Blog Posting page that appears, click the
   Post Blog button.

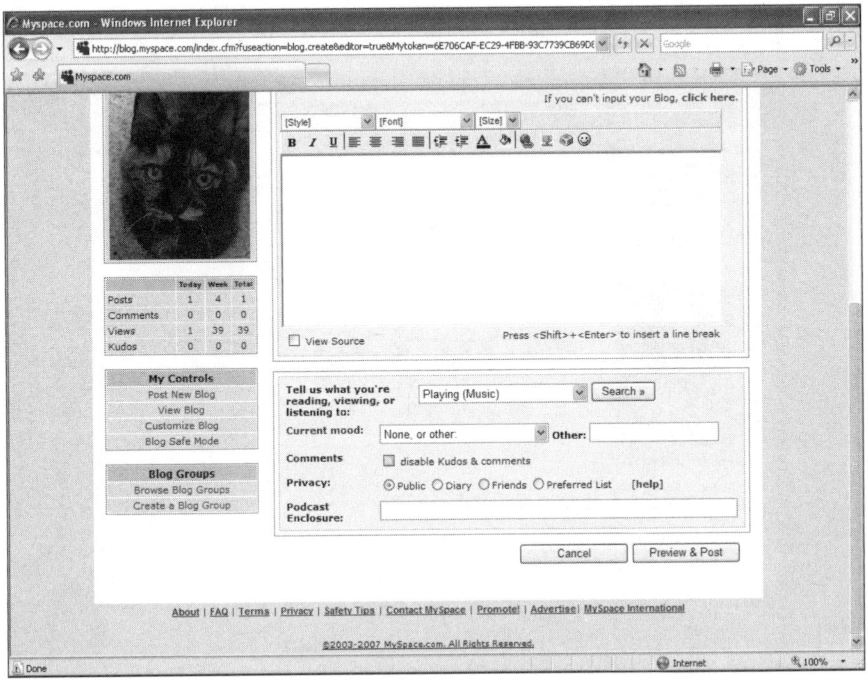

FIGURE 8-24 The Disable Kudos & Comments check box

You'll still see the Comments and Kudos links, but when you click on either the Comments or Kudos, a new page opens and shows the comments and kudos unlinked so you know that you (or anyone else) can add a comment or kudo to your blog post.

LINK TO OTHER BLOGS

If you find a blog post and you want to link to it in your own blog, it's an easy process: You need to copy the web address and add just a little HTML to your page to create the link. Here's how:

1. Click the Blog link in the menu bar.

2. Open the post from your favorite blog. In this example I'll click the topic from the blog I subscribed to at the beginning of the chapter (it's Figure 8-3 if you want to check). A new browser window opens and displays the blog post.

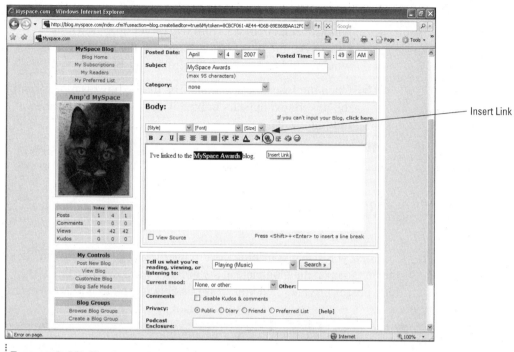

Insert Link

FIGURE 8-25 The Insert Link button

3. Click the web site address in the browser's Address bar and then press CTRL+C to copy the address.

4. Type a new blog post as you did in the "Add Blog Posts" section earlier in this chapter.

5. In the Body box, highlight the text that will contain the link.

6. Click the Insert Link button in the toolbar, as shown in Figure 8-25.

7. In the link dialog box that appears, shown in Figure 8-26, click in the URL box and then press CTRL+V. The web site address appears in the box.

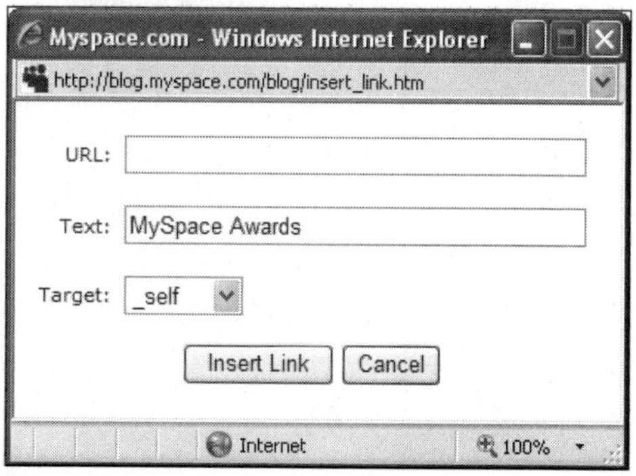

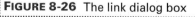

FIGURE 8-26 The link dialog box

8. If you want the link to open the blog post in a new browser window, select _blank from the Target drop-down list. Otherwise, the blog post will open in the same browser window and take users away from your blog.

9. Click the Insert Link button. The dialog box disappears and the linked text appears in blue with an underline, as shown in Figure 8-27.

10. Click the Preview & Post button. You'll see the linked text in the blog post so you can test it and confirm that it works the way you expect.

11. In the Confirm Blog Posting page that appears, click the Post Blog button.

Now you'll see your blog post in the blog page and you can click the link to open the blog page in the browser window. Note that if the blog post is private, then you won't be able to link to it unless you're

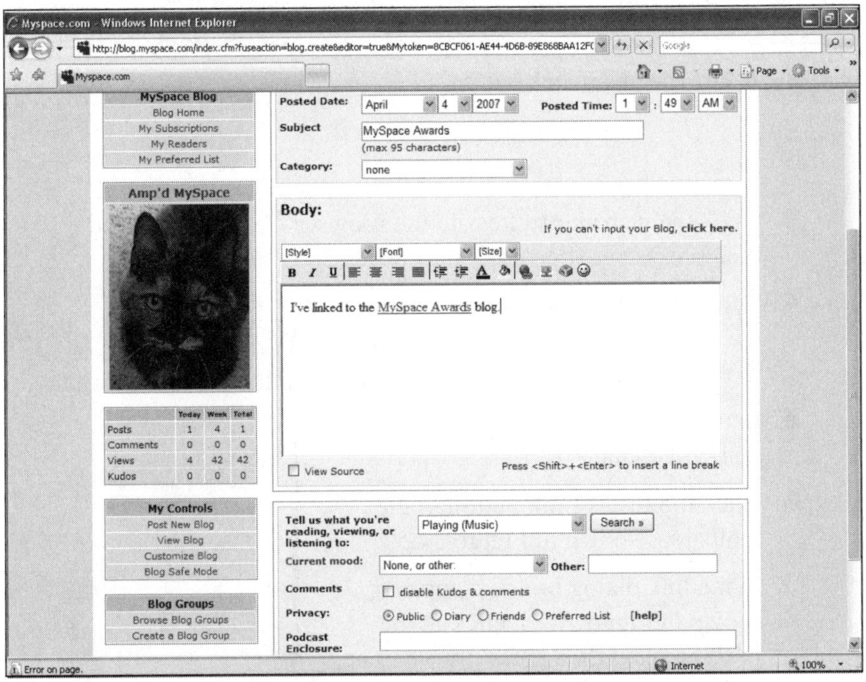

FIGURE 8-27 The linked text

one of the blogger's friends, and you should also get permission from the blogger to link to their private blog post.

EVALUATE AND JOIN THE RIGHT BLOG GROUPS

There are so many blogs in MySpace that the good people at MySpace have put all the blogs into different categories so you can join the category (or categories) that best fits your blog. You can then decide to add your blog to that blog group so other MySpace users can find your blog more easily. Here's how to review and join a blog group.

1. Click the Blog link in the menu bar.

2. In the Blog Control Center page, scroll down to the bottom of the page and click the Browse Blog Groups link in the Blog Groups area, shown in Figure 8-28.

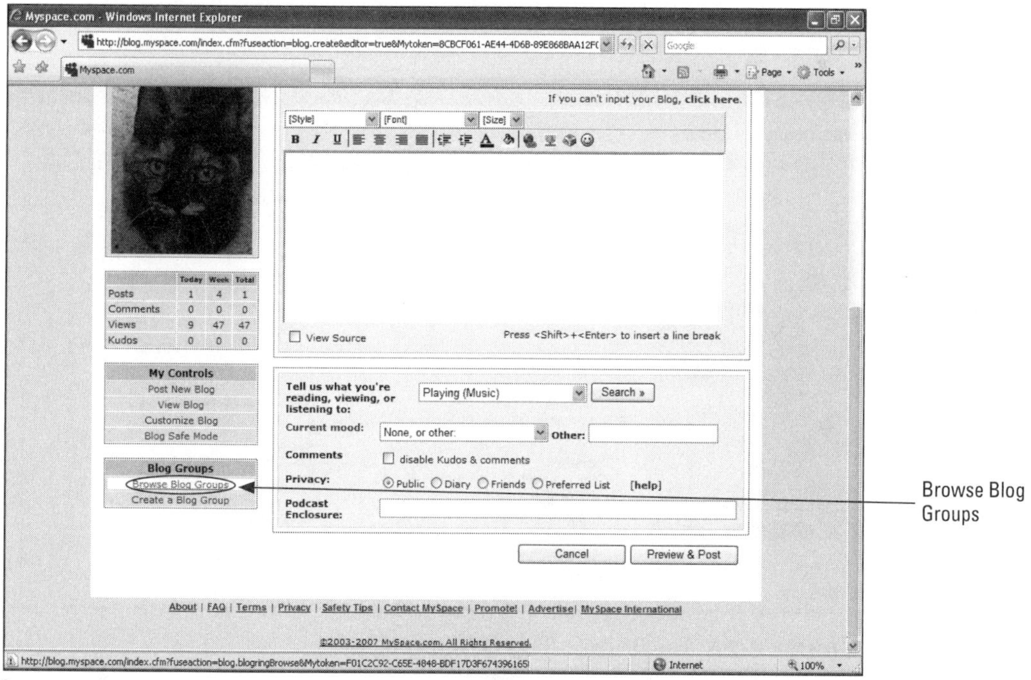

FIGURE 8-28 The Browse Blog Groups link

3. The Browse Blog Groups page appears, as shown in Figure 8-29 and displays 15 group categories with a number of subcategory links under each category heading.

4. When you click one of the blog groups, you'll see the latest blog posts that fall into that area. For example, if you click the Physics link within the Science & Nature section, a new page appears that shows all the blog groups in the category, as shown in Figure 8-30.

5. Click the blog group name you want to see. The group contains a number of blogs, so you can visit those blogs and see what those users are talking about, as shown in Figure 8-31.

6. If you want to join the blog group, click the Join Blog Group link. Your blog will be added to the list immediately unless the blog group leader requires that he or she approve your application. In that case you will be contacted by the group leader to let you know about his or her decision.

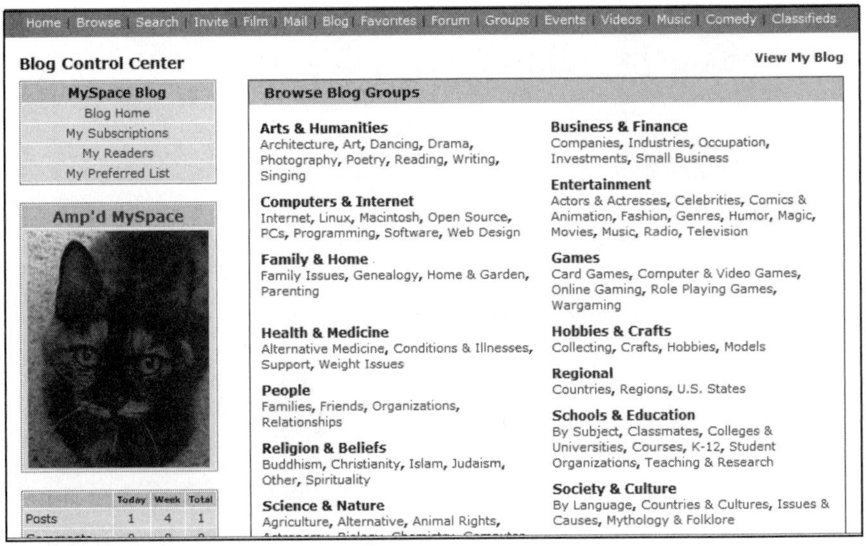

FIGURE 8-29 The Browse Blog Groups page

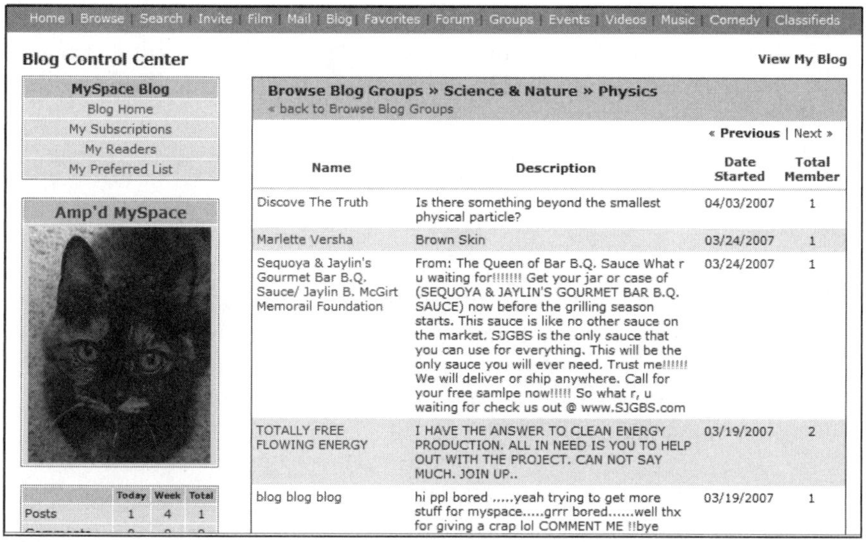

FIGURE 8-30 The blog groups in the Physics category

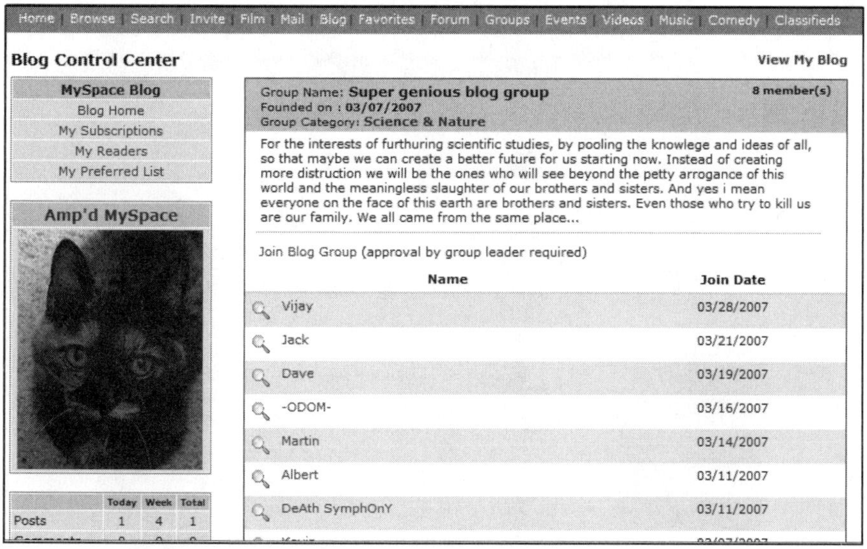

FIGURE 8-31 A blog group that has eight members

When you read a user's blog and you want to go back to browsing blog groups, scroll down the page and click the Browse Blog Groups link at the left side of the blog page. You'll return to the Browse Blog Groups page.

FAQS

How do I turn off blog e-mail notifications?   If you subscribe to a lot of blogs or blogs that have a lot of postings, you may not want to get a post in your e-mail but would prefer to visit the Blog Control Center instead to catch up. Here's how you turn off blog notification messages:

1. Click the Blog link in the menu bar. The Blog Control Center page appears.

2. In the MySpace Blog section, click My Subscriptions, shown in Figure 8-32.

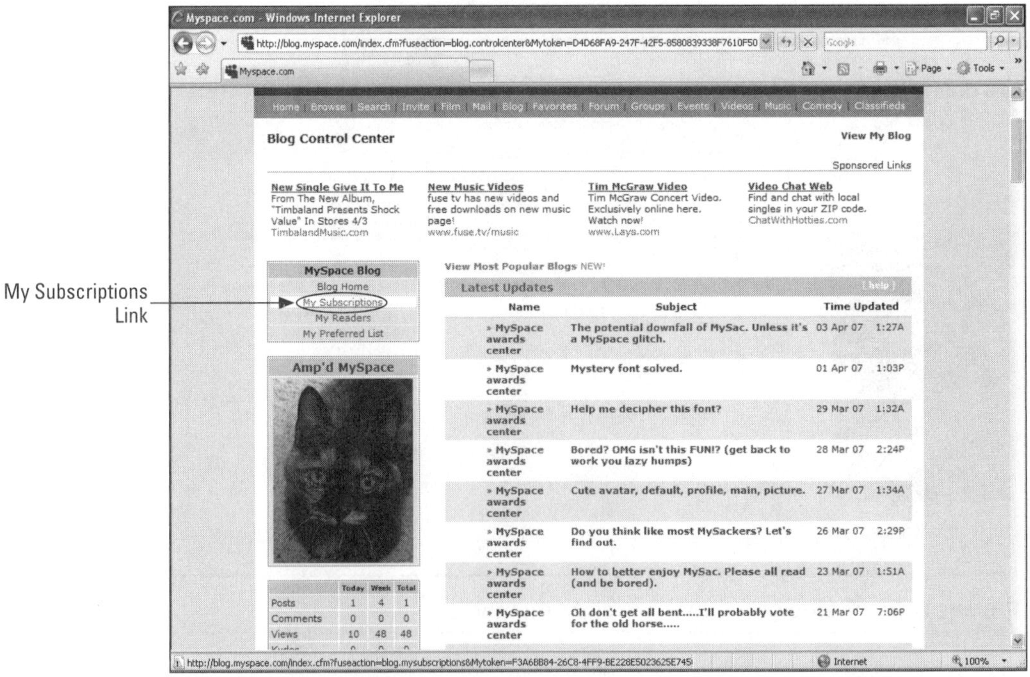

FIGURE 8-32 The My Subscriptions link

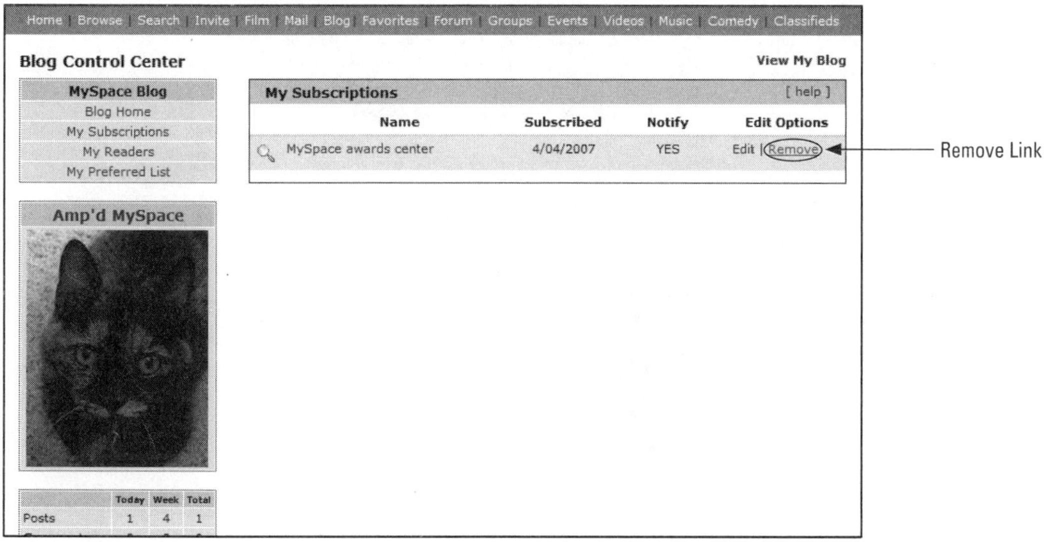

FIGURE 8-33 The Remove link

3. In the My Subscriptions table that appears, click the Remove link within the row containing the blog as shown in Figure 8-33.

4. In the dialog box that appears, shown in Figure 8-34, click the OK button.

5. The Blog Control Center page appears, shown in Figure 8-35. Notice how NO appears in the Notify column.

FIGURE 8-34 Click the OK button in the dialog box.

Can my blog header be an image that's on my web site? Yes. In the Page Header section of Customizing Your Blog, select the Your Own HTML Header radio button, and in the box provided, type the following:

```
<img src="http://www.mywebsite.com/myimage.jpg">
```

FIGURE 8-35 You will not be notified by e-mail any more for this blog.

Replace *www.mywebsite.com* with the name of your web site, and replace *myimage.jpg* with the name of your image.

I'm adding CSS code to my blog page, but I can't add any more characters. Why not? The limit for adding code is 8,000 characters, including spaces. If you can't add any more characters in the box, then you have exceeded the 8,000-character limit. In this case, one option you may want to consider is to change some of the blog settings in the other areas of the Customize My Blog page and remove those matching lines of your CSS code to conform to the 8,000-character limit.

Chapter 9

Nine More Ways to Update Your Profile

Unlike the last chapter, this chapter will be short and sweet. We're going to give you quick and easy instructions for updating your profile in nine different ways, from hiding certain sections from public view to dialing in to your page from your cell phone.

We're going to update your profile from the Change Account Settings page. Get there from your home page by clicking the Account Settings link to the right of your profile picture. The Change Account Settings page appears, as shown in Figure 9-1.

You'll be clicking links in the My Account Settings table to make these changes. Ready? As my mother would say every time she would go on an amusement park ride with me, here we gooooo....

HIDE CERTAIN SECTIONS FROM PUBLIC VIEW

Here's how to hide certain sections from public viewing:

1. Click the Change Settings link in the Privacy Settings row. The Privacy Settings page appears, as shown in Figure 9-2.

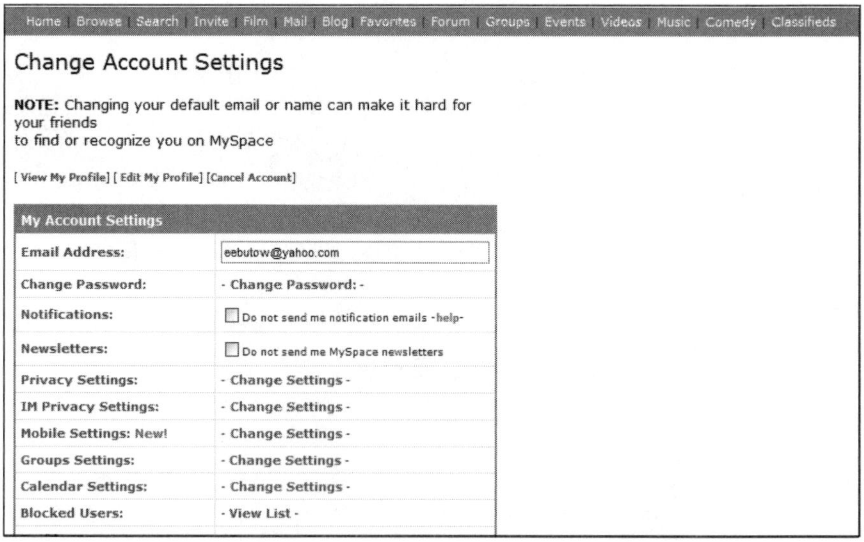

FIGURE 9-1 The Change Account Settings page

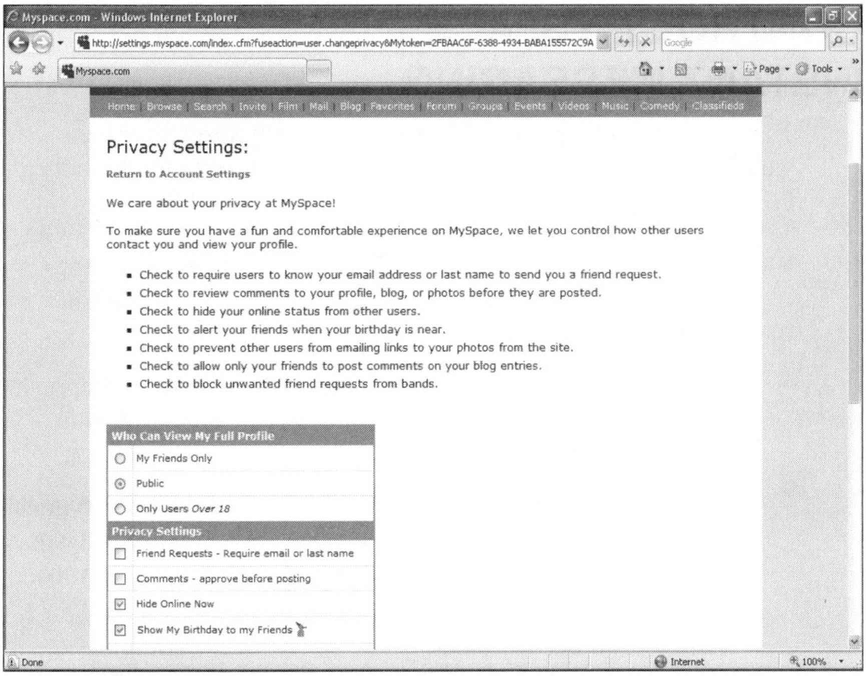

FIGURE 9-2 The Privacy Settings page

2. In the Who Can View My Full Profile section, click the appropriate radio button to make your full profile public (which is the default selection), make your full profile visible only to friends, or make your full profile visible to MySpace users who claim they are 18 or older.

3. If you want to keep your privacy settings private, keep the Hide Online Now check box selected.

4. Click the Change Settings button. A message appears above the table that states your privacy settings have been updated.

5. Click the Return to Account Settings link at the top of the page.

CONTROL MYSPACE INSTANT MESSAGING

To receive instant messages from anyone on MySpace over the web, you must have the Hide Online Now check box cleared in the Privacy Settings page. Here's how to control who can IM you:

1. Click the Change Settings link in the IM Privacy Settings row. The IM Privacy Settings page appears, as shown in Figure 9-3.

2. In the My IM Privacy Settings section, click the appropriate radio button to have no one IM you (which is the default selection), have friends IM you, or have anyone IM you.

3. In the IM Invite Privacy Settings section, select the appropriate check boxes to tell MySpace to block IM invites from one or more groups. If you want to block IM invites from everyone, select the Everyone check box.

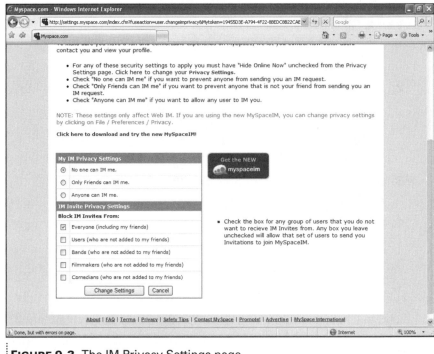

FIGURE 9-3 The IM Privacy Settings page

4. Click the Change Settings button. A message appears above the table that states your privacy settings have been updated.

5. Click the Return to Account Settings link at the top of the page.

CONTROL ACCESS TO COMMENTS

MySpace makes it easy for you to control who can leave comments in your blog and whether you want to read the comments before posting them. Here's how:

1. Click the Change Settings link in the Privacy Settings row. The Privacy Settings page appears, as shown in Figure 9-4.

2. In the Privacy Settings section, select the Comments – Approve Before Posting check box to tell MySpace to send you the comment so you can approve it before posting it for everyone to see.

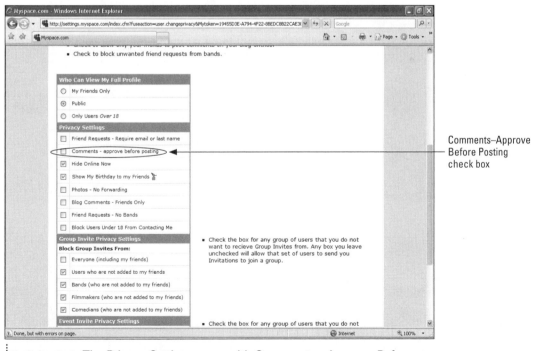

FIGURE 9-4 The Privacy Settings page with Comments – Approve Before Posting check box

3. Restrict comment posting to friends only by selecting the Blog Comments – Friends Only check box.

4. Click the Change Settings button. A message appears above the table that states your privacy settings have been updated.

5. Click the Return to Account Settings link at the top of the page.

CONTROL ACCESS TO INVITES

As a MySpace user you'll get invitations to many events. If you find them a nuisance and want to filter out the invitations to only get invitations from friends, or if you don't want any invitations whatsoever, here's how you control access to invites:

1. Click the Change Settings link in the Privacy Settings row. The Privacy Settings page appears, as shown in Figure 9-5.

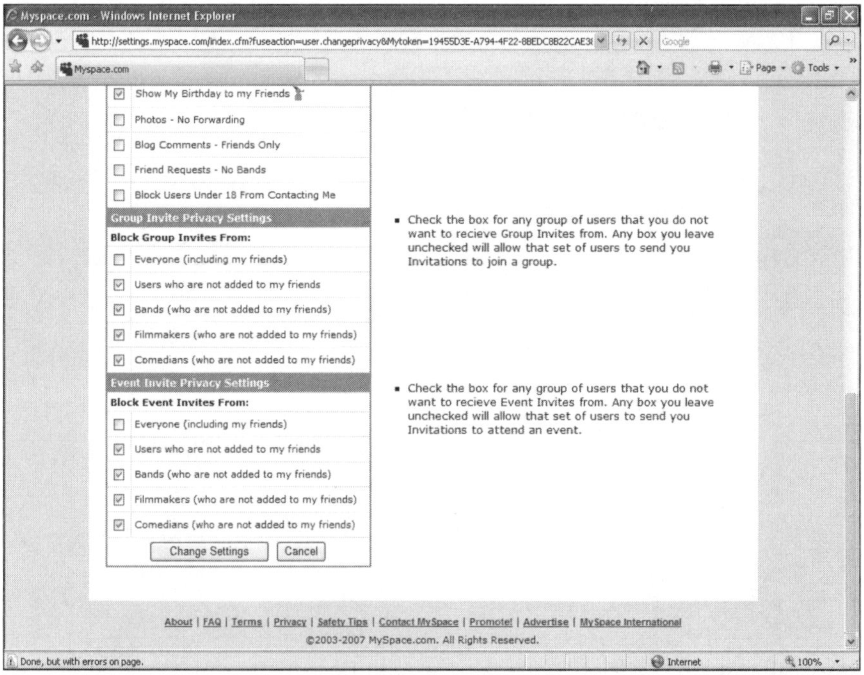

FIGURE 9-5 The Privacy Settings page with Group Invite and Event Invite privacy settings

2. In the Group Invite Privacy Settings section, by default every group of users except your friends is blocked from sending you group invitations, as shown by the selected check box next to the group name. You can block invitations altogether by selecting the Everyone check box.

3. In the Event Invite Privacy Settings section, by default every group of users except your friends is blocked from sending you event invitations, as shown by the selected check box next to the group name. You can block invitations altogether by selecting the Everyone check box.

4. Click the Change Settings button. A message appears above the table that states your privacy settings have been updated.

5. Click the Return to Account Settings link at the top of the page.

Note that if you want to block IM event requests, you can do this as described in the "Control MySpace Instant Messaging" section earlier in this chapter.

BLOCK FRIEND REQUESTS

If you decide you don't want someone to become your friend because they don't know you and/or you don't want musical bands to be your friends, you can block friend requests. Here's how:

1. Click the Change Settings link in the Privacy Settings row. The Privacy Settings page appears, as shown in Figure 9-6.

2. In the Privacy Settings section, select the Friend Requests – Require Email or Last Name check box to tell MySpace that you won't consider accepting a friend unless you know the user's e-mail address or last name.

3. Block friend requests from musical bands by selecting the Friend Requests – No Bands check box.

4. Click the Change Settings button. A message appears above the table that states your privacy settings have been updated.

5. Click the Return to Account Settings link at the top of the page.

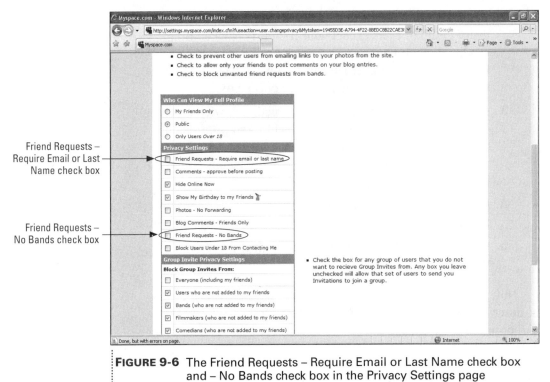

FIGURE 9-6 The Friend Requests – Require Email or Last Name check box and – No Bands check box in the Privacy Settings page

BLOCK A USER

There may be one or more reasons why you would want to block a user from contacting you at all. The person may not be able to take no for an answer, may be creeping you out, or may not seem interesting, and you want that user to move on.

Block an Underage User

Here's how to block a user from contacting you because they're under the age of 18:

1. Click the Change Settings link in the Privacy Settings row. The Privacy Settings page appears, as shown in Figure 9-7.

2. In the Privacy Settings section, select the Block Users Under 18 From Contacting Me check box to tell MySpace that you won't accept communication from any user who is under the age of 18.

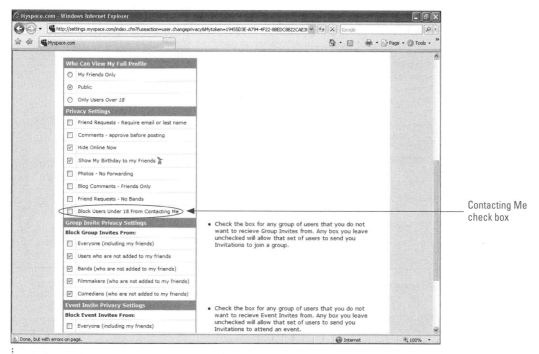

FIGURE 9-7 The Block Users Under 18 From Contacting Me check box in the Privacy Settings page

3. Click the Change Settings button. A message appears above the table that states your privacy settings have been updated.

4. Click the Return to Account Settings link at the top of the page.

Block a User Entirely

Here's how to block a user entirely:

1. Click the Mail link in the menu bar. The Mail Center window appears, as shown in Figure 9-8.

2. Click the Friend Requests link. The Friend Request Manager page appears, as shown in Figure 9-9.

3. Click the user's picture (or picture placeholder if they don't have one) in the From column. The user's profile page appears, as shown in Figure 9-10.

Friend Requests Link ——→

FIGURE 9-8 The Mail Center window

4. In the Contacting area, click the Block User link.

5. In the dialog box that appears, click the OK button to block the user.

FIGURE 9-9 The Friend Request Manager page

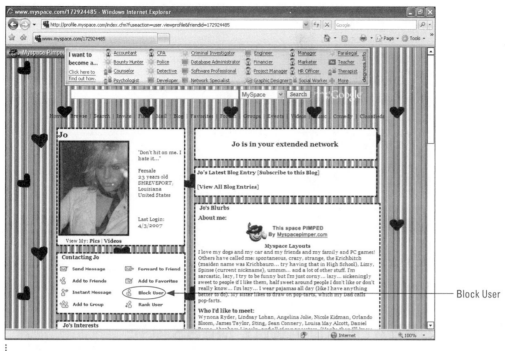

FIGURE 9-10 The user's profile page

TELL OTHERS YOUR GROUPS OF INTEREST

If you want to tell visitors to your profile about your groups of interest so you can try to connect with other users who share your interests, here's how you can tell MySpace to add your groups of interest to your profile:

1. Click the Change Settings link in the Profile Settings row. The Profile Settings page appears, as shown in Figure 9-11.

2. Select the Display Groups I Belong To check box.

3. Click the Change Settings button. A message appears above the table that states your privacy settings have been updated.

4. Click the Return to Account Settings link at the top of the page.

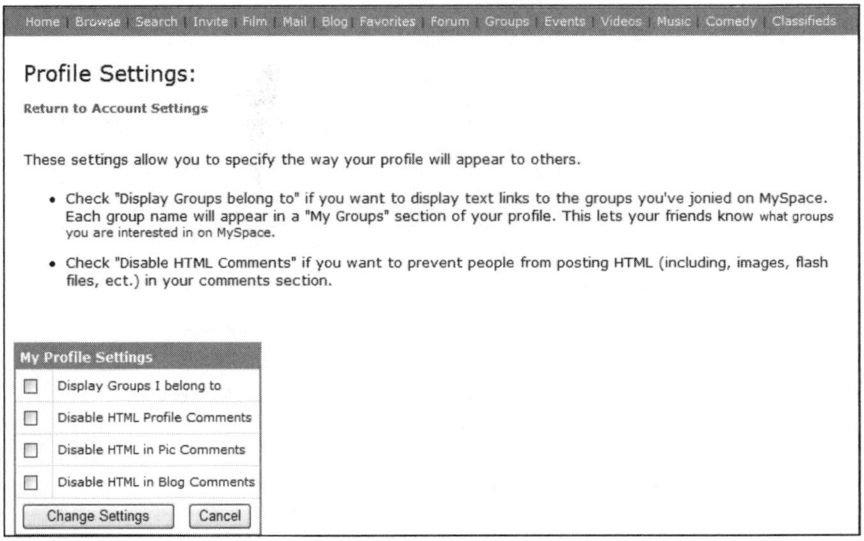

Home | Browse | Search | Invite | Film | Mail | Blog | Favorites | Forum | Groups | Events | Videos | Music | Comedy | Classifieds

Profile Settings:

Return to Account Settings

These settings allow you to specify the way your profile will appear to others.

- Check "Display Groups belong to" if you want to display text links to the groups you've jonied on MySpace. Each group name will appear in a "My Groups" section of your profile. This lets your friends know what groups you are interested in on MySpace.
- Check "Disable HTML Comments" if you want to prevent people from posting HTML (including, images, flash files, ect.) in your comments section.

My Profile Settings

☐ Display Groups I belong to
☐ Disable HTML Profile Comments
☐ Disable HTML in Pic Comments
☐ Disable HTML in Blog Comments

[Change Settings]   [Cancel]

FIGURE 9-11 The Profile Settings page

CREATE AN AWAY MESSAGE

If you know you're going to be away from your MySpace account for a while and you get messages from your friends and other profile visitors, you can create an away message thanking them for contacting you and letting them know when you'll return. Here's how:

1. From the My Account Settings page, click the View/Edit Away Message link in the Away Message row. The Away Message page appears, as shown in Figure 9-12.

2. Type the away message in the Message box.

3. Select the check box to show the away message when someone sends you a message.

4. Click the Save button. The Change Account Settings window appears. The next time someone sends you a message, they'll receive your away message right away.

If you want to keep your message for later use but you don't want to have MySpace display the message when someone tries to send you a message, clear the check box. When you're ready to go away again and want to display the away message, select the check box.

FIGURE 9-12 The Away Message page

SET UP MYSPACE ALERTS FOR YOUR CELL PHONE

MySpace realizes that you may want to log in to your MySpace account from your AT&T or Helio cell phone or other mobile device to find out who wants to talk with you. So MySpace includes text messaging capabilities so you can have MySpace alert you when you receive text messages.

1. Click the Change Settings link in the Mobile Settings row. The Mobile Alerts Settings page appears, as shown in Figure 9-13.

2. In the My Mobile Notification Settings table, clear any check boxes if you don't want a text message when you receive a friend request, comment, message, and/or event invite.

3. Click the Apply Settings button. The My Mobile Number table appears, as shown in Figure 9-14.

4. Type the phone number in the Number box.

5. Select your mobile phone carrier from the Carrier drop-down list.

FIGURE 9-13 The Mobile Alerts Settings page

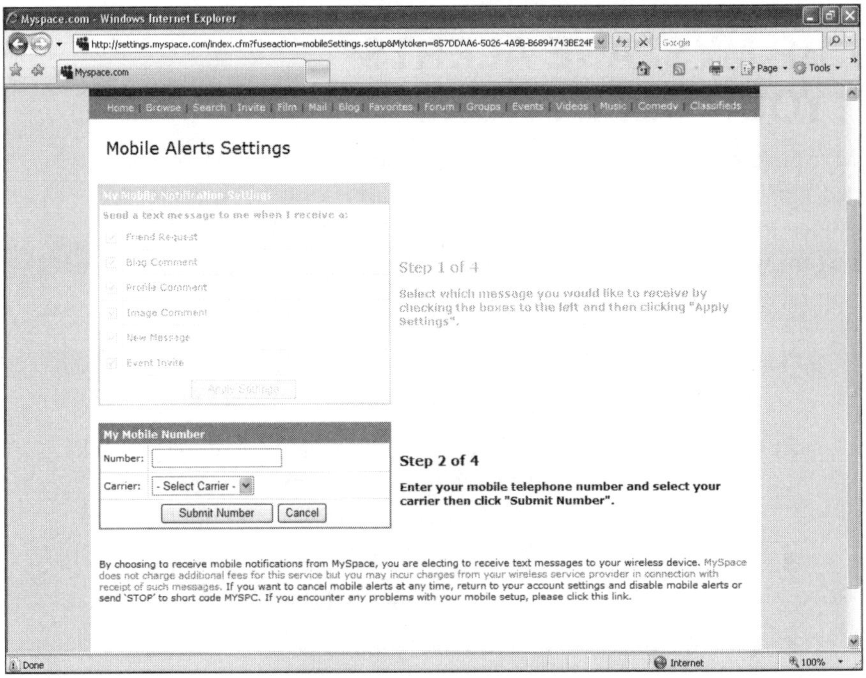

FIGURE 9-14 The My Mobile Number table

6. Click the Submit Number button. A second My Mobile Number table appears below the first My Mobile Number table, as shown in Figure 9-15. At this point, MySpace is going to verify the phone number you entered by sending a text message with an activation code to your phone. Please note that this may take up to ten minutes to arrive.

7. Type the activation code you receive in the text message on your mobile device in the Activation Code box.

NOTE
If your activation code does not arrive within ten minutes, click the link marked [send new code] next to the Activation Code box, or go back to Step 4 to re-enter your mobile phone number.

8. Click the Activate button. A congratulations page appears that tells you that you are now receiving MySpace alerts.

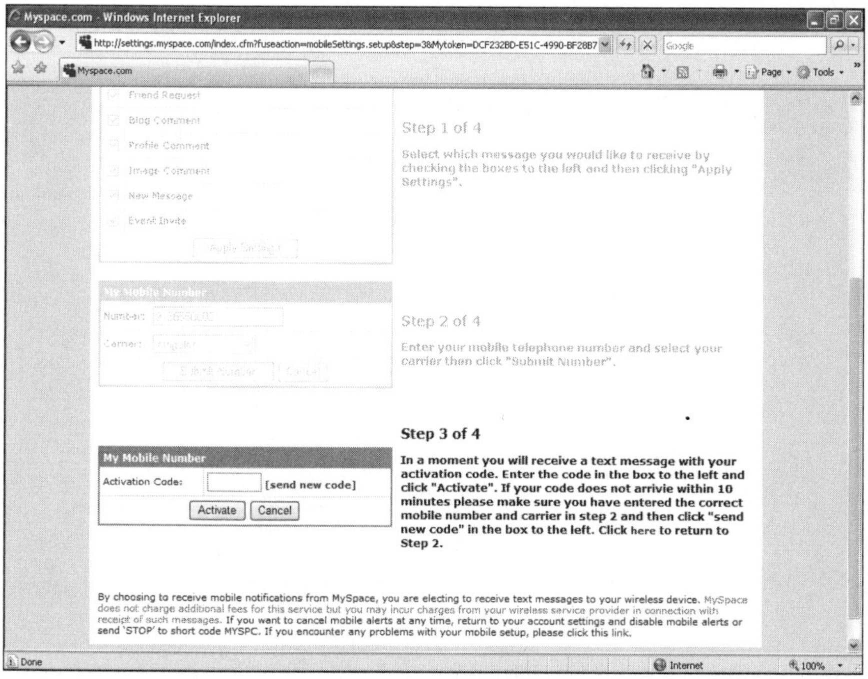

FIGURE 9-15 The second My Mobile Number table

Part III
Making Your MySpace Presence Extreme!

Chapter 10

Growing Your Circle of Friends

Everyone needs friends, and MySpace is a great way to meet them. When you join MySpace you immediately pick up one friend: Tom. Tom is actually Tom Anderson, the president of MySpace. You can find many more as MySpace has nearly 170 million potential friends on the network as of the writing of this book. You can search on MySpace, you can import your list of friends from your e-mail program, and you can invite people you know to join your friends network. Once you have friends, you can send them bulletins, maintain their information in your MySpace address book, and connect to your friends' friends to keep building your friends network.

FIND YOUR FRIENDS ON MYSPACE

In Chapter 1 you read about adding schools to your profile, which is a good way to find new friends on MySpace because you're looking to contact (or catch up with) people you know from school. But it's not the only way to find friends. You can also browse for friends, search for friends by typing a partial or full name into MySpace, or search for users based on your interests. First let's search for friends by browsing the MySpace network.

Browsing MySpace

When you browse MySpace for new friends, you can make your search as general or as specific as you want. Here's how to set your browse criteria:

1. Click the Browse link in the main menu bar. The Browse Users page appears, as shown in Figure 10-1, and displays the list of users based on the default MySpace browse settings.

2. In the Set Browse Criteria table, select the criteria for your search. You can search for other MySpace users with specific characteristics (such as an age range), users with specific reasons for being on MySpace, or only users who have photos. You can also sort your results by those who recently updated their profile, those who recently logged in, those who are new to MySpace, and those users who are closest to you in case you want to meet your MySpace friend in person someday.

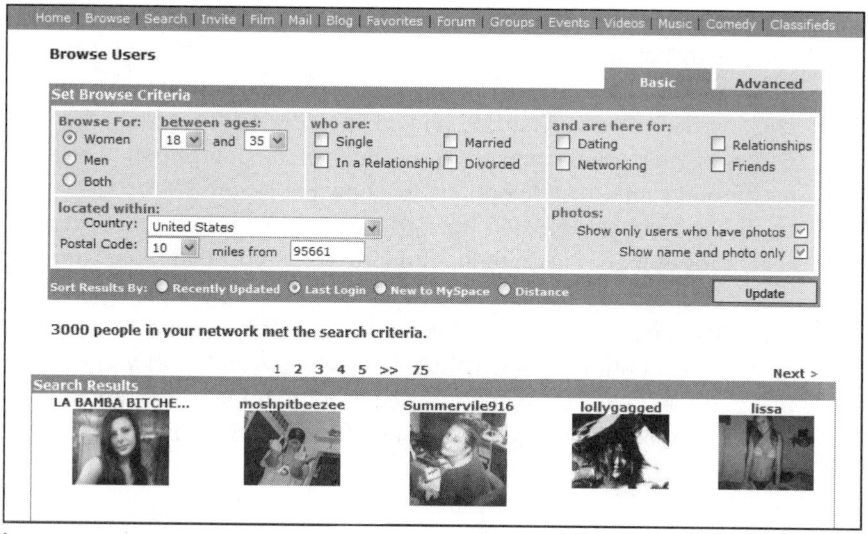

FIGURE 10-1 The Browse Users page

3. Click the Update button. The updated results appear below the table, as shown in Figure 10-2. If you want to view a user's profile (such as one whose user is currently online), click the user's name or picture to open the profile.

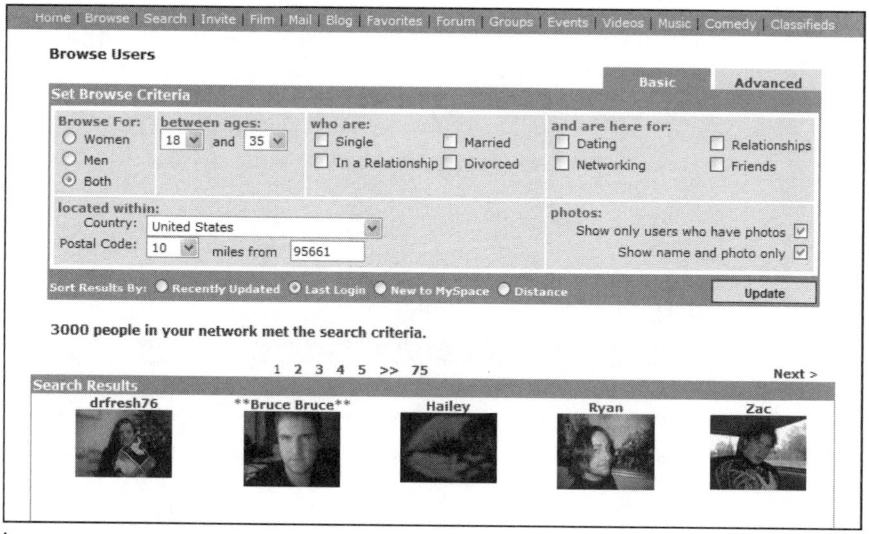

FIGURE 10-2 The updated results

The Set Browse Criteria table has two tabs. The Basic tab appears by default and gives you some basic options. If you want to search for a more specific person on MySpace, you can do so by clicking the Advanced tab. When you click the Advanced tab, the Set Browse Criteria table expands to include personal information and background and lifestyle options, as shown in Figure 10-3.

In the Personal Info and Background & Lifestyle areas, you can search for users based on their ethnicity, body type, their education, and even more specific questions such as their religion and whether they have kids, want kids, or don't want kids. When you finish selecting the options you want, click the Update button. If you decide that you don't need to search for such specific information, click the Basic tab to hide the Personal Info and Background & Lifestyle areas.

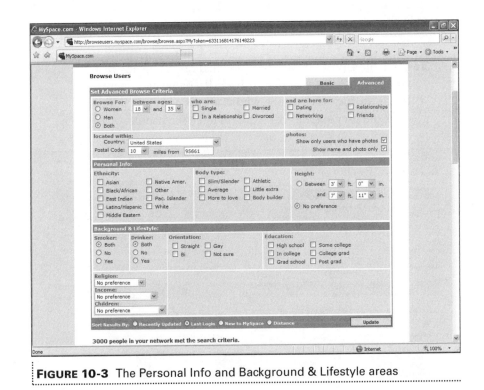

FIGURE 10-3 The Personal Info and Background & Lifestyle areas

Searching for a Specific MySpace User

You can search for a specific MySpace user by their own name, their profile display name, or their e-mail address. If you're not sure what the user's name is, you can type partial information and MySpace will return all user names, profile names, or their e-mail addresses that match that partial information. Here's how you search for a specific MySpace user:

1. Click the Search link in the main menu bar. The Search page appears, as shown in Figure 10-4.

2. Search for your friend in the Find a Friend box. The default search criteria is by name, but you can also search by display name by clicking the Display Name button or search by e-mail address by clicking the Email button. For this example, type the name of the user you want to find in the box.

3. Click the Find button. The Find a Friend page appears and displays the results of your search, as shown in Figure 10-5.

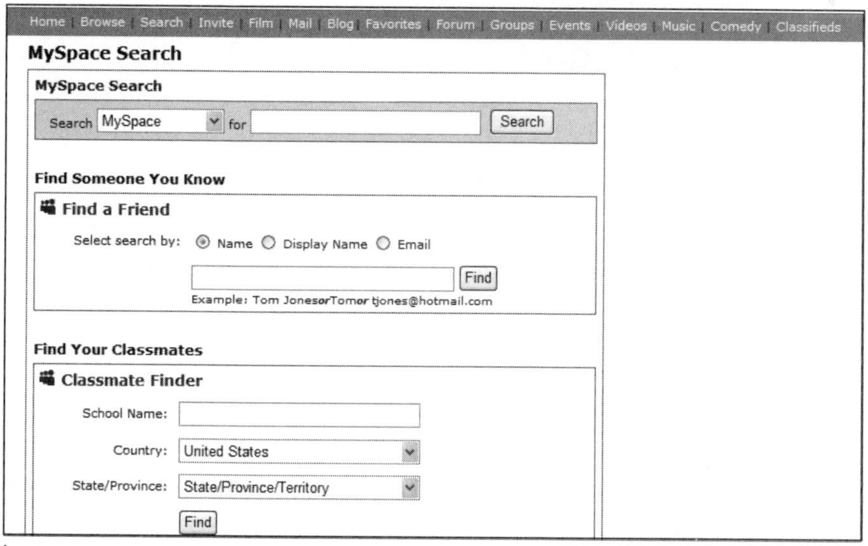

FIGURE 10-4 The MySpace Search page

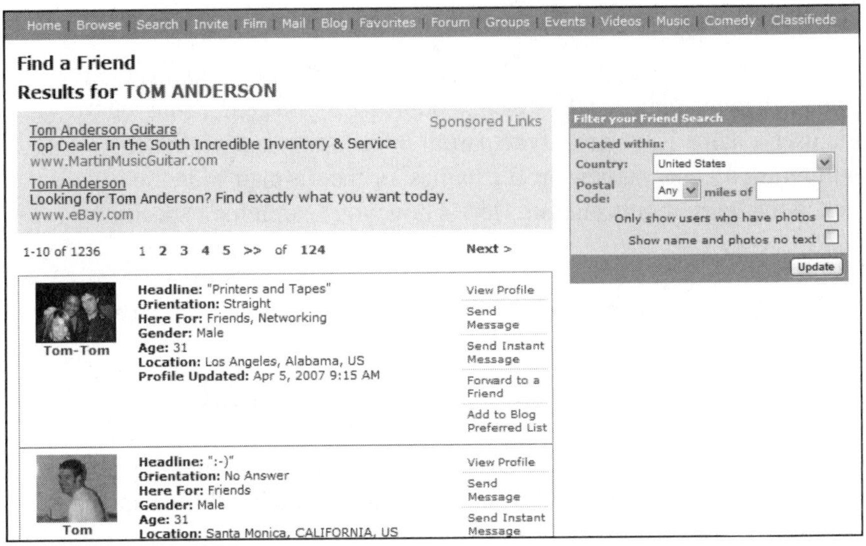

FIGURE 10-5 The Find a Friend page with the results

You can scroll down the list or click the Next link to move to the next page of results to find the user you're looking for. Ten results appear on each page.

Searching Based on Networking Affiliation

If you would rather search for friends based on their interests that are the same or similar to your own, you can search based on your networking affiliation.

1. Click Search in the main menu bar. The MySpace Search page appears.

2. Scroll down to the Affiliation for Networking box, as shown in Figure 10-6, and then select the Networking field from the Field drop-down list.

3. Select a sub-field from the Sub-Field drop-down list.

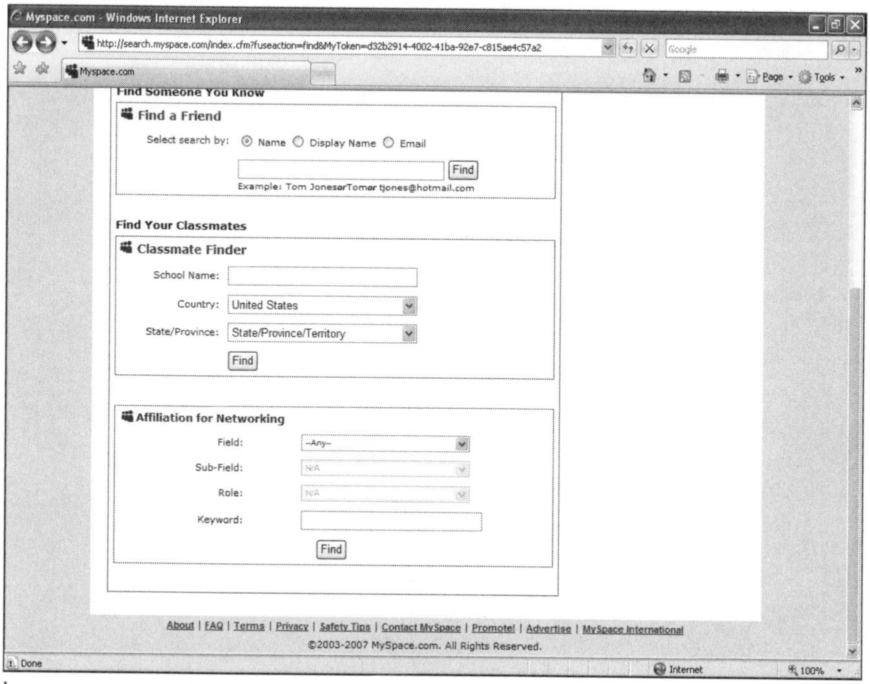

FIGURE 10-6 The Affiliation for Networking box

4. If there is a role you play in your field, such as a network engineer in the IT field, select the role from the Role drop-down list. If you don't see a role that fits you, you can select Other in the list or simply leave the selection as Any.

5. Type the search keyword in the Keyword box. If there is no keyword you can think of, then leave the box blank.

6. Click the Find button. The Find a Friend page appears and lists the results of your search, as shown in Figure 10-7.

As with the Find a Friend page that appears after you search for a specific MySpace user, ten results appear on each page when you search for someone who has the same networking interests. You can scroll down the list or click the Next link to move to the next page of results.

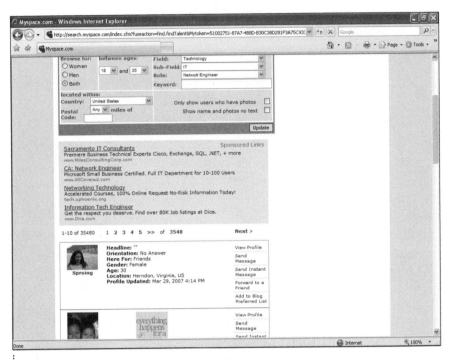

FIGURE 10-7 The Find a Friend page lists the results.

SEND A MYSPACE INVITATION TO YOUR FRIENDS

If you want people you know to join your MySpace friends network, invite those people to join your network—when they accept, they automatically join your Friends list. There are two ways you can invite to people you know to join MySpace: Through the MySpace site or through an e-mail program such as Outlook. Let's start by sending an invitation through MySpace.

Through MySpace

MySpace makes it easy to send an invitation to people you know to join MySpace and your Friends list.

1. Click the Invite link in the menu bar. The Invite Your Friends to MySpace page appears, as shown in Figure 10-8.

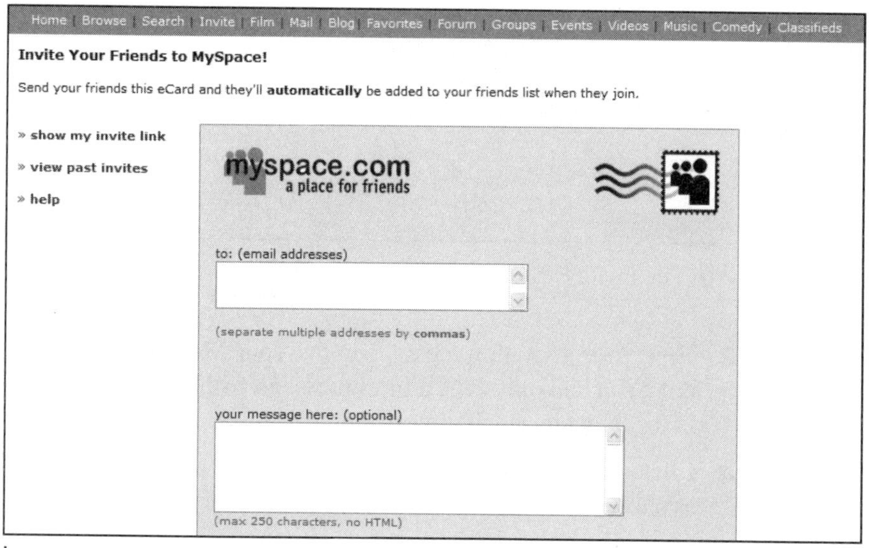

FIGURE 10-8 The Invite Your Friends to MySpace page

2. Type the e-mail address in the To box. If you want to add more than one address, separate each address with a comma, as shown in Figure 10-9.

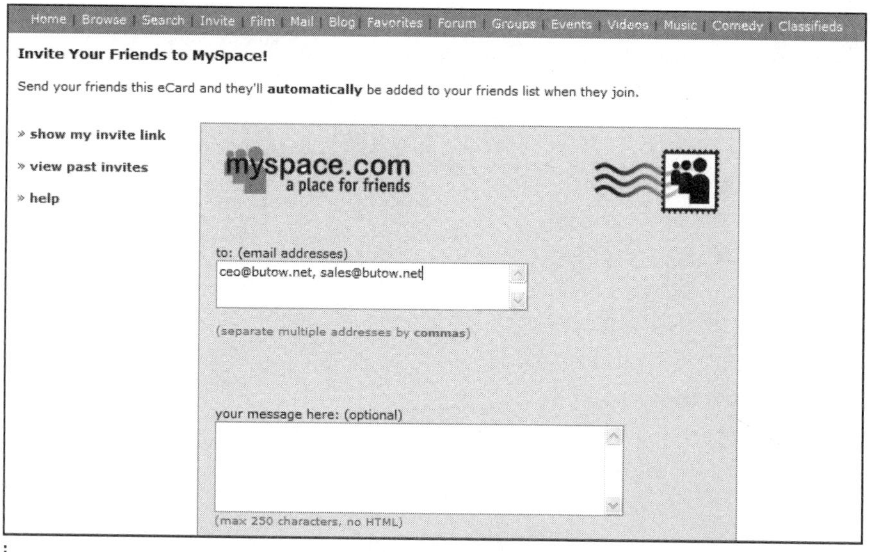

FIGURE 10-9 E-mail addresses separated by a comma

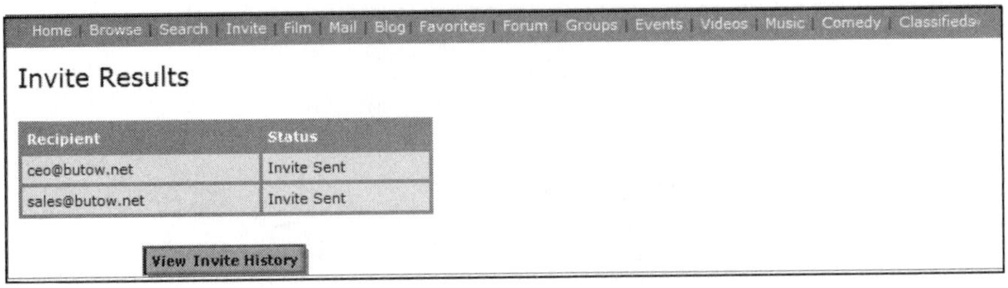

FIGURE 10-10 The Invite Results page

3. Type your invitation message in the Your Message Here box. You can only type a brief message with no more than 250 characters (including spaces).

4. Click the Send Invite button. The Invite Results page appears, as shown in Figure 10-10.

5. You can view your invitation history by clicking the View Invite History button. The Invite History page appears, as shown in Figure 10-11.

The Invite History table shows the current status of your invitations and gives you the options of sending a reminder to an invitee by clicking the Remind link or deleting the invitation by clicking the Delete link.

FIGURE 10-11 The Invite History page

Through Your E-mail System

When MySpace sends an invitation to your friends, it uses your profile display name, which others may not recognize. You can get around this problem by sending e-mail to your friends and copying the invitation link from MySpace into your message.

1. Click the Invite link in the main menu bar. The Invite Your Friends to MySpace page appears, as shown in Figure 10-12.

2. Click the link that states Show My Invite Link. The Personal Invite Link page appears, as shown in Figure 10-13.

3. Click the Click Here link to automatically open an e-mail message. In this example, MySpace has opened an e-mail message in Outlook and has included some generic text in the message as well. Now you can add your friends' e-mail addresses in the To box and change the message text to meet your needs. When you're finished, click the Send button.

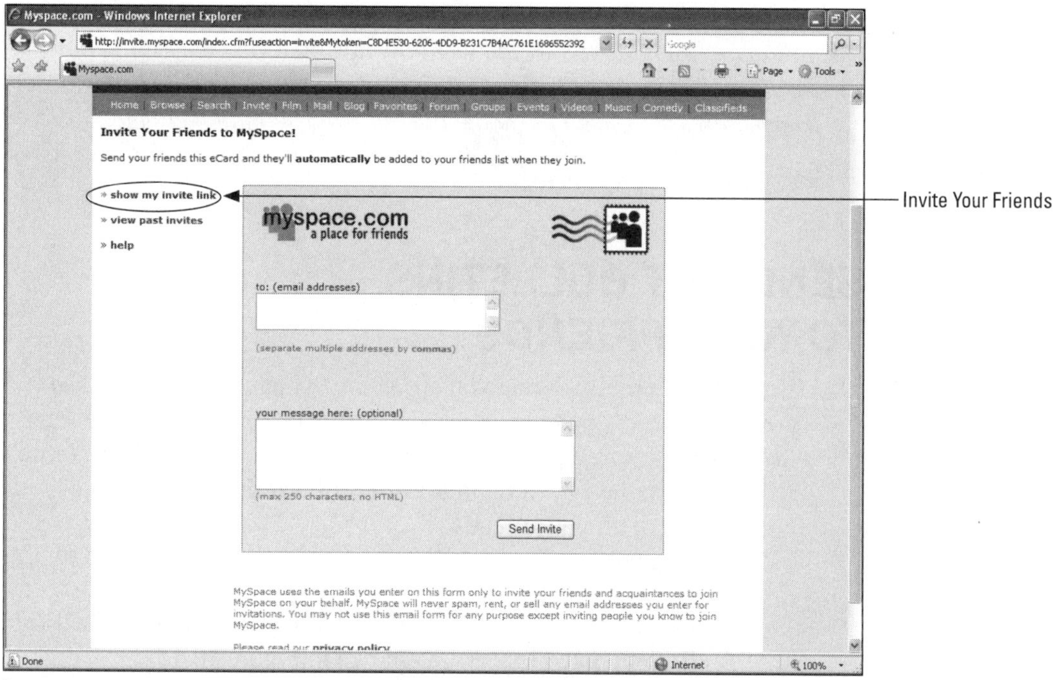

FIGURE 10-12 The Invite Your Friends to MySpace page

NOTE
If you do not use Outlook or if you use a web-based e-mail system like Yahoo or Hotmail, you would want to click the Copy button to copy the link into the Clipboard. Then, when you're writing an e-mail to your friends, press CTRL-V to paste the link into your e-mail message.

That's all there is to it!

SEND OUT BULLETINS TO YOUR FRIENDS

If you have a message that you absolutely want your friends to see, create and send a bulletin. After you create a bulletin, MySpace sends the bulletin to you and all your friends at the same time. The bulletin will appear in the My Bulletin Space section at the bottom of the home pages of all your friends.

Adding a bulletin is easy:

1. In the My Mail section, click the Post Bulletin link. The Post Bulletin page appears, as shown in Figure 10-14.

2. Type the subject of the bulletin in the Subject box.

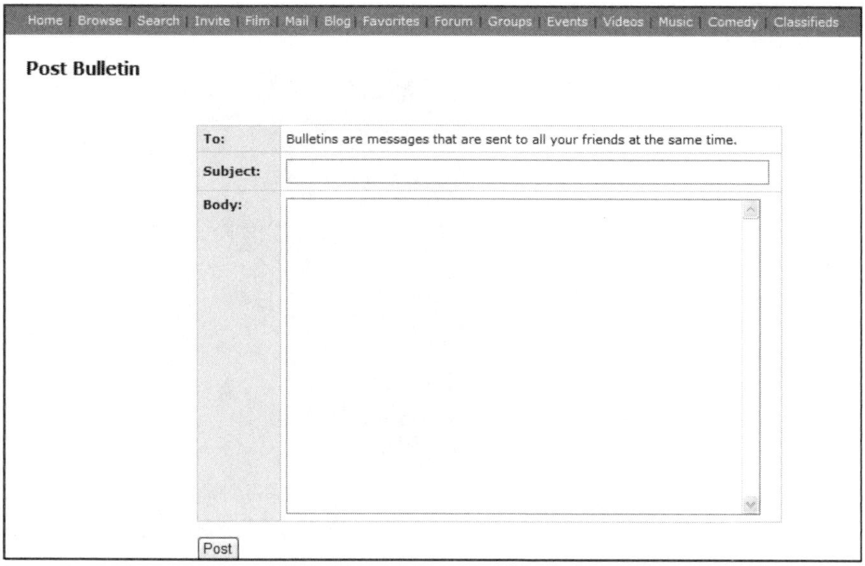

FIGURE 10-14 The Post Bulletin page

3. Type your bulletin in the Body box. Be respectful of your friends by keeping the bulletin as brief as possible.

4. Click the Post button. The Confirm Bulletin page appears and displays the subject and body of the bulletin you wrote.

5. You can take one of three actions from here:

■ Delete the bulletin without posting it by clicking the Cancel button.

■ If you want to edit the bulletin further, click the Edit button to return to the Post Bulletin page.

■ Post the bulletin by clicking the Post Bulletin button.

After you click the Post Bulletin button, the Bulletin Has Been Posted page appears, as shown in Figure 10-15, and informs you that it may take up to five minutes to post the bulletin, though in my experience it hardly takes that long.

Click the Home link to return to your profile summary page, and then scroll down to the bottom of the page. Your bulletin appears in the My Bulletin Space area, as shown in Figure 10-16.

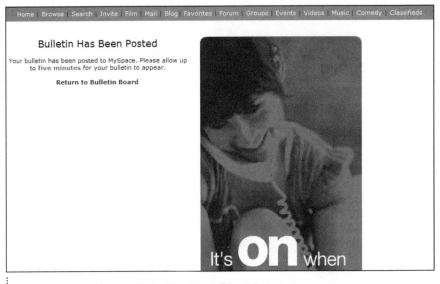

FIGURE 10-15 The Bulletin Has Been Posted page

FIGURE 10-16 The My Bulletin Space area

View the bulletin by clicking the bulletin subject. The Read Bulletin page appears. Delete the bulletin by clicking the Delete button, or return to your profile summary page by clicking the Home link.

NOTE *You can only delete the bulletin postings that you created. Everyone else's bulletin postings will stay on your Bulletin Board.*

UPDATE AND MAINTAIN YOUR MYSPACE ADDRESS BOOK

MySpace comes with its own address book, so you can use MySpace as the one source for maintaining your friends' contact information either on your computer or, your cell phone or PDA (if you log in using it). Here's how you can access your address book and maintain it by adding new friends' contact information:

1. Click the Mail link in the main menu bar. The Mail Center page appears, as shown in Figure 10-17.

2. Click the Address Book link. The Address Book page appears, as shown in Figure 10-18, and lists all contacts. If there are no contacts in your address book, the text "No contacts listed" appears in the table.

Address Book Link

FIGURE 10-17 The Mail Center page

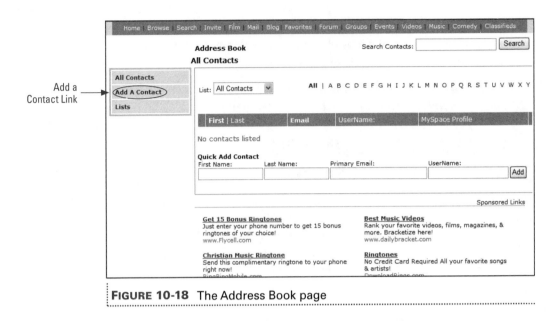

Add a
Contact Link

FIGURE 10-18 The Address Book page

3. Click the Add A Contact link. The Add Contact page appears, as shown in Figure 10-19.

4. Type the user's name and profile username in the Name area.

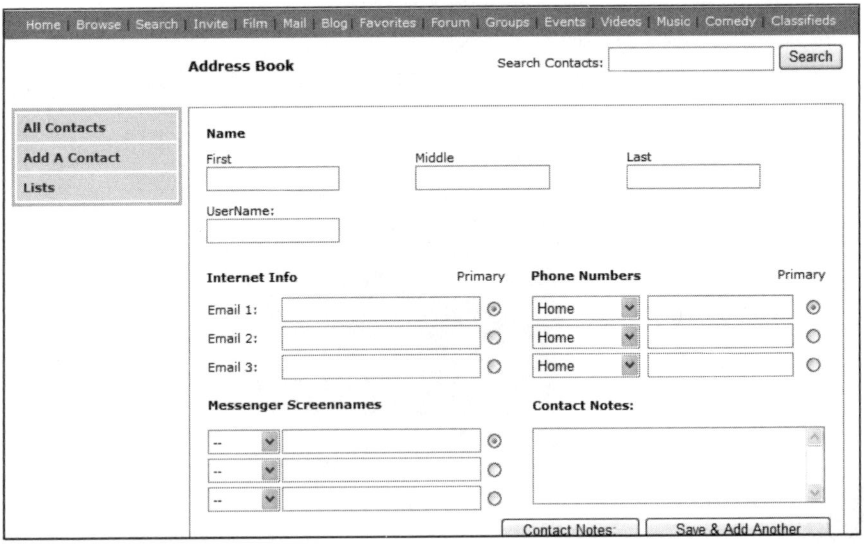

FIGURE 10-19 The Add Contact page

5. Type the user's e-mail addresses in the Internet Info area. You can add as many as three addresses. If one of these addresses is the primary address, click the button under the Primary column to the right of the e-mail address boxes. The first e-mail address you add is the primary e-mail address by default. Note that if you don't add an e-mail address for the user, you can't save the entry in the address book.

6. Type the user's phone numbers in the Phone Numbers area. You can add different types of phone numbers (like home, work, and mobile) by selecting the type from the drop-down list to the left of the phone number. If one of these phone numbers is the primary number, click the button under the Primary column to the right of the phone number boxes. The first phone number you add is the primary phone number by default.

7. If the user has instant messaging screen names on the Yahoo, MSN, or AIM service, select the service type and then type the screen name in the box. If the instant messaging service is the primary service, click the button to the right of the screen name box. The first instant messaging screen name you add is the primary screen name by default.

8. Type any contact notes in the Contact Notes box.

9. Click the Save & Add Another button and then click the All Contacts link. The new contact appears in the Address Book page, as shown in Figure 10-20. Simple, isn't it?

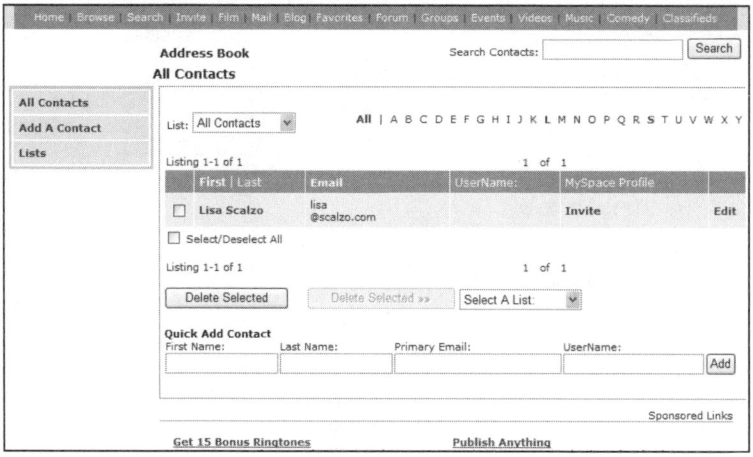

FIGURE 10-20 The new contact in the Address Book page

CONNECT TO YOUR FRIENDS' FRIENDS ON MYSPACE

When you view your friends' profiles, you'll see that they list their friends as well. If you're curious, you can find out more about those friends by scrolling down the user's page to their Friend Space area and then clicking the View All Of [name's] Friends (where [name's] is the name of the MySpace user). For example, in Figure 10-21 I've scrolled down to Tom Anderson's Friend Space area.

When I click the View All of Tom's Friends link, the View All Friends page appears, as shown in Figure 10-22, and lists all of Tom's friends so you can click on their photo or their username and learn more about them. Tom is not an example of the typical MySpace user because most users don't have nearly 170 million friends. You will be able to look at your friend's friends list in considerably less time than the years (if not decades) it would take to view all of Tom's friends.

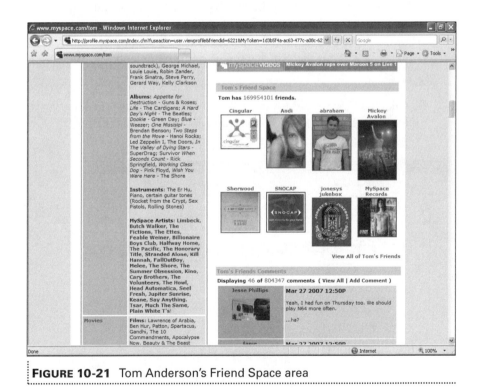

FIGURE 10-21 Tom Anderson's Friend Space area

FIGURE 10-22 The View All Friends page

FAQS

Do I have to include a message when I send an invitation? No. Including a message is optional. MySpace automatically generates text in the invitation that lets you know that you're a member of MySpace and you're inviting the recipient to join.

Can I add more than one contact in the address book without going back to the Address Book page? Yes. After you add the contact information, click the Save & Add Another button. MySpace saves the contact information and refreshes the Add Contact page so you can add another contact. After you add the last contact, click the Save & Add Another button, then click the All Contacts link to see all the people you've added.

Chapter 11

Contributing to the MySpace Community

With nearly 170 million users as of this writing, MySpace is a bigger community than any city in the world. Like any large city, MySpace contains many smaller communities. The most immediate of these communities is your own network of friends. As you venture out into the larger MySpace "neighborhoods," you can join groups of users who communicate and collaborate about different interests, from musical artists and bands to the meaning of life. If you don't like any of the groups you see, start your own. Then you can use the participation in your groups to add to your friends network. You can make the group public or keep it private and send invitations to your friends inviting them to join your group.

If your group is geographically based, you can also use MySpace to advertise local upcoming events in your area such as a school event, a band that's going to be making an appearance in your area, or any other type of gathering. Then you can add your event and any other events broadcasted to you into your MySpace calendar so you have one place to keep track of your busy social schedule.

EVALUATE THE GROUPS ON MYSPACE

There are literally millions of groups on MySpace. Fortunately MySpace categorizes these groups into 34 different categories—and those are just the English-language groups. Here's how you can search for MySpace groups so you can evaluate them and join the ones that fit your needs:

1. Click the Groups link in the main menu bar. The Groups Home page appears, as shown in Figure 11-1.

2. Click the group category that interests you. For this example I'll choose Business & Entrepreneurs since I have my own business. The Business & Entrepreneurs group page appears, as shown in Figure 11-2, and lists the first few groups MySpace finds.

3. You can search for more specific groups in the Search Groups box. In this box you can search by keyword or for

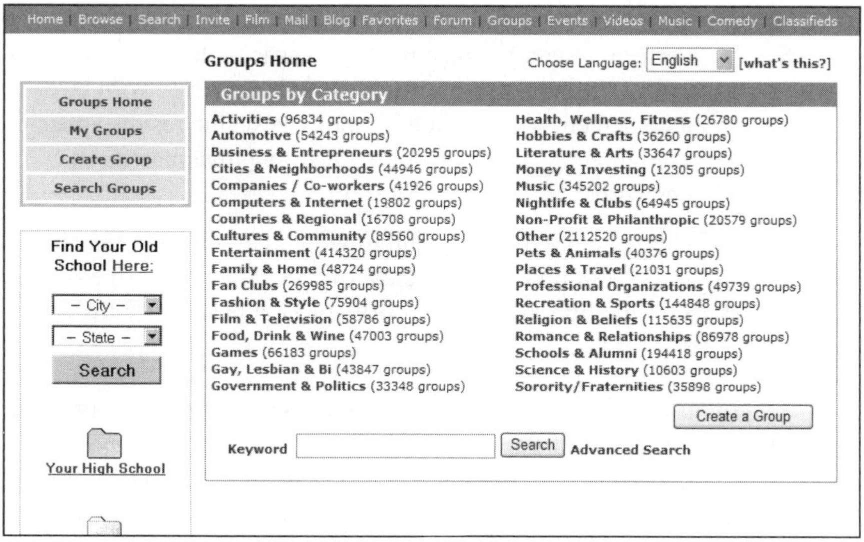

| Home | Browse | Search | Invite | Film | Mail | Blog | Favorites | Forum | Groups | Events | Videos | Music | Comedy | Classifieds |

Groups Home   Choose Language: English ▾ [what's this?]

Groups Home
My Groups
Create Group
Search Groups

Find Your Old School Here:

– City – ▾
– State – ▾
Search

Your High School

Groups by Category

Activities (96834 groups)
Automotive (54243 groups)
Business & Entrepreneurs (20295 groups)
Cities & Neighborhoods (44946 groups)
Companies / Co-workers (41926 groups)
Computers & Internet (19802 groups)
Countries & Regional (16708 groups)
Cultures & Community (89560 groups)
Entertainment (414320 groups)
Family & Home (48724 groups)
Fan Clubs (269985 groups)
Fashion & Style (75904 groups)
Film & Television (58786 groups)
Food, Drink & Wine (47003 groups)
Games (66183 groups)
Gay, Lesbian & Bi (43847 groups)
Government & Politics (33348 groups)

Health, Wellness, Fitness (26780 groups)
Hobbies & Crafts (36260 groups)
Literature & Arts (33647 groups)
Money & Investing (12305 groups)
Music (345202 groups)
Nightlife & Clubs (64945 groups)
Non-Profit & Philanthropic (20579 groups)
Other (2112520 groups)
Pets & Animals (40376 groups)
Places & Travel (21031 groups)
Professional Organizations (49739 groups)
Recreation & Sports (144848 groups)
Religion & Beliefs (115635 groups)
Romance & Relationships (86978 groups)
Schools & Alumni (194418 groups)
Science & History (10603 groups)
Sorority/Fraternities (35898 groups)

Create a Group

Keyword [_____] Search **Advanced Search**

FIGURE 11-1 The Groups Home page

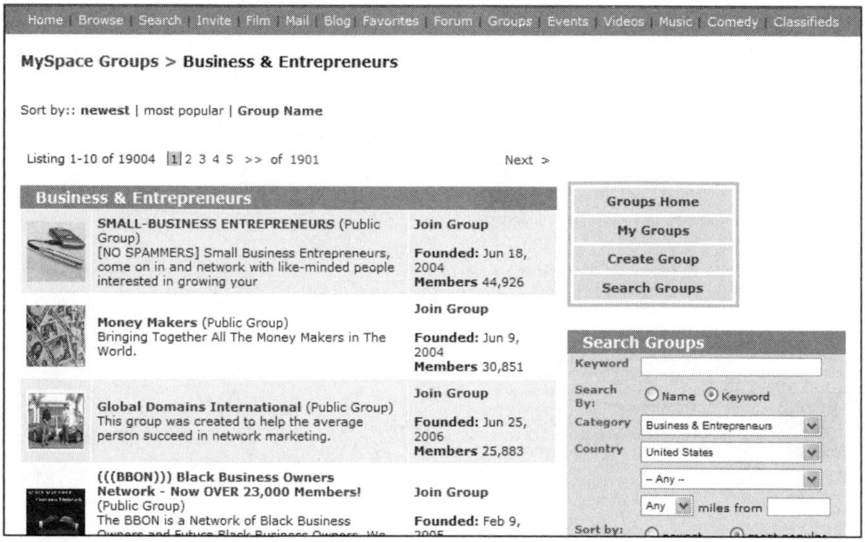

| Home | Browse | Search | Invite | Film | Mail | Blog | Favorites | Forum | Groups | Events | Videos | Music | Comedy | Classifieds |

MySpace Groups > Business & Entrepreneurs

Sort by:: **newest** | most popular | **Group Name**

Listing 1-10 of 19004 [1] 2 3 4 5 >> of 1901   Next >

Business & Entrepreneurs

SMALL-BUSINESS ENTREPRENEURS (Public Group)
[NO SPAMMERS] Small Business Entrepreneurs, come on in and network with like-minded people interested in growing your
Join Group
Founded: Jun 18, 2004
Members 44,926

Money Makers (Public Group)
Bringing Together All The Money Makers In The World.
Join Group
Founded: Jun 9, 2004
Members 30,851

Global Domains International (Public Group)
This group was created to help the average person succeed in network marketing.
Join Group
Founded: Jun 25, 2006
Members 25,883

(((BBON))) Black Business Owners Network - Now OVER 23,000 Members! (Public Group)
The BBON is a Network of Black Business Owners and Future Black Business Owners. We
Join Group
Founded: Feb 9, 2005

Groups Home
My Groups
Create Group
Search Groups

Search Groups
Keyword [_____]
Search By: ○ Name ● Keyword
Category [Business & Entrepreneurs ▾]
Country [United States ▾]
[– Any – ▾]
[Any ▾] miles from [____]
Sort by: ○ newest ● most popular

FIGURE 11-2 The Business & Entrepreneurs group page

groups in a specific area. You need to add a keyword to perform a search. Since my business is in the Sacramento area, I'll type **Sacramento business** in the Keyword box and then click the Search button. The search results appear in Figure 11-3—there is only one group that matches the keywords.

4. Click the title of the group to view more information about it. For example, when I click the Sacramento Business Leaders title, the group profile page appears, as shown in Figure 11-4.

If you're dissatisfied with your search and you want to start over, click the MySpace Groups link at the top of the page just below the menu bar, as you see in Figure 11-3. You can also click the Groups link in the main menu bar. Either way, you'll end up back at the Groups Home page.

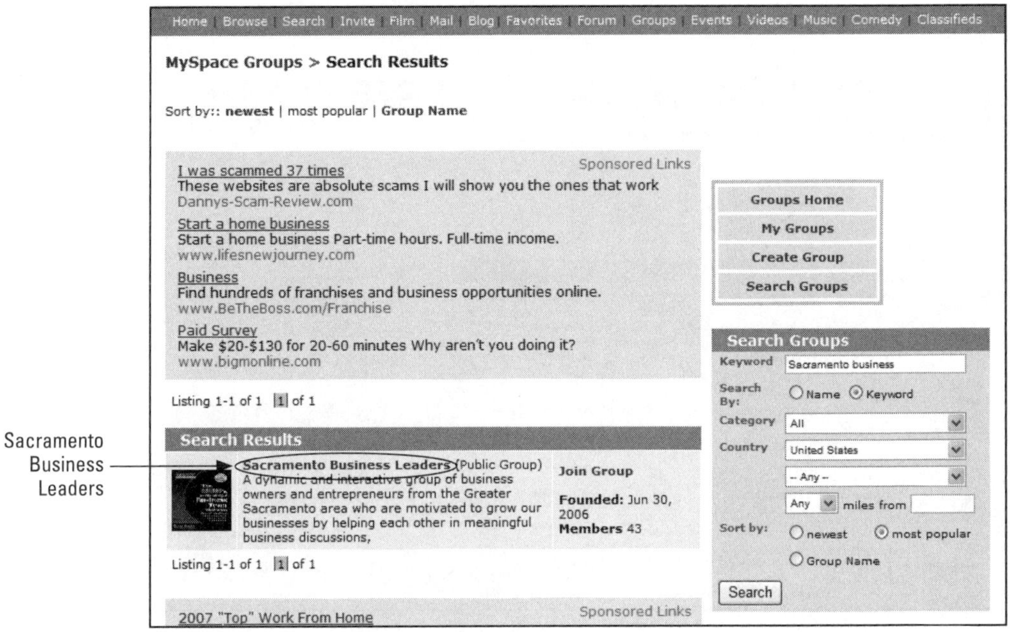

FIGURE 11-3 The search results

FIGURE 11-4 The Sacramento Business Leaders group profile page

JOIN A MYSPACE GROUP

So now that you've had a chance to evaluate the available MySpace groups, how do you join? It's simple. For this example I'll open up the Business & Entrepreneurs group category as I did in the previous section.

1. Click the Join Group link for the group you want to join, as shown in Figure 11-5.

2. The Confirm Join Group page appears, as shown in Figure 11-6. Click the Join button.

3. MySpace confirms that you're a member, as shown in Figure 11-7. That's it! Click the Back to Group Profile link to open the group profile page. You'll need to do this for the task in the next section.

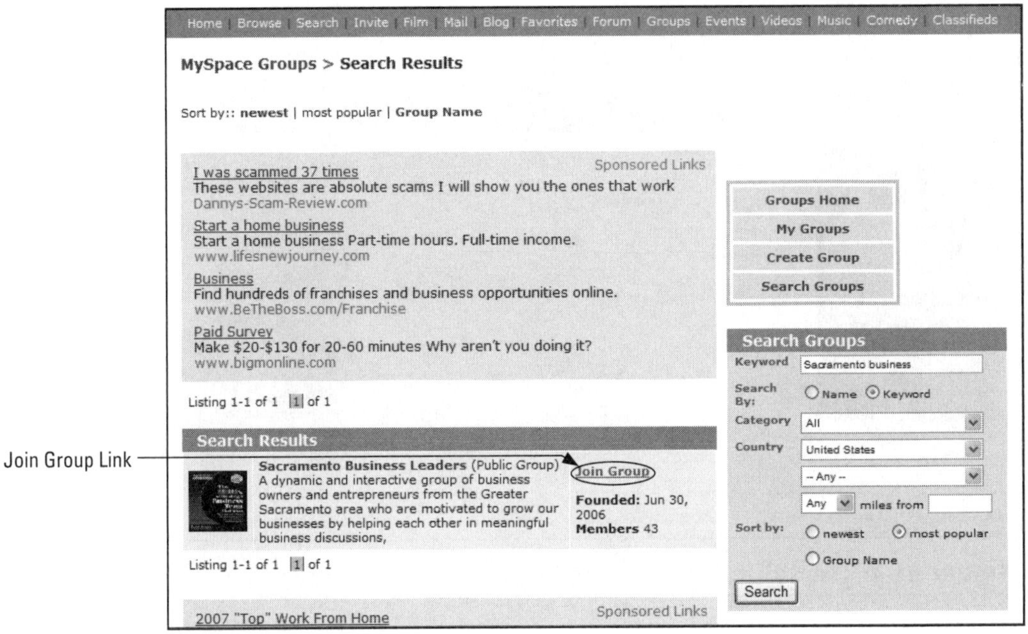

Join Group Link ———

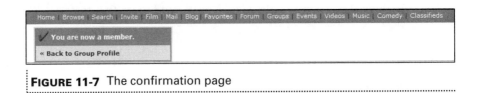

FIGURE 11-5 The Join Group link

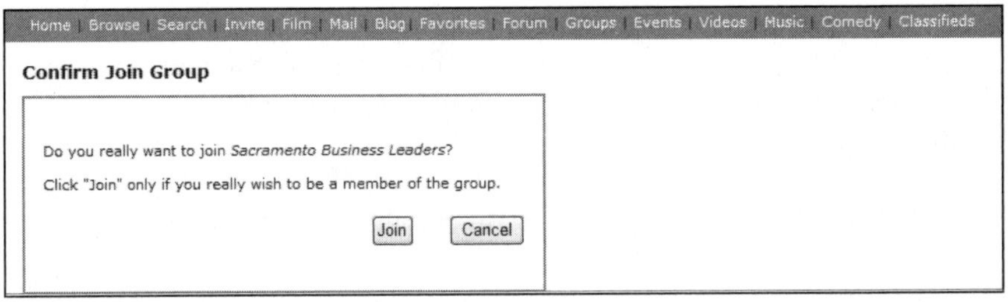

FIGURE 11-6 The Confirm Join Group page

FIGURE 11-7 The confirmation page

GET BULLETINS FROM
YOUR MYSPACE GROUP

Now that you're a part of a MySpace group, you'll automatically get
bulletins from them that you can read when you visit the Groups Home
page. You can change your bulletin privacy settings to hide any bulletins
in the Groups Home page as well as receive bulletins from your group
members and/or the moderator in your group. At the end of the previous
section, you opened the group profile for the profile you just joined—in
this example it's the Sacramento Business Leaders group, and we'll
continue to use this example to change bulletin settings.

1. In the group profile page, click the Privacy button, as shown
   in Figure 11-8.

2. The Group Privacy Settings page appears, as shown in
   Figure 11-9. In the Settings table, select one (or more) of the
   three check boxes to tell MySpace to post bulletins from the
   moderator and/or other group members in your bulletin space
   on your profile home page and to display (or hide) indicators
   on the Groups Home page about new bulletins for you.

Privacy Button

| Home | Browse | Search | Invite | Film | Mail | Blog | Favorites | Forum | Groups | Events | Videos | Music | Comedy | Classifieds |

Group URL: http://groups.myspace.com/sacbizleaders   ★ Back to Groups Directory

Sacramento Business Leaders

Category: Business &
Entrepreneurs

Type: Public Membership [help]
Founded: Jun 30, 2006
Location:: Sacramento,
California - US
Members: 44

Invite Others
Resign
Post Bulletin
Post Topic
Privacy

Group Leader:
Karen - SalesPartners

» View Group Photos

Under Construction!!!! Please be patient for a day or two. :-)

The Sacramento Business Leaders group is a dynamic and interactive group of business owners and entrepreneurs from the Greater
Sacramento area who are motivated to grow our businesses by helping each other in meaningful business discussions, networking, and

FIGURE 11-8 The Privacy button

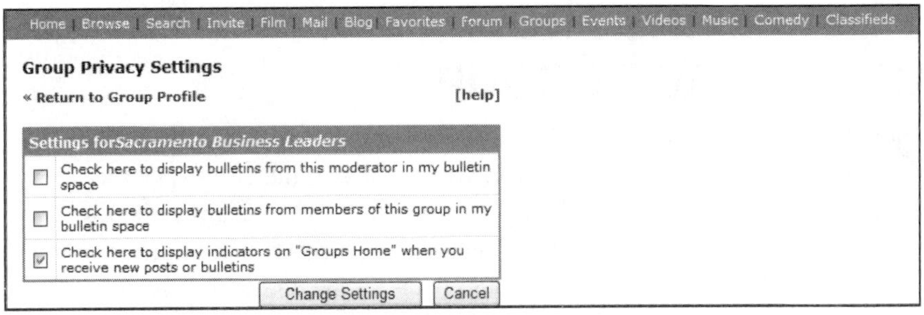

FIGURE 11-9 The Group Privacy Settings page

3. Click the Change Settings button. The text "Your settings have been updated" appears above the settings table. You can return to the group profile by clicking the Return to Group Profile link.

CREATE YOUR OWN MYSPACE GROUP

If you don't like any of the groups that you find—or you find that there aren't any groups that talk about what you want to talk about—you can create your own group. Here's how to do it:

1. Click the Groups link in the main menu bar. The Groups Home page appears, as shown in Figure 11-10.

2. Click the Create Group button. The Create a Group on MySpace page appears, as shown in Figure 11-11, so you can add information about your group in the Create a Group table.

3. Type the group name in the Group Name box.

4. Select the category your group belongs to from the Category drop-down list.

5. In the next seven rows you can click the appropriate buttons to change the group options to the ones you prefer. For example, if you want your group members to be able to post bulletins, click the Yes button in the Members Can Post Bulletins row.

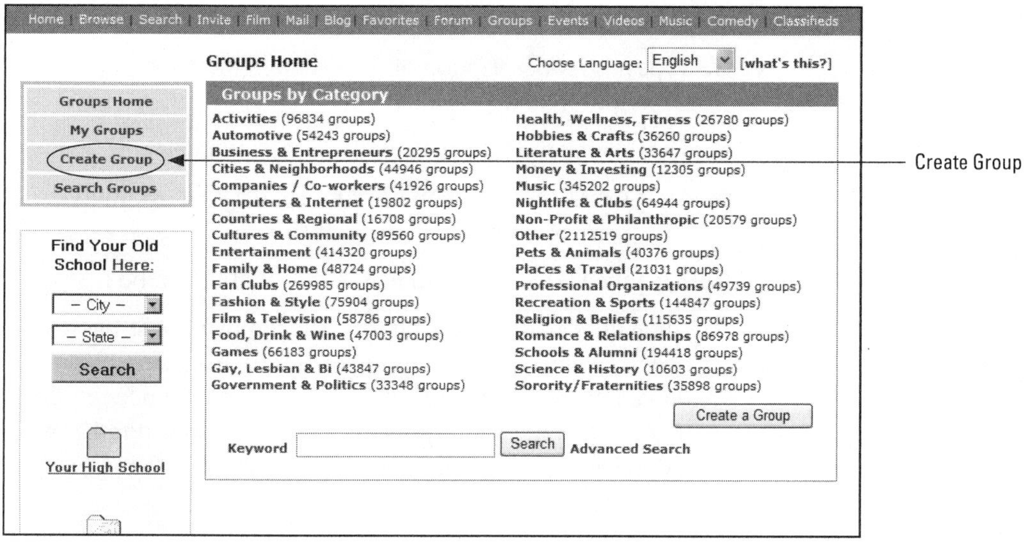

FIGURE 11-10 The Groups Home page with the Create Group button

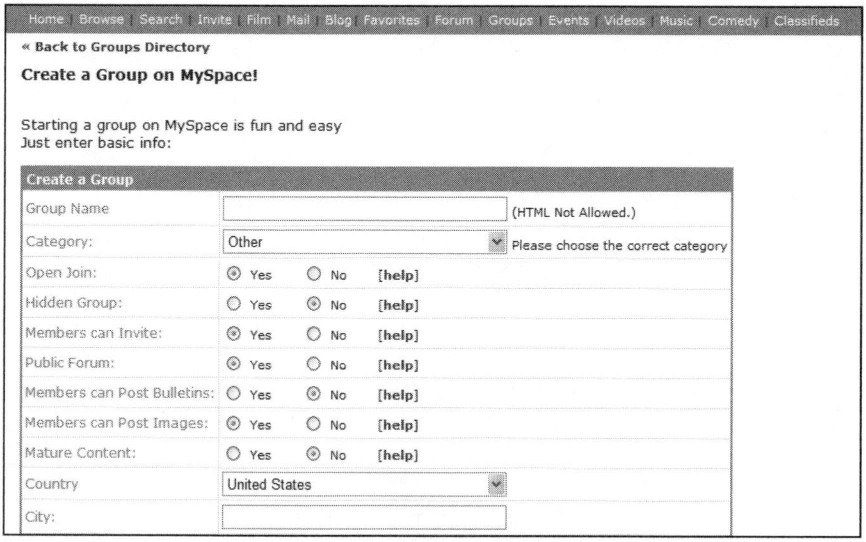

FIGURE 11-11 The Create a Group on MySpace page

6. Select the Country, City, State/Region, and ZIP Code.

7. Type a brief description of the group in the Short Description box.

8. Type a longer description in the Description box.

9. Type the URL name you want to use for your group in the URL box, as shown in Figure 11-12.

10. Type the text from the image in the Verification box.

11. Click the Create Group button. The Upload Some Photos page appears, as shown in Figure 11-13. You can upload photos by clicking the Browse button and then opening the image file in the appropriate folder. If you would rather not upload any photos right now, click the Skip & Go Directly to Group Profile page link.

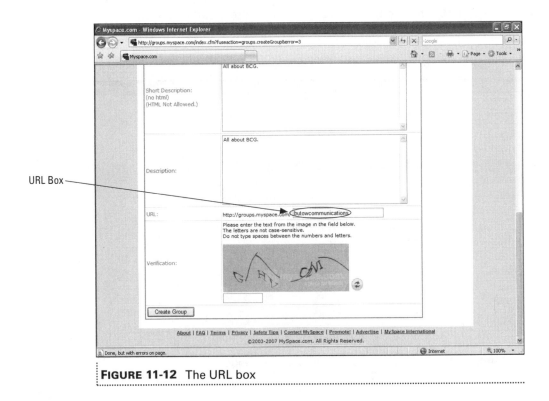

FIGURE 11-12 The URL box

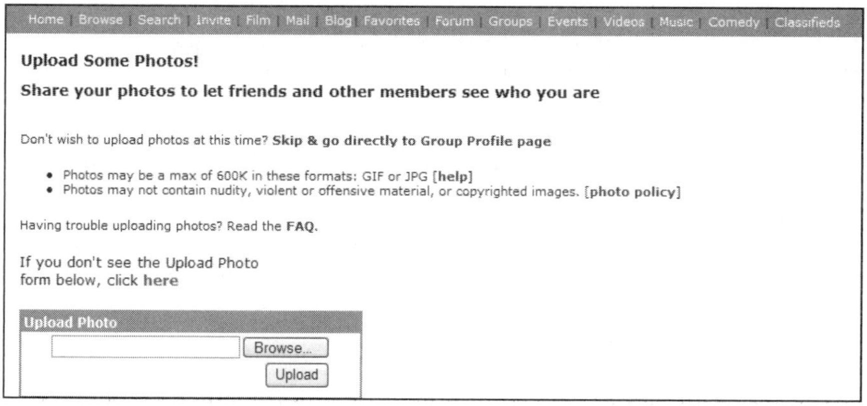

Home | Browse | Search | Invite | Film | Mail | Blog | Favorites | Forum | Groups | Events | Videos | Music | Comedy | Classifieds

Upload Some Photos!

Share your photos to let friends and other members see who you are

Don't wish to upload photos at this time? **Skip & go directly to Group Profile page**

- Photos may be a max of 600K in these formats: GIF or JPG [**help**]
- Photos may not contain nudity, violent or offensive material, or copyrighted images. [**photo policy**]

Having trouble uploading photos? Read the **FAQ.**

If you don't see the Upload Photo
form below, click **here**

Upload Photo
[_____] Browse...
Upload

FIGURE 11-13 The Upload Some Photos page

The group profile page appears, as shown in Figure 11-14. Now that you've created the group, you're the moderator of the group. You get to set the group rules, invite others to join your group, post forum and bulletin messages, and you also get to kick people out of the group if they violate those rules.

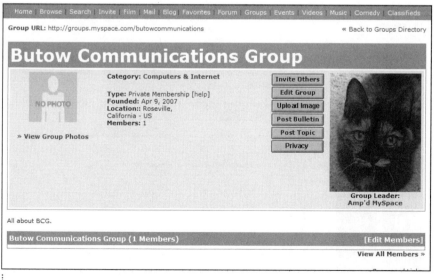

Home | Browse | Search | Invite | Film | Mail | Blog | Favorites | Forum | Groups | Events | Videos | Music | Comedy | Classifieds

Group URL: http://groups.myspace.com/butowcommunications   « Back to Groups Directory

Butow Communications Group

NO PHOTO

Category: Computers & Internet

Type: Private Membership [help]
Founded: Apr 9, 2007
Location:: Roseville, California - US
Members: 1

» **View Group Photos**

Invite Others
Edit Group
Upload Image
Post Bulletin
Post Topic
Privacy

Group Leader:
Amp'd MySpace

All about BCG.

Butow Communications Group (1 Members)   **[Edit Members]**

View All Members »

FIGURE 11-14 The group profile page

MAKE ANNOUNCEMENTS TO YOUR GROUP

If you want to let your group know about something that's going on with you, here's how to post a bulletin to all the members in your group:

1. Click the Post Bulletin button. The Post Group Bulletin page appears, as shown in Figure 11-15.

2. Type the subject and body in the Subject and Body boxes.

3. Click the Post button. The Confirm Bulletin page appears, as shown in Figure 11-16.

4. Click the Post Bulletin button. MySpace sends the bulletin to everyone in the group.

Before you type your information, take time to read the posting rules that appear above the Subject box. If you send a bulletin that violates the rules, it's within the group moderator's power to kick you out of the group.

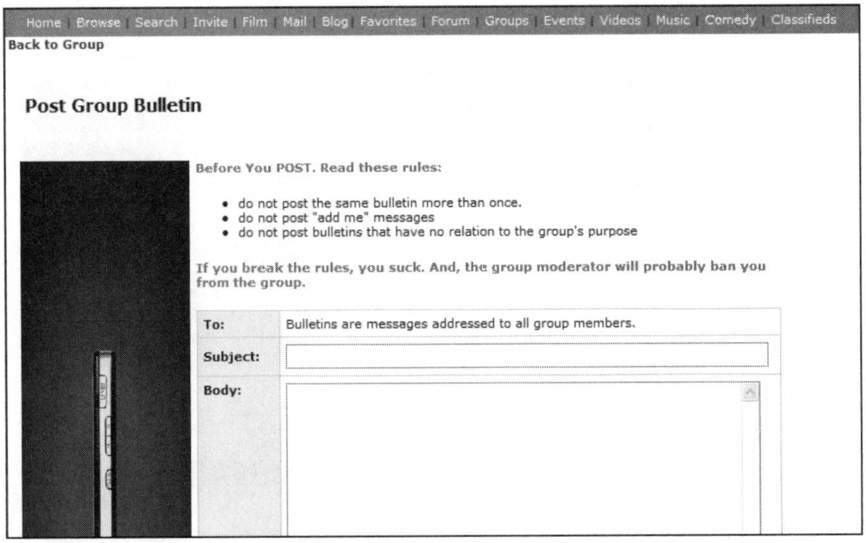

FIGURE 11-15 The Post Group Bulletin page

FIGURE 11-16 The Confirm Bulletin page

CREATE MYSPACE EVENTS

If you have a public event that you want to promote, such as a fundraising event for your school, it's easy to post an event notice on MySpace so everyone can view the event on the Events page. You can also create private events such as a New Year's party with friends that you can deliver only to your invitees. Before you post your event, you should add the event to your calendar and add a reminder about the event so you don't forget about it as you go about your busy life. We'll start by adding the event to the calendar first.

Add the Event to Your Calendar

Here's how to access your MySpace calendar and add an event (as well as a reminder) to it:

1. In your profile home page, click Manage Calendar to the right of your profile photo. The My Calendar page appears, as shown in Figure 11-17.

2. Click the Add button to the left of the time when the event will start. The Add Entry to Calendar page appears, as shown in Figure 11-18.

3. Type the event title in the Title box.

4. Enter information about the event in the rest of the page. For Reminders, click the Send a Reminder button and specify

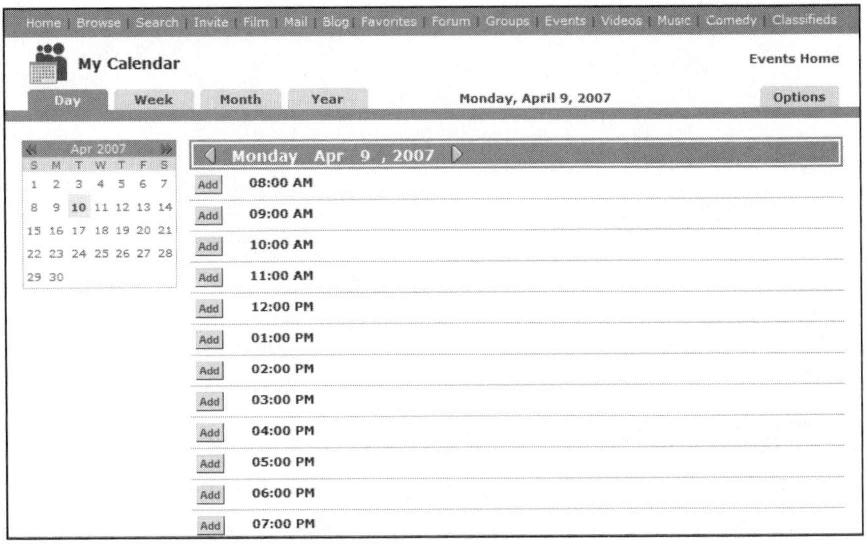

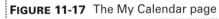

FIGURE 11-17 The My Calendar page

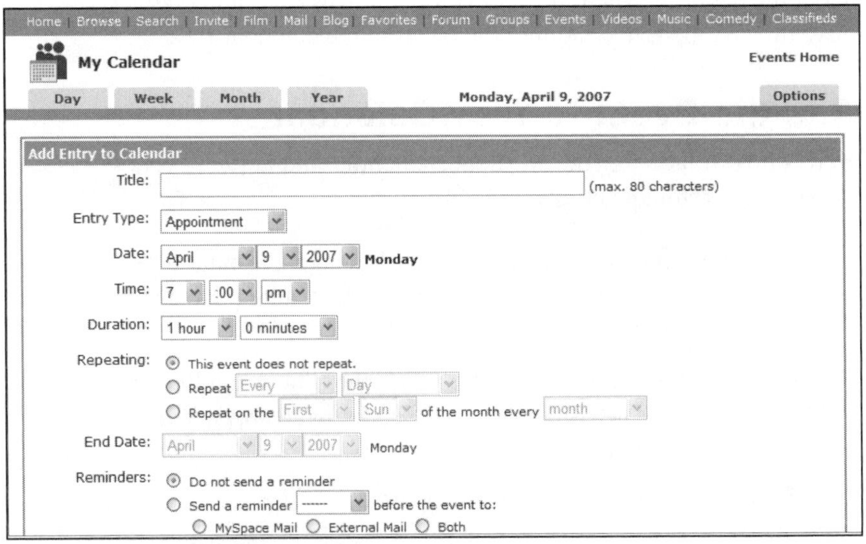

FIGURE 11-18 The Add Entry to Calendar page

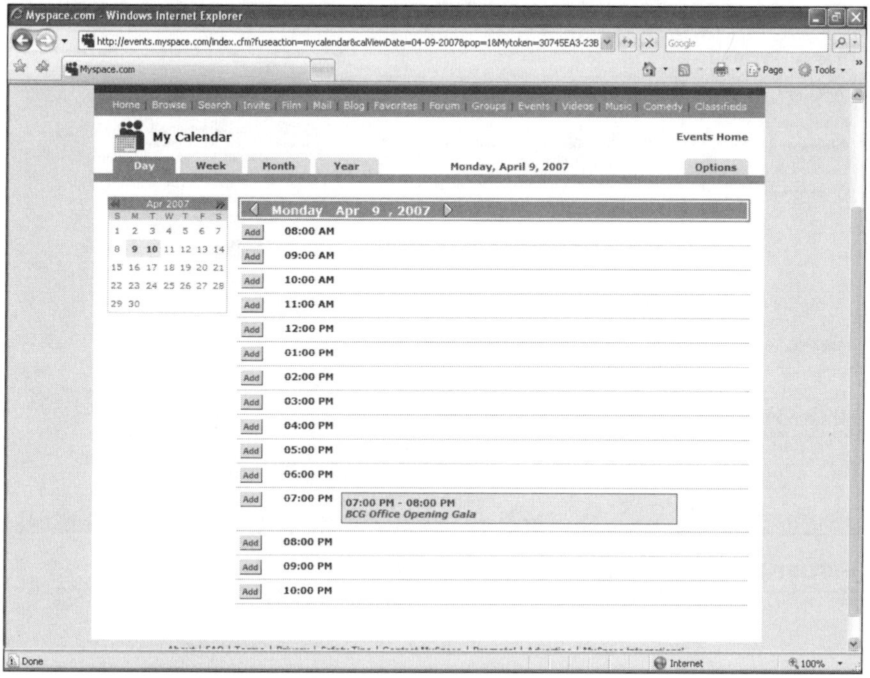

FIGURE 11-19 The event appears in the calendar.

how many days in advance of the event you want MySpace to remind you about the event. Then select whether you want the reminder to come to your MySpace e-mail inbox, your regular e-mail inbox, or both.

5. Click the Save button. Your event appears in the calendar, as shown in Figure 11-19.

Post the Event

Now let's post the event.

1. Click the Events link in the main menu bar. The MySpace Events page appears, as shown in Figure 11-20.

2. Click the Create New Event link. The Create An Event page appears, as shown in Figure 11-21.

Create New Event ────▶

FIGURE 11-20 The MySpace Events page

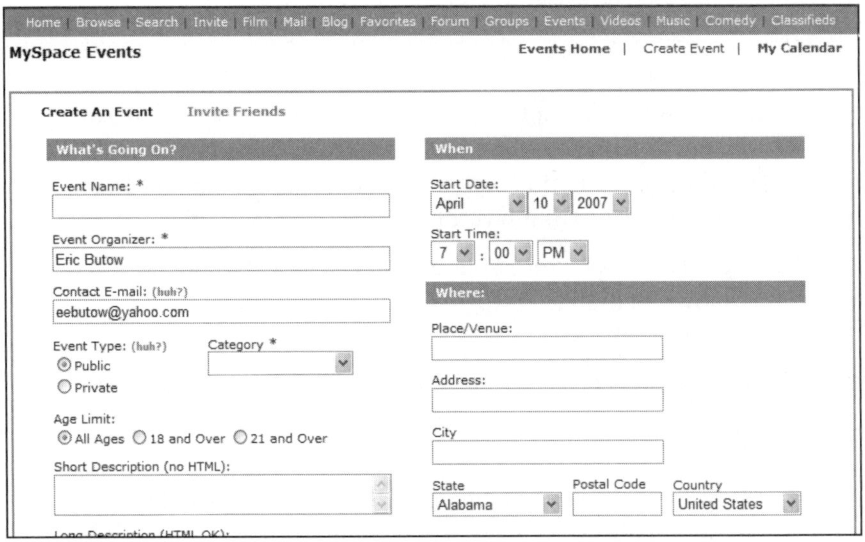

FIGURE 11-21 The Create An Event page

3. Enter information about the event in the What's Going On? section. You need to provide information in boxes and lists with titles that include a red asterisk.

4. Specify information about when the event will take place in the When section.

5. Enter information about where the event will take place in the Where section.

6. Type the information from the image into the box above the Save Event button.

7. Click the Save Event button. The Edit This Event page appears and lets you determine the invitation details and who you want to invite to the event.

You can click the Invite & Update button after you send out your invitations. If you'd rather not send invitations out yet but just want to look at what you've added for your event, click the View This Event page link. The Events page appears, as shown in Figure 11-22. If you want to edit the event, click the Edit Event link.

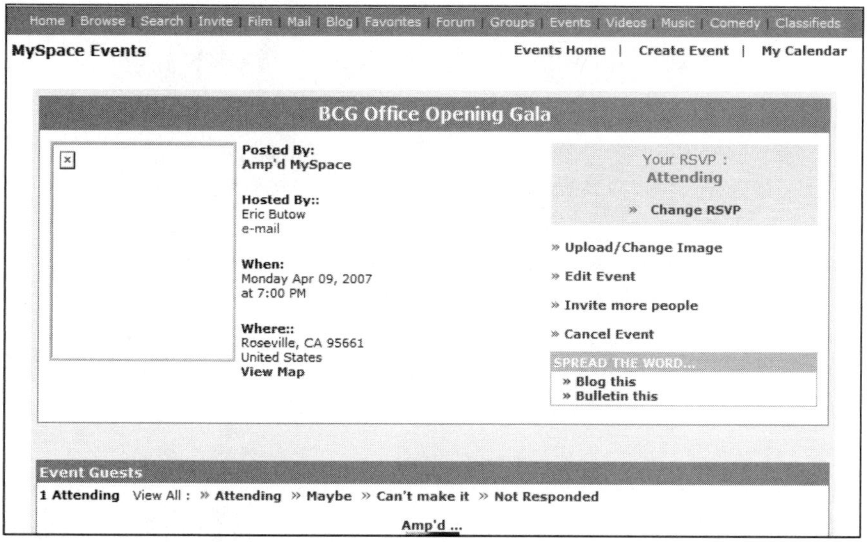

FIGURE 11-22 The Events page

ADD EVENTS TO YOUR CALENDAR

There are plenty of events going on in MySpace all the time, and you can add events you want to be a part of in your calendar quickly and easily so you can be reminded of what's going on in your neighborhood and online soon. Here's how to add an event to your calendar:

1. Click the Events link in the main menu bar.

2. In the MySpace Events page you can select one of the featured events in the Featured Events area, or you can select one of the events in the Search Events list, as shown in Figure 11-23.

3. Click the event name in the list. The event page appears, as shown in Figure 11-24.

4. Add the event to your calendar by clicking the Add to My Calendar button.

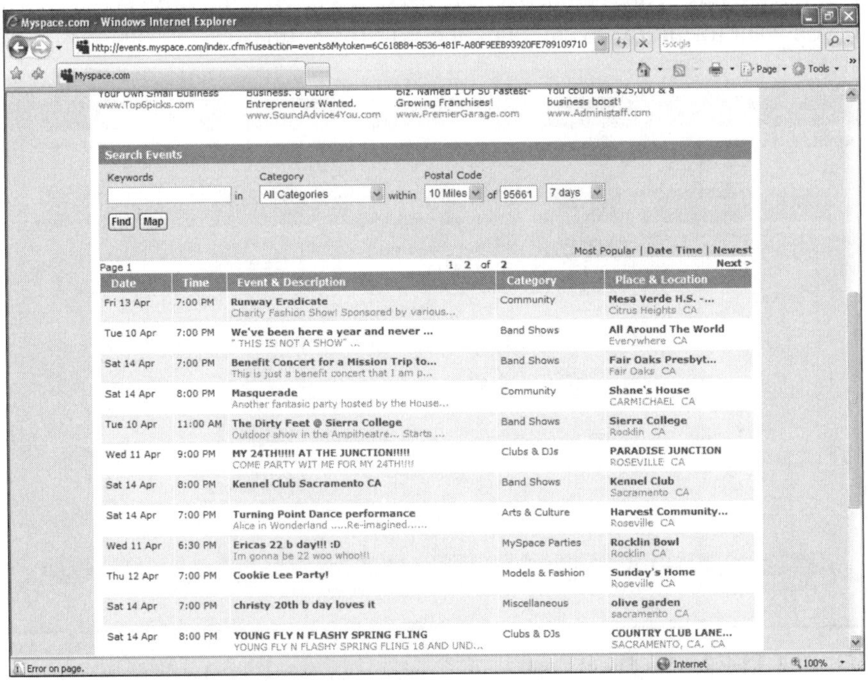

FIGURE 11-23 The Search Events list

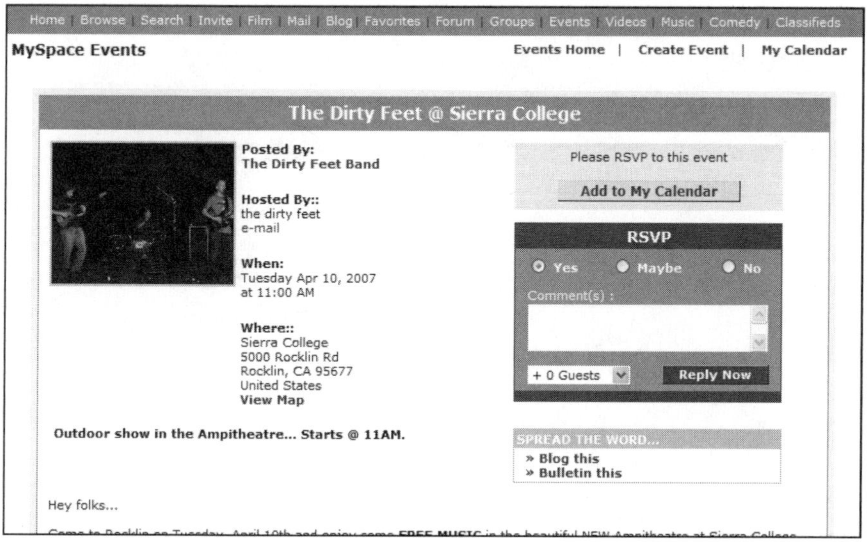

FIGURE 11-24 The event page

And that's it. Really. The event page refreshes, and if you want to remove the event from your calendar, click the Remove from My Calendar button.

BLOG YOUR EVENT

Invitations are all well and good, but you need to keep your event in front of people's eyes repeatedly for them to get the message that you want them to be there. MySpace makes it easy for you to type blog messages related to your event. For this example we'll use the event we created in the "Create MySpace Events" section earlier in this chapter to access the blog tool.

1. Click the Events link in the main menu bar.

2. In the MySpace Events page, click the Events I've Posted link, as shown in Figure 11-25.

3. In the Upcoming Events table, click the title of the event, as shown in Figure 11-26.

Events I've
Posted Link

FIGURE 11-25 The Events I've Posted link

4. In the event information page, click the Blog This link in the Spread the Word section, as shown in Figure 11-27.

The Post a New Blog Entry page appears and MySpace immediately adds the subject text "Check out this event" and the name of the event in the Subject box. You can add the text for your blog in the Body box.

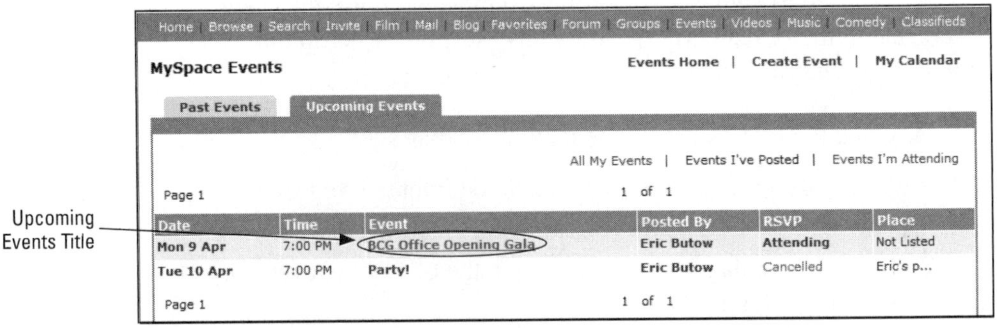

Upcoming
Events Title

FIGURE 11-26 The title in the Upcoming Events table

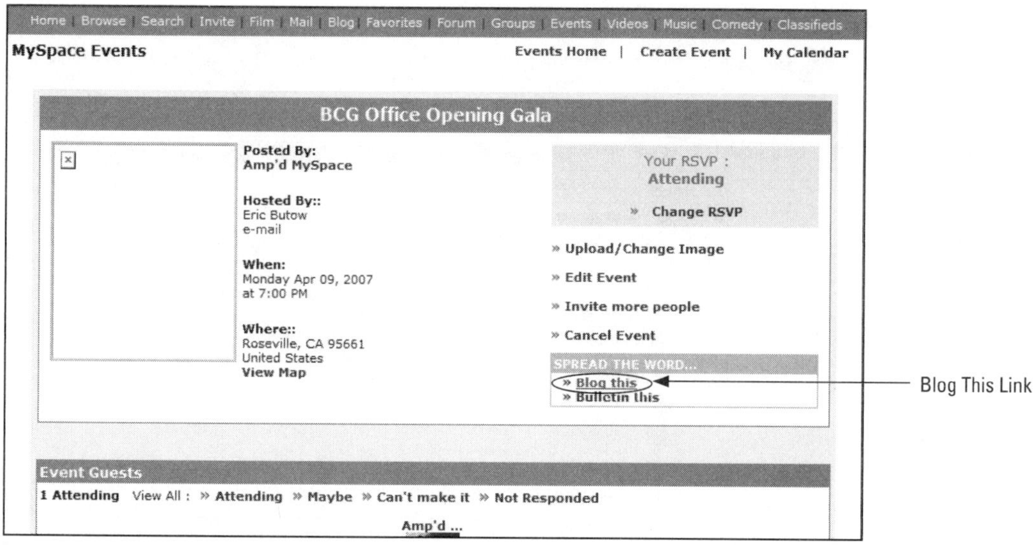

FIGURE 11-27 The Blog This link

FAQS

Can I have the MySpace calendar automatically remind me about all events? Yes. You can set automatic reminders for all events in the MySpace calendar. In the My Calendar page, click the Options tab, as shown in Figure 11-28.

The My Calendar Options page appears, as shown in Figure 11-29, and you can change the reminder settings in the Default Reminder Settings area.

Can I also send bulletins to people about my event? Yes. When you open your event information page, click the Bulletin This link in the Spread the Word section. MySpace automatically adds the text for the bulletin in the Post Bulletin page so all you have to do is make any changes and then post the bulletin.

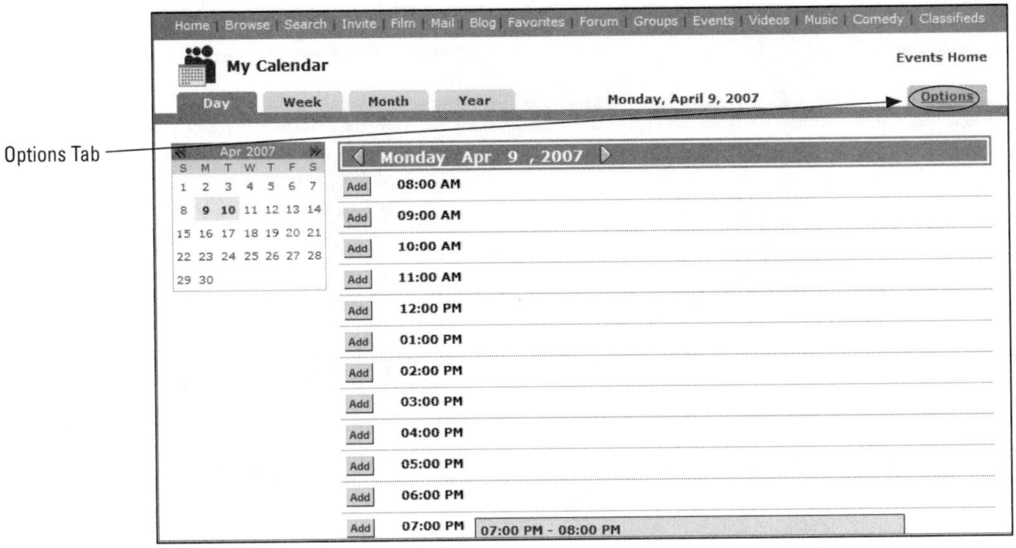

Options Tab

FIGURE 11-28 The Options tab

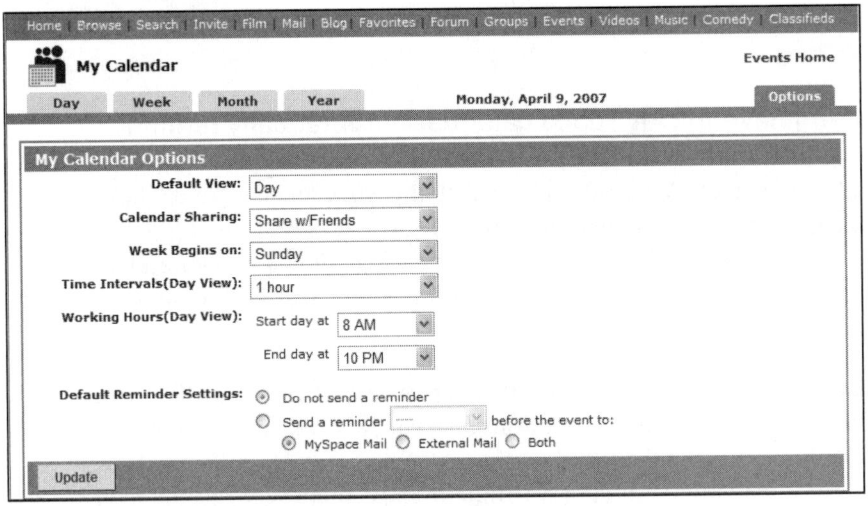

FIGURE 11-29 The My Calendar Options page

Chapter 12

Unleash Your Inner Artist

In the past, MySpace has long proven its worth as a networking site to musicians by opening up a whole new way to promote new music. In fact, it could be argued that for today's up-and-coming bands, a MySpace page with tour dates and a custom-made friends list ready for the latest e-mail touting the next concert date is as much a must as a good-quality amp. And with the explosion of higher-quality film clips available over the web, it's likely that having a MySpace page will soon be as indispensable to the indie filmmaker as a top-notch camera and a cell phone with a speed-dial setting are for their Hollywood agent.

NOTE *For more details on how important this really is for the music artist, skip ahead to Chapters 15 and 16.*

WHY IS MYSPACE YOUR IDEAL AUDIENCE SITE?

There are other sites out there for the independent filmmaker. For example, Ifilm.com hosts many "viral marketing" videos, and it was arguably the first of these types of sites to go big. As a matter of fact, in October 15, 2005, it was purchased by MTV Networks in a multimillion dollar deal. Another possibility was Google video—and of course, Google stands in its own field when it comes to searches and the ability to find things online.

But no site—and really, I mean there is literally no other site on the Internet—comes close in its ability to help you get the word out. With the launch of MySpace Film in mid-2006, MySpace has clearly targeted the film world as its next media entry point. This has really been a no-brainer for MySpace to move into, for three reasons.

First, it's always been part of the whole media-savvy focus of MySpace from the start. Back in early 2006, MySpace cofounder Tom Anderson told *Filmmaker* magazine that "I went with music and film on MySpace because I was a musician who went to film school… It's both what interested me personally and what seemed to make the most sense within MySpace." And indeed it does—which brings us to points and 3.

Second, the rise of MySpace was lucky to take place around the same time as two other developments. One was the mass acceptance of higher bandwidth due to DSL and cable modems, among other things—that allow people to download bit-rich videos as opposed to simple text. The other was the emergence of short-time videos as a major force, thanks to the site YouTube. What MySpace has that YouTube or the Google and Yahoo video sites do not is the linked-in networking where someone can propagate a video clip to more people than exist on most users' e-mail lists.

Third and finally is the audience that makes up MySpace. Not only are there lots of users who are from and around the entertainment communities of Los Angeles and other places, but also, MySpace users are overwhelmingly young, hip, media-savvy, and above all tech-savvy. MySpace members like to chat and discuss the content on the pages they design and personalize themselves. It's a way to get into the indie filmmaking scene without having to do a lot of driving or networking over yet another house party. Whatever the magic combination is, the site has attracted much of its media buzz precisely because of its success as a promotional powerhouse.

> **NOTE** *Still doubt us as to the kind of "buzz" you can generate on MySpace? Consider what happened with 2008 presidential hopeful Barack Obama. At the cost of losing 160,000 friends, in early 2007 the candidate's presidential campaign took over control of the MySpace page listed under his name. For two and a half years, the page had been run by an Obama supporter from Los Angeles. But as the site exploded in popularity, Obama's campaign took over control of the page, and had to rebuild the friends list. Although he had to start all over again with zero friends, within three days, it was already back to 17,000 and climbing!*
>
> *No, Obama's not an artist per se. But that's the kind of networking power that artists would want on their side when they create their own works of art.*

CREATE A FILMMAKER PROFILE ON MYSPACE

Signing up for a MySpace Filmmaker profile is available at the perfect price for the struggling filmmaker who is trying to put their vision on celluloid with their lunch money and their credit cards. It's free! And for the grand price of nothing down, nothing per month, you essentially get a free web site with a built-in audience where you can upload your short film or trailer so it can spread virally all over the Internet.

As an added bonus, uploading your film to your MySpace filmmaker profile doesn't require any technical knowledge of the complex and ever-changing world of streaming video.

To create your filmmaker's profile, begin by creating an account on MySpace.com. But don't just sign up with a regular MySpace account. Instead, make sure you do this the right way, and follow these steps:

1. Begin by navigating to www.myspace.com and click on Film in the navigation bar. You'll be taken to the MySpace Film page, as shown in Figure 12-1.

NOTE *Be careful! Be sure to click the Film link in the MySpace.com navigation bar, not the Videos link, which is also in the navigation bar, but more toward the right.*

2. Next, click on Filmmaker Signup in the MySpace Film toolbar toward the right. Again, be careful! Don't click on the Sign Up link at the top of the screen or you'll simply be

FIGURE 12-1 The main Film page on MySpace

getting a regular user account. By clicking on Filmmaker Signup, you'll be taken to the signup page shown in Figure 12-2.

3. Fill in the appropriate fields, agree to the MySpace Terms of Service and Privacy Policy by selecting the check box, and click Sign Up. You'll have to verify yourself by entering a special combination of letters and numbers, as shown in Figure 12-3, and then fill out or select information to flesh out your profile in the profile page, as shown in Figure 12-4.

4. Click Continue and then post a picture to your profile, as shown in Figure 12-5, if you want to do so at this time. You can always come back to this step later by clicking Skip for Now if you are one of those filmmakers who only wants to stay on one side of the lens.

5. In the next step, add your audience by adding your existing friends' e-mails as in Figure 12-6. Click Invite to add their e-mail addresses or click Skip for Now if you want to add this later.

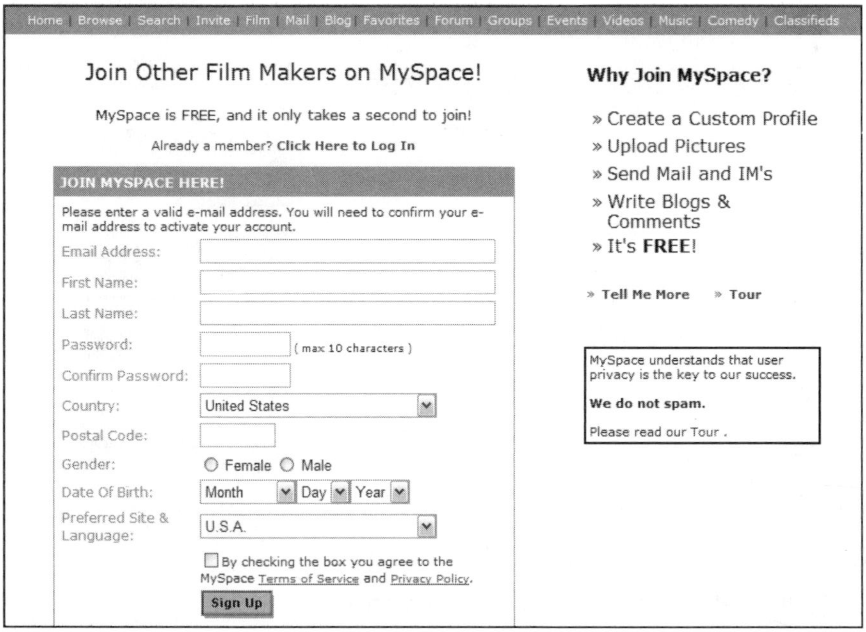

FIGURE 12-2 The MySpace Filmmaker page

Home | Browse | Search | Invite | Film | Mail | Blog | Favorites | Forum | Groups | Events | Videos | Music | Comedy | Classifieds

Verify Account

MySpace.com takes abuse seriously. Keeping MySpace.com free of abuse and spam ensures a fun and safe experience for everyone.

Requiring users to correctly enter the text from the image below is one of the ways MySpace can protect it's users from spam.

Please enter the text from the field below Letters are not case sensitive Do not type spaces between the numbers and letters

Please enter the text from the image in the field below.
The letters are not case-sensitive.
Do not type spaces between the numbers and letters.

Continue to My Account

FIGURE 12-3 The MySpace Filmmaker Verify Account page

Home | Browse | Search | Invite | Film | Mail | Blog | Favorites | Forum | Groups | Events | Videos | Music | Comedy | Classifieds

is a member of MySpace and would like you to join

ADDITIONAL INFO

Role 1:	Director
Role 2:	Producer
Role 3:	Editor
Status:	Student
Website:	www.myfilmrocks.com
Influences:	Anime, Rockumentaries
Favorite Directors:	Tarantino, Hitchcock
Awards:	Working on it!
Festivals:	Raindance 2005
Professional Affiliations:	N/A

Continue

Professional Affiliations: privacy policy .

Meet Your Friends' Friends & See How You're Connected!

Create Your Personal Profile...

Invite Your Friends & View Their Profiles...

Meet Your Friends' Friends & Their Friends' Friends!

FIGURE 12-4 The MySpace Filmmaker profile

Skip for Now

FIGURE 12-5 The MySpace Filmmaker Profile–Upload Some Photos page

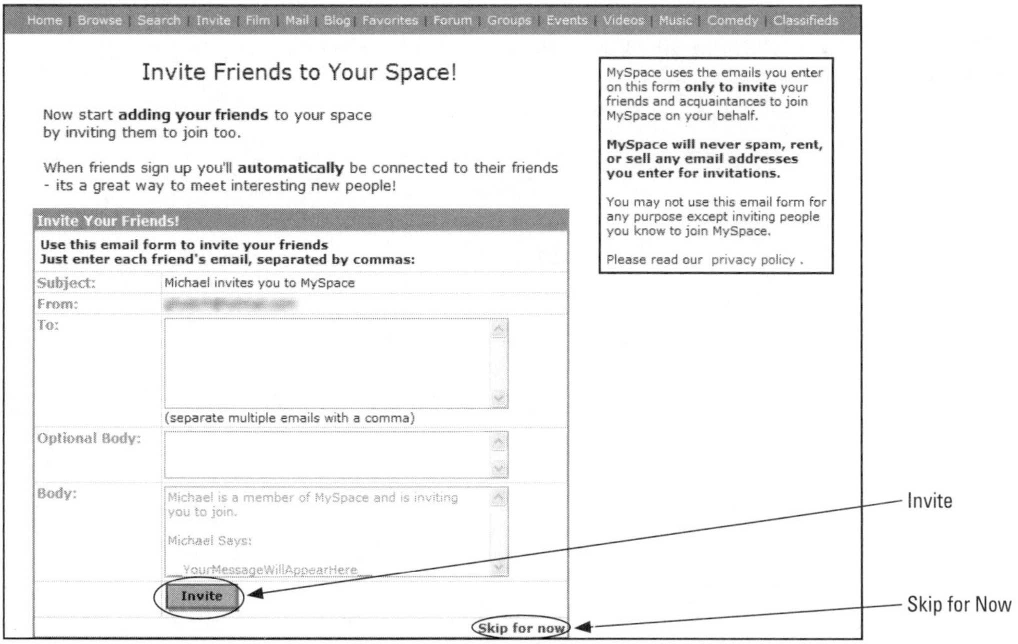

Invite

Skip for Now

FIGURE 12-6 The MySpace Filmmaker Profile–entering e-mail addresses

6. MySpace asks a couple more questions before you upload your video clip. Note the warning at the top of the page: If you upload porn or unauthorized copyrighted material, your MySpace.com account will be deleted (see Figure 12-7). And while MySpace might take its time getting around to spotting a film that is in violation of its edicts, it will enforce them quickly and without recourse. Answer the questions MySpace offers, which will enable the right kind of audience to find you.

Although it is off the bottom of the screen in Figure 12-7, be sure to scroll down and answer the question of whether you want your video available for public consumption by the MySpace community. Once you answer that question, you should next agree to the Terms and Conditions by selecting the check box, and click Continue.

7. Finally, the moment of truth: You are now allowed to upload your video clip, as shown in Figure 12-8. Luckily, the space and format restrictions are pretty loose.

NOTE   *Your film can be in Windows Media, AVI, MPEG/MPG, MP4, FLV, RealMedia, or QuickTime format. The maximum size is 100MB.*

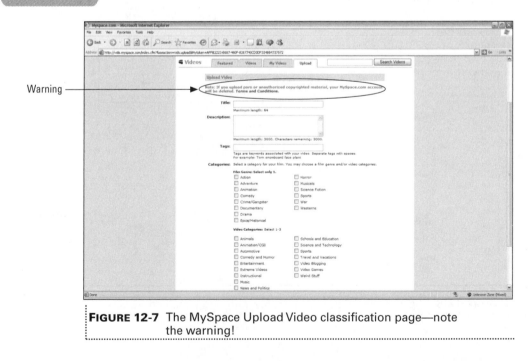

FIGURE 12-7 The MySpace Upload Video classification page—note the warning!

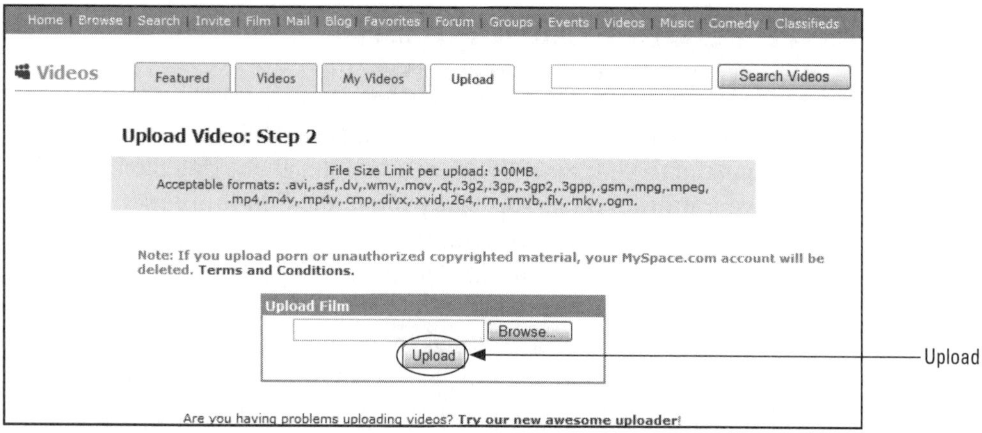

FIGURE 12-8 The MySpace Upload Video page

Navigate to your video with the Browse button and click Upload.

8. As your video is being processed, you'll see a screen similar to Figure 12-9. When the upload is finished, MySpace will inform you that your video has been uploaded to one of the main MySpace servers. Once the upload is completed (this can take up to 24 hours during high-traffic times), you'll see the video appear on your Profile page. To visit your profile at any time, simply click on Home in the MySpace main menu bar above.

FIGURE 12-9 MySpace as it processes your clip

EDIT YOUR FILMMAKER PROFILE ON MYSPACE

Editing your profile is extremely easy. Basically, it amounts to logging in to your new MySpace account and clicking the Edit link by your profile name. This takes you to the Edit Profile screen, which will look like Figure 12-10.

It's here that you can add, delete, or change your profile's markers by clicking on the Film Maker Details tab. On the Manage Videos tab, you can add your latest creations to the page.

Perhaps most importantly, as shown in Figure 12-11, you can also add screening dates to your events calendar by clicking the Screenings tab so that people will know when they can go to see your film and add dates to their personal calendars so that they don't forget.

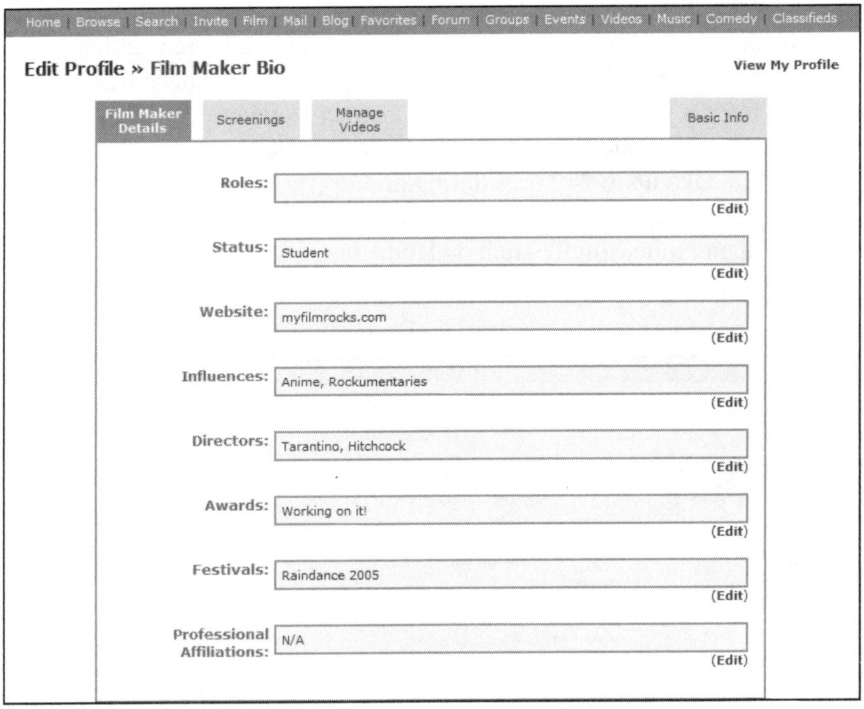

FIGURE 12-10 The Edit Profile screen for your filmmaker profile

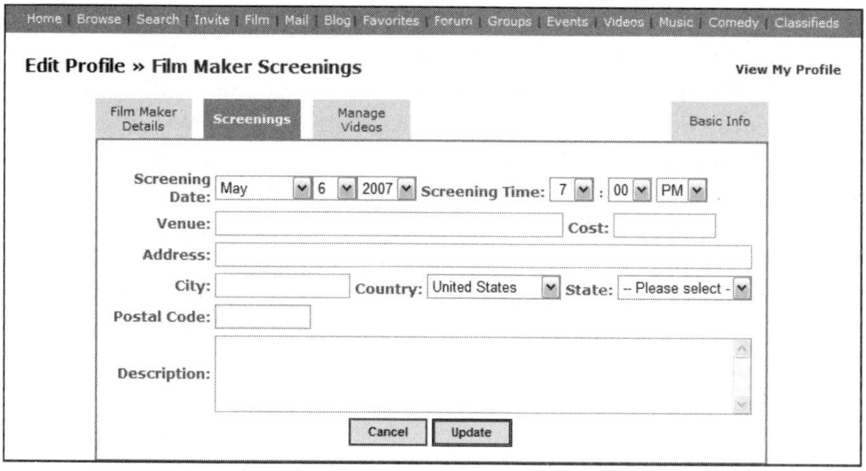

FIGURE 12-11 The Screenings tab for your filmmaker profile

By filling out the fields here and clicking Update, you can post bulletins to your friends list to let them know about the progress of your film. You can also use the bulletins to remind people of upcoming screenings, festivals, reviews, and so on. And of course, make sure you check your page on a regular basis to accept friend requests as you build your audience.

WHAT IF YOU'RE REALLY, REALLY JUST STARTING OUT?

This is a surprisingly common question when it comes to aspiring— and we do mean "aspiring"—filmmakers when they're looking into MySpace. The answer is no—you don't need to already have a film "in the can" to sign up. You can just be interested in film school. Or you could have a screenplay and you're trying to line up the right people to put it to celluloid. Or you could be a backyard filmmaker with aspirations to become the next Spielberg. It doesn't matter one bit.

In fact, if you're at this stage, MySpace can still assist you. Other amateur (and not a few professional) filmmakers will usually be happy to give you tips on filmmaking and even suggest methods for making your film. This type of advice is common only to the few sites (MySpace, eBay, and "niche interest" sites) that have taken the time to build a community forum.

For MySpace, this information can be found in the imaginatively named "Filmmaker Forum." In the forum you can pretty much find all aspects of discussion that pertain to filmmaking: financing, casting calls, camera tricks—the entire gamut of the industry is talked about. And best of all, thanks to MySpace, it's no further away from your browsing needs than your fingertips. Just click on the Forum link in the top MySpace menu bar, and scroll down to click the Filmmaker Forum to enter and read posts from aspiring filmmakers, amateurs, and professionals alike.

Chapter 13

Developing an Online Following

It's not enough just to have a profile on MySpace. You want to drive people to your profile so you will develop an online following among other MySpace users. After all, having other users wanting to know what you're doing and wanting to be your friend is better than waiting for others to visit your profile. To drive users, you need to get involved in the MySpace community.

This chapter gives you seven ways to get involved in your MySpace community right away. Some of what's in this chapter reviews what's been in other chapters and some of it is new, but if you find that you're not getting the attention you want from other MySpace users, bookmark this chapter and turn to it when you feel you need to better develop your online following.

PREMIERE NEW CONTENT EXCLUSIVELY ON MYSPACE

If you have new content, whether it's a new blog or new multimedia such as a song or movie, you can premiere your new content exclusively on your MySpace profile. After you post your new content on your profile, be sure to tell everyone about your new content by following this checklist:

- Post information about your content in the appropriate MySpace forum.
- Send a bulletin to your friends.
- Post information in your groups.
- Start your own blog and post to your blog regularly.
- If your content is part of an event, post your event on the Events page.
- Use pictures to tell event stories.

The following sections tell you more about how to check off each one of these items on your checklist.

INVOLVE YOURSELF IN THE COMMUNITY

There's a huge community of MySpace users not only in groups but also in forums. It's easy to find the forum that's right for you and post information about your new content and your profile for everyone to read—well, everyone who reads messages on that forum, anyway.

1. Click the Forum link in the main menu bar. The Forum Home page appears, as shown in Figure 13-1. There are 22 forum categories you can choose from in the list.

2. Click the title of the forum you want to visit. For this example I'll click Business & Entrepreneurs. Four subcategories for Business & Entrepreneurs appear, as shown in Figure 13-2.

3. Click the subcategory forum name you want. I'll click the Business subcategory name. The forum page appears, as shown in Figure 13-3. The forum table shows each forum topic, how many posts there have been in that topic, who last posted, and who started the topic by posting the first message.

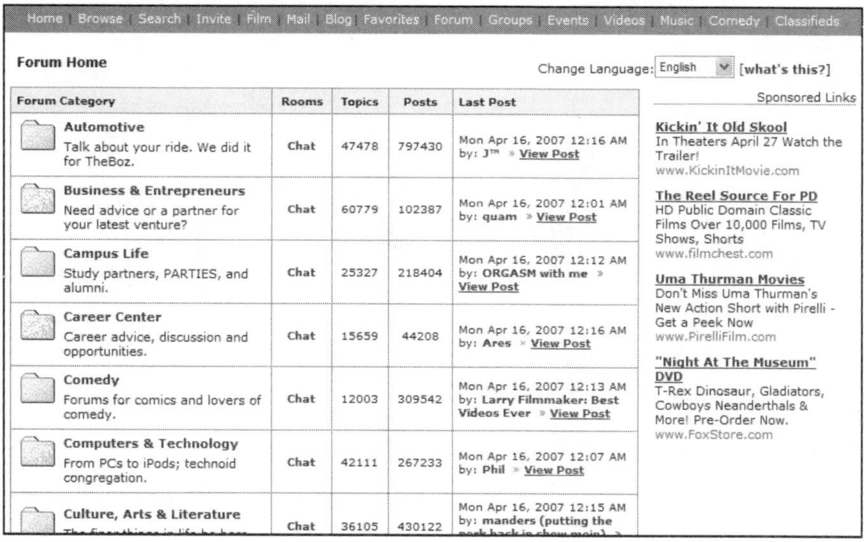

Forum Category	Rooms	Topics	Posts	Last Post
Automotive Talk about your ride. We did it for TheBoz.	Chat	47478	797430	Mon Apr 16, 2007 12:16 AM by: J™ » **View Post**
Business & Entrepreneurs Need advice or a partner for your latest venture?	Chat	60779	102387	Mon Apr 16, 2007 12:01 AM by: **quam** » **View Post**
Campus Life Study partners, PARTIES, and alumni.	Chat	25327	218404	Mon Apr 16, 2007 12:12 AM by: **ORGASM with me** » **View Post**
Career Center Career advice, discussion and opportunities.	Chat	15659	44208	Mon Apr 16, 2007 12:16 AM by: **Ares** » **View Post**
Comedy Forums for comics and lovers of comedy.	Chat	12003	309542	Mon Apr 16, 2007 12:13 AM by: **Larry Filmmaker: Best Videos Ever** » **View Post**
Computers & Technology From PCs to iPods; technoid congregation.	Chat	42111	267233	Mon Apr 16, 2007 12:07 AM by: **Phil** » **View Post**
Culture, Arts & Literature The finest things in life be here.	Chat	36105	430122	Mon Apr 16, 2007 12:15 AM by: **manders (putting the neck back in chow mein)** »

Sponsored Links

Kickin' It Old Skool
In Theaters April 27 Watch the Trailer!
www.KickinItMovie.com

The Reel Source For PD
HD Public Domain Classic Films Over 10,000 Films, TV Shows, Shorts
www.filmchest.com

Uma Thurman Movies
Don't Miss Uma Thurman's New Action Short with Pirelli - Get a Peek Now
www.PirelliFilm.com

"Night At The Museum" DVD
T-Rex Dinosaur, Gladiators, Cowboys Neanderthals & More! Pre-Order Now.
www.FoxStore.com

FIGURE 13-1 The Forum Home page

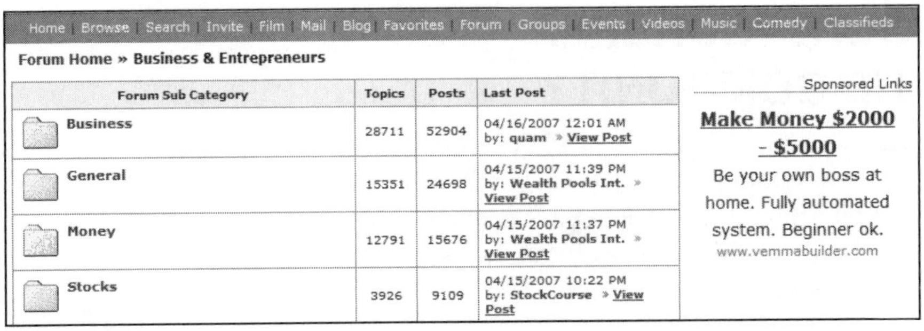

FIGURE 13-2 The Business & Entrepreneurs forum subcategory page

4. Click the forum title name in the Forum Topic column. The topic page appears, as shown in Figure 13-4, and displays the first message in the topic at the top of the page. You need to scroll down to view all the messages in the forum, and each message is contained within its own table row.

5. Reply to a message by clicking the Reply button in the upper-right corner of the message row or by clicking the Post a Reply link on the left side of the page. The Message Board: Reply page appears, as shown in Figure 13-5.

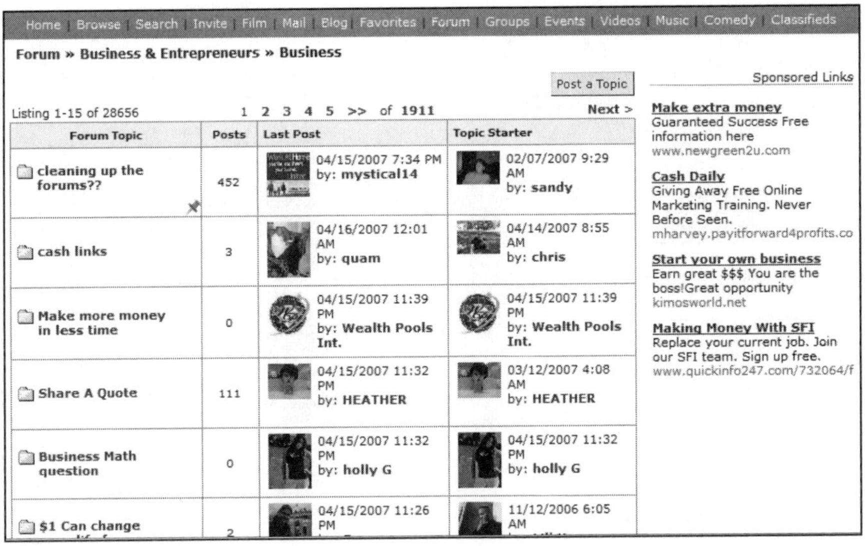

FIGURE 13-3 The forum page

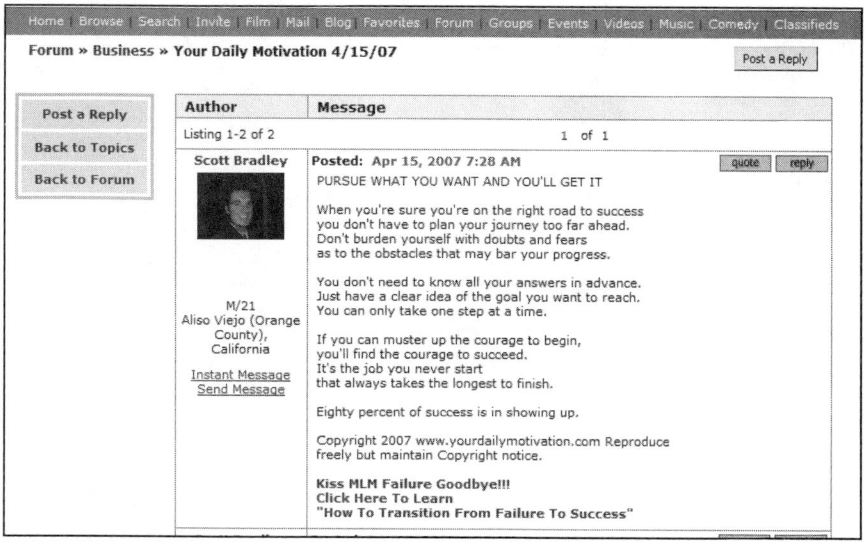

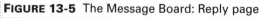

Home | Browse | Search | Invite | Film | Mail | Blog | Favorites | Forum | Groups | Events | Videos | Music | Comedy | Classifieds

Forum » Business » Your Daily Motivation 4/15/07

Post a Reply

	Author	Message
Post a Reply		Listing 1-2 of 2 — 1 of 1
Back to Topics	**Scott Bradley**	**Posted:** Apr 15, 2007 7:28 AM quote reply
Back to Forum		PURSUE WHAT YOU WANT AND YOU'LL GET IT

Scott Bradley

M/21
Aliso Viejo (Orange County),
California

Instant Message
Send Message

Posted: Apr 15, 2007 7:28 AM   quote reply

PURSUE WHAT YOU WANT AND YOU'LL GET IT

When you're sure you're on the right road to success
you don't have to plan your journey too far ahead.
Don't burden yourself with doubts and fears
as to the obstacles that may bar your progress.

You don't need to know all your answers in advance.
Just have a clear idea of the goal you want to reach.
You can only take one step at a time.

If you can muster up the courage to begin,
you'll find the courage to succeed.
It's the job you never start
that always takes the longest to finish.

Eighty percent of success is in showing up.

Copyright 2007 www.yourdailymotivation.com Reproduce
freely but maintain Copyright notice.

**Kiss MLM Failure Goodbye!!!
Click Here To Learn
"How To Transition From Failure To Success"**

FIGURE 13-4 The topic page

6. Click the Post Reply button when you finish typing your reply. The topic page reappears and your reply appears as the last message in the forum.

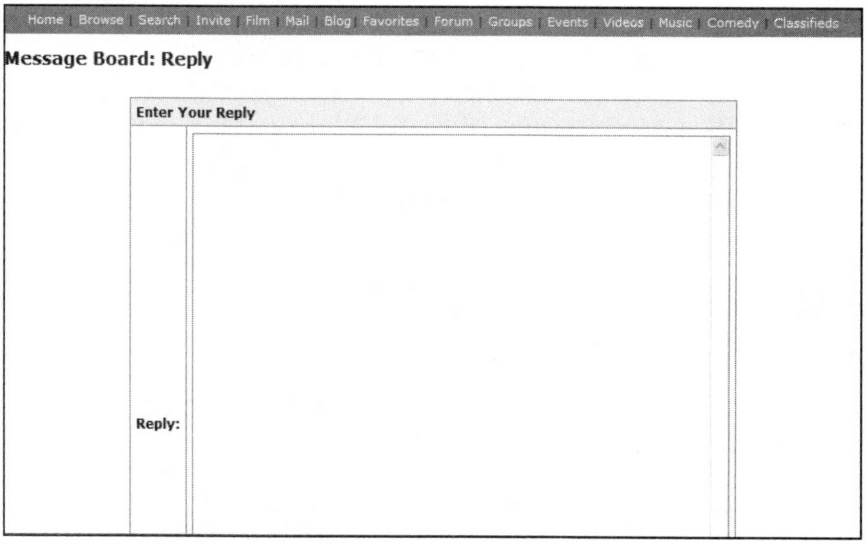

Home | Browse | Search | Invite | Film | Mail | Blog | Favorites | Forum | Groups | Events | Videos | Music | Comedy | Classifieds

Message Board: Reply

Enter Your Reply

Reply:

FIGURE 13-5 The Message Board: Reply page

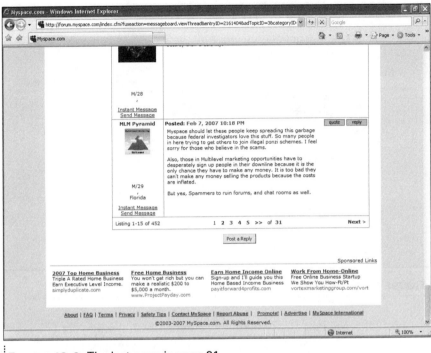

FIGURE 13-6 The last page is page 31.

Note that if there are more than 15 messages on a page, you need to click the Next link at the bottom of the page to move to the next page. If you want to see the last page of messages, click the last page number at the bottom of the page. For example, in Figure 13-6, the last page is page 31 because there are 452 total messages in the forum, so clicking on 31 would take you to the end of that forum discussion.

USE MYSPACE GROUPS... START YOUR OWN!

If you want to start your own MySpace group to drive people there, let's review how to create a group:

1. Click the Groups link in the main menu bar. The Groups Home page appears, as shown in Figure 13-7.

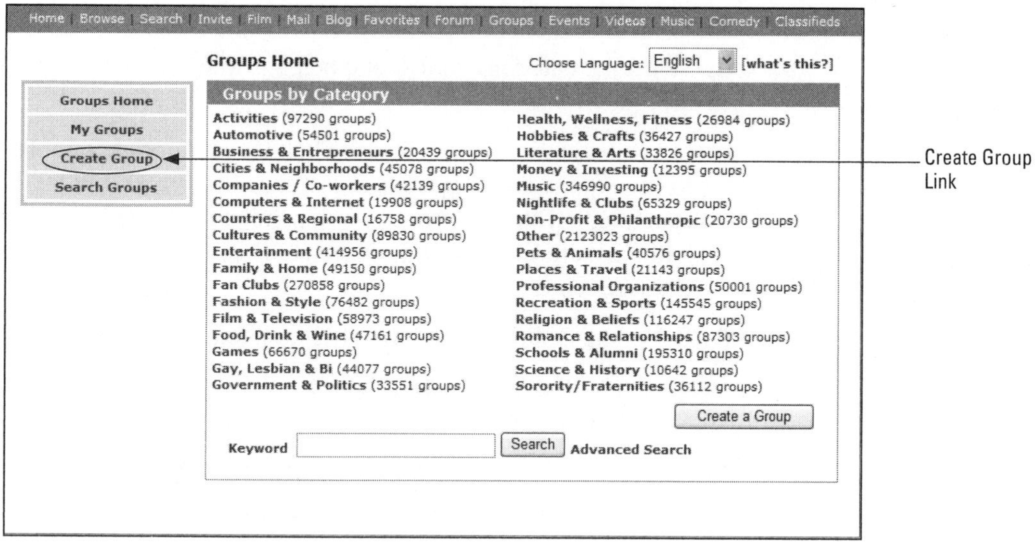

FIGURE 13-7 The Groups Home page

2. Click the Create Group link. The Create a Group on MySpace page appears, as shown in Figure 13-8, so you can add information about your group in the Create a Group table.

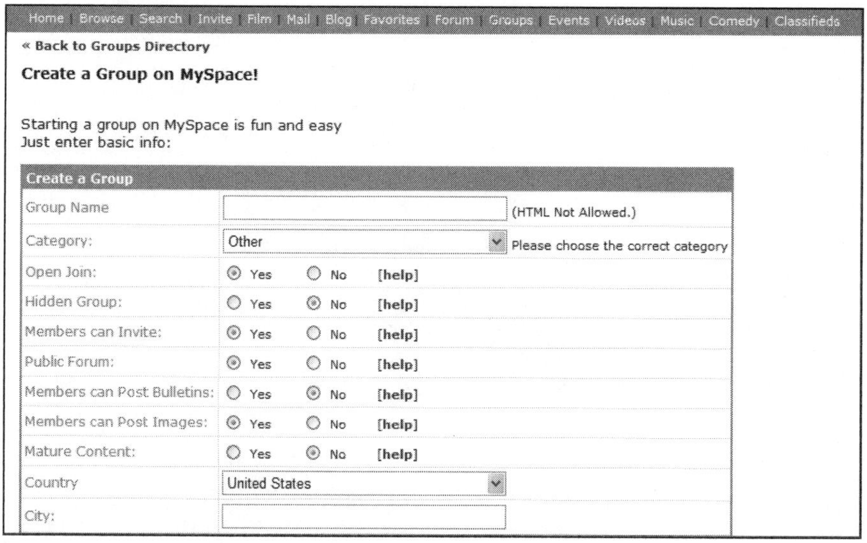

FIGURE 13-8 The Create a Group on MySpace page

3. Type the group name in the Group Name box.

4. Select the category your group belongs to from the Category drop-down list.

5. In the next seven rows you can click the appropriate buttons to change the group options to the ones you prefer. For example, if you want your group members to be able to post bulletins, click the Yes button in the Members Can Post Bulletins row.

6. Select the Country, City, State/Region, and ZIP Code.

7. Type a brief description of the group in the Short Description box.

8. Type a longer description in the Description box.

9. Type the URL name you want to use for your group in the URL box, as shown in Figure 13-9.

10. Type the text from the image in the Verification row box.

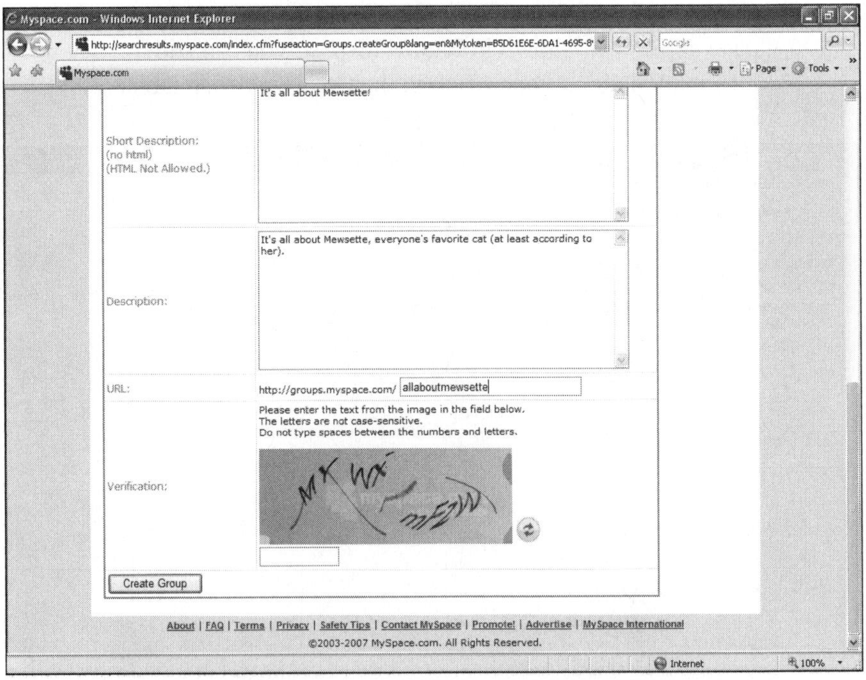

FIGURE 13-9 The URL box

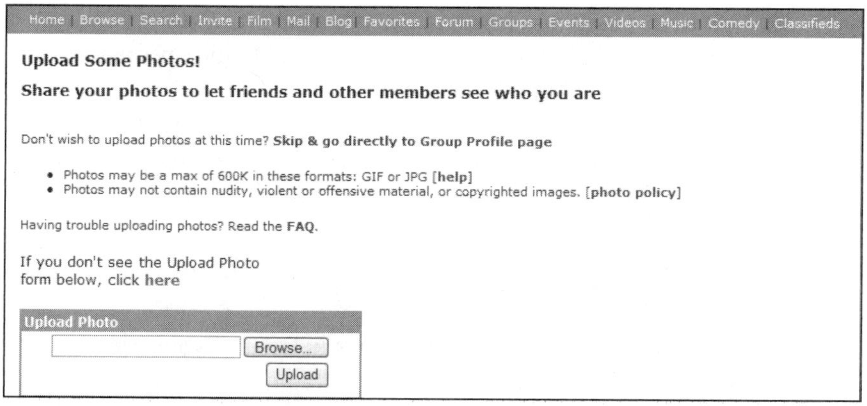

Home | Browse | Search | Invite | Film | Mail | Blog | Favorites | Forum | Groups | Events | Videos | Music | Comedy | Classifieds
Upload Some Photos!
Share your photos to let friends and other members see who you are
Don't wish to upload photos at this time? Skip & go directly to Group Profile page
Photos may be a max of 600K in these formats: GIF or JPG [help]
Photos may not contain nudity, violent or offensive material, or copyrighted images. [photo policy]
Having trouble uploading photos? Read the FAQ.
If you don't see the Upload Photo form below, click here
Upload Photo
Browse...
Upload

FIGURE 13-10 The Upload Some Photos page

11. Click the Create Group button. The Upload Some Photos page appears, as shown in Figure 13-10. You can upload photos if you want by clicking the Browse button and then opening the image file in the appropriate folder. If you would rather not upload any photos right now, click the Skip & Go Directly to Group Profile page link.

The group profile page appears, as shown in Figure 13-11. Now that you've created the group, you're the moderator of the group.

Home | Browse | Search | Invite | Film | Mail | Blog | Favorites | Forum | Groups | Events | Videos | Music | Comedy | Classifieds
Group URL: http://groups.myspace.com/allaboutmewsette
« Back to Groups Directory
All About Mewsette
NO PHOTO
» View Group Photos
Category: Pets & Animals
Type: Public Membership [help]
Founded: Apr 16, 2007
Location:: Roseville, California - US
Members: 1
Invite Others
Edit Group
Upload Image
Post Bulletin
Post Topic
Privacy
Group Leader: Amp'd MySpace
It's all about Mewsette, everyone's favorite cat (at least according to her).
All About Mewsette (1 Members)
[Edit Members]
View All Members »

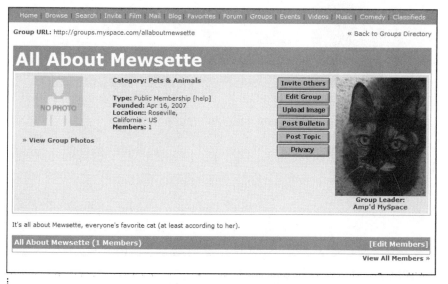

FIGURE 13-11 The group profile page

You get to set the group rules, invite others to join your group, post forum and bulletin messages, and you also get to kick people out of the group if they violate those rules.

If you want to learn more about MySpace groups, go back to Chapter 11, which talks about evaluating groups you may want to join, how to join them, and how to contribute to them.

START YOUR OWN BLOG

A blog is a great way to keep your news in front of your friends, and MySpace gives you your own blog by default when you create your profile. So let's review how to create a blog post.

1. In your profile home page, click the Blog link in the menu bar. The Blog Control Center page appears.

2. Scroll down the page until you see the My Controls section, as shown in Figure 13-12. Then click the Post New Blog link.

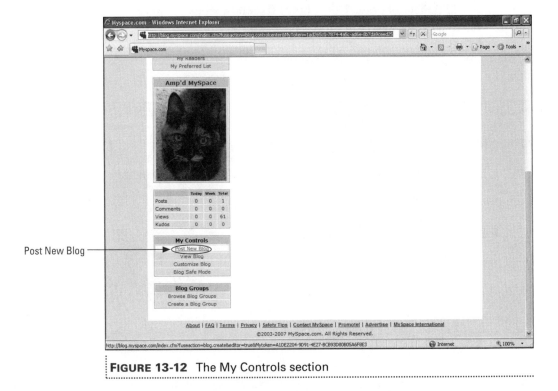

FIGURE 13-12 The My Controls section

3. In the Post a New Blog Entry page that appears, if you don't want your entry to have the current date and time you can specify the blog post date and time in the Posted Date and Posted Time drop-down lists, as shown in Figure 13-13. The default post date and time are the current date and time.

4. Type the subject of the blog post in the Subject box.

5. Select the category from the Category drop-down list if you want this post to fall within a specific category. If you don't, leave the selection as "none."

6. Type the post in the Body box, as shown in Figure 13-14. You can use the formatting tools above the box to edit your text. For example, you can change the font, style, and text size.

7. If you want to control the look of your blog post using HTML and/or CSS code, select the View Source check box. Otherwise leave this check box blank. You can go back to Chapter 2 (for HTML) or Chapter 3 (for CSS) if you want a refresher.

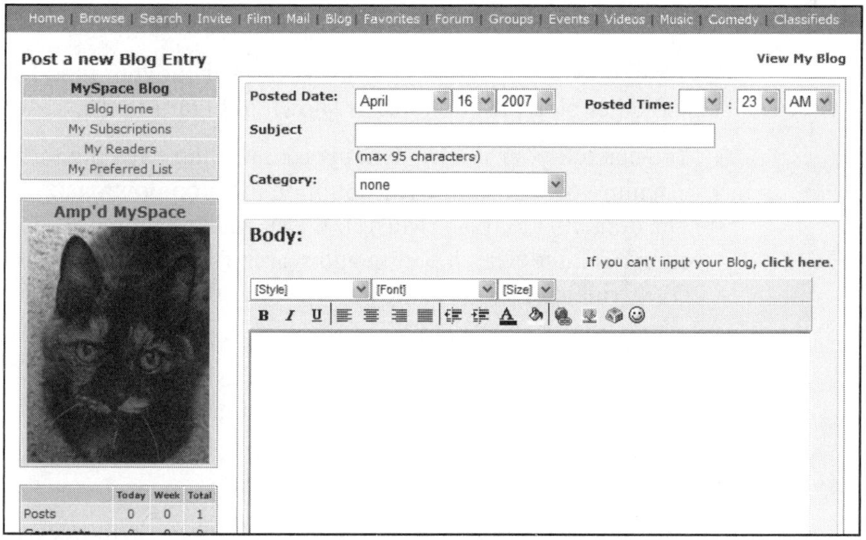

FIGURE 13-13 The Posted Date and Posted Time drop-down lists

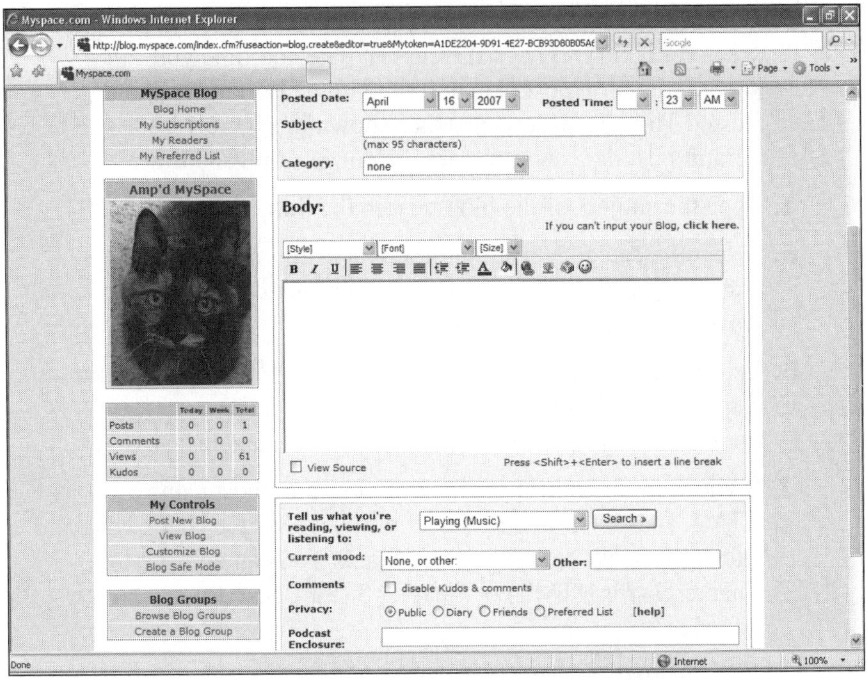

FIGURE 13-14 The Body box

8. Scroll down the page to view the section about your mood and other blog post options, as shown in Figure 13-15.

9. You can tell your readers what you're reading, viewing, or listening to by selecting the option in the drop-down list. The default is Playing (Music). If you want to get more specific, click the Search button and search for the music, book, DVD/video, or video game you're currently reviewing.

10. Select your current mood in the Current Mood drop-down list. If you are in another mood that isn't shown in the drop-down list (like a combination of several moods), type the mood in the Other box.

11. For Privacy click the button that tells MySpace who you want to see your blog. The default selection is Public, but you can also make the blog your own private diary, have the post visible only to your friends, or make the post available only to your preferred list.

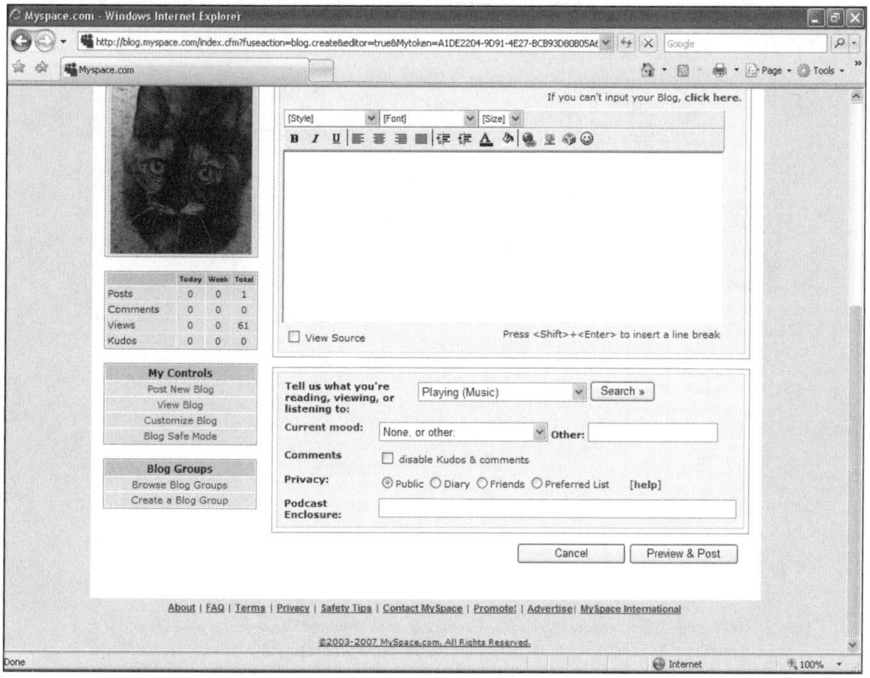

FIGURE 13-15 The bottom section of the Post a New Blog Entry page

12. Click the Preview & Post button.

13. In the Confirm Blog Posting page that appears, as shown in Figure 13-16, click the Post Blog button. If you decide that you would rather edit your blog post some more instead, click the Edit button to return to the Post a New Blog Entry page.

FIGURE 13-16 The Confirm Blog Posting page

Edit and Remove

FIGURE 13-17 The blog post with the Edit and Remove links

After you publish your blog, your blog with the new post appears in your blog page, as shown in Figure 13-17. If you decide that you want to tweak your post a bit more after reading it, click the Edit link below the blog post. Don't like the post at all? Just click the Remove link below the blog post and then click the OK button in the dialog box that appears asking if you really want to remove the post. Simple as that.

If you want more information about blogging, including how to lay out your blog and how to add audio and video to your blog, flip back to Chapter 8 for all the details.

SENDING BULLETINS

Creating blogs won't help unless you send out bulletins to your friends letting them know that you have a new blog entry. Here's a review of how to send a bulletin to your friends.

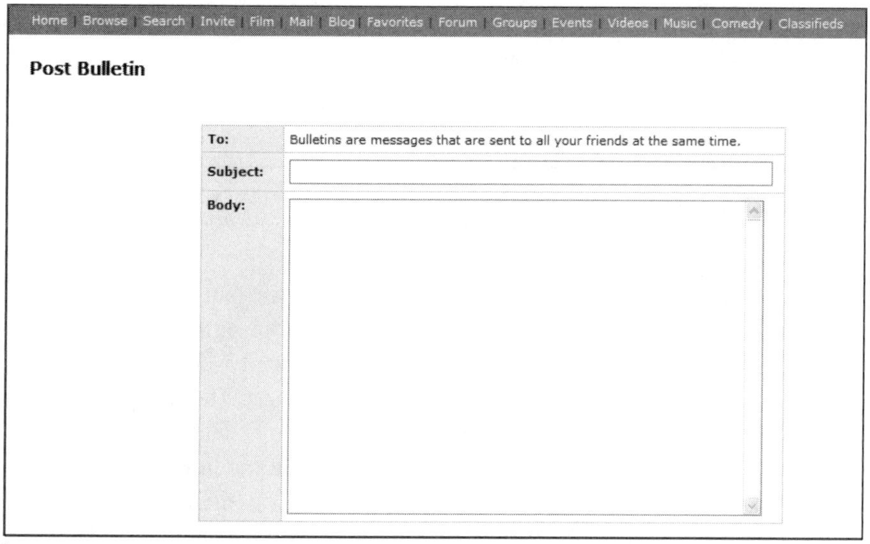

Post Bulletin

To:	Bulletins are messages that are sent to all your friends at the same time.
Subject:	
Body:	

FIGURE 13-18 The Post Bulletin page

1. In the My Mail section, click the Post Bulletin link. The Post Bulletin page appears, as shown in Figure 13-18.

2. Type the subject of the bulletin in the Subject box.

3. Type your bulletin in the Body box. Be respectful of your friends by keeping the bulletin as brief as possible.

4. Click the Post button. The Confirm Bulletin page appears and displays the subject and body of the bulletin you wrote.

5. You can take one of three actions from here:

   - Delete the bulletin without posting it by clicking the Cancel button.

   - Click the Edit button to return to the Post Bulletin page, if you want to edit the bulletin further.

   - Post the bulletin by clicking the Post Bulletin button.

After you click the Post Bulletin button, the Bulletin Has Been Posted page appears, as shown in Figure 13-19, and informs you that it may take up to five minutes to post the bulletin, although in my experience it doesn't usually take that long.

FIGURE 13-19 The Bulletin Has Been Posted page

Click the Home link to return to your profile summary page, and then scroll down to the bottom of the page. Your bulletin appears in the My Bulletin Space area, as shown in Figure 13-20.

View the bulletin by clicking the bulletin subject. The Read Bulletin page appears. Delete the bulletin by clicking the Delete button, or return to your profile summary page by clicking the Home link.

Chapter 10 has more information about growing your circle of friends beyond sending bulletins, including finding new friends, sending invitations, and updating and maintaining your address book.

FIGURE 13-20 The My Bulletin Space area

POSTING EVENTS

If you have events that you want to tell your friends or the entire MySpace community about, you can post events to MySpace. In this section we'll review how to do that.

1. Click the Events link in the main menu bar. The MySpace Events page appears, as shown in Figure 13-21.

2. Click the Create New Event link. The Create an Event page appears, as shown in Figure 13-22.

3. Enter information about the event in the What's Going On? section. You need to provide information in boxes and lists with titles that include a red asterisk.

4. Specify information about when the event will take place in the When section.

5. Enter information about where the event will take place in the Where section.

6. Type the information from the image into the box above the Save Event button.

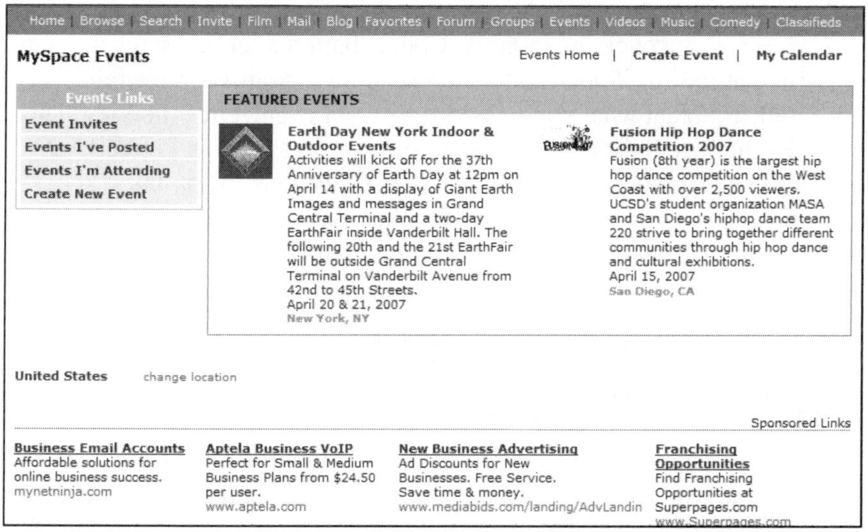

FIGURE 13-21 The MySpace Events page

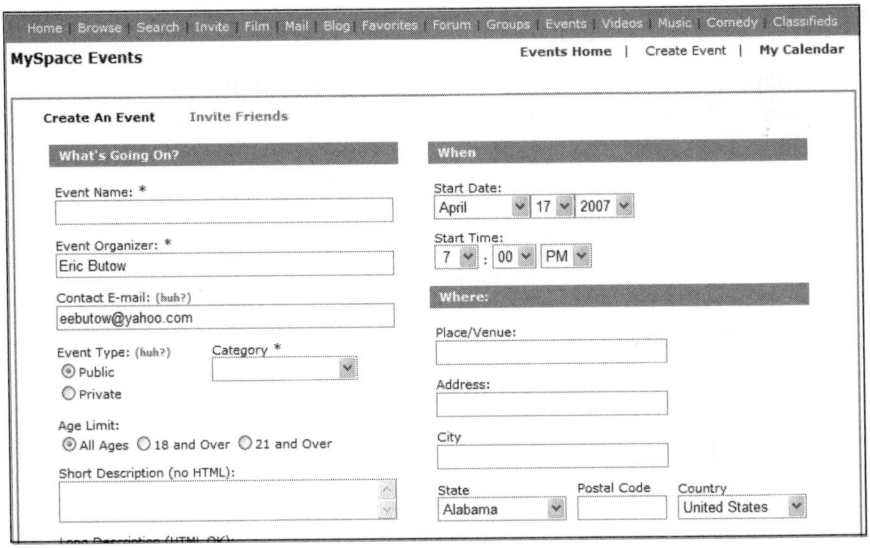

FIGURE 13-22   The Create an Event page

7. Click the Save Event button. The Edit This Event page appears and lets you determine the invitation details and who you want to invite to the event.

You can click the Invite & Update button after you send out your invitations, or if you'd rather not send invitations yet but would rather look at what you've added for your event, click the View This Event Page link. The event page appears, as shown in Figure 13-23. If you want to edit the event, click the Edit This Event link.

You can learn more about creating events as well as adding events to your calendar and blogging your event in Chapter 11.

USE PICTURES TO TELL EVENT STORIES

If you want to use pictures to help tell your story of an event for people who missed it or are interested in what you do at your events, you can create a photo album, add pictures to it, and then give your photos a caption. Let's review how to do that.

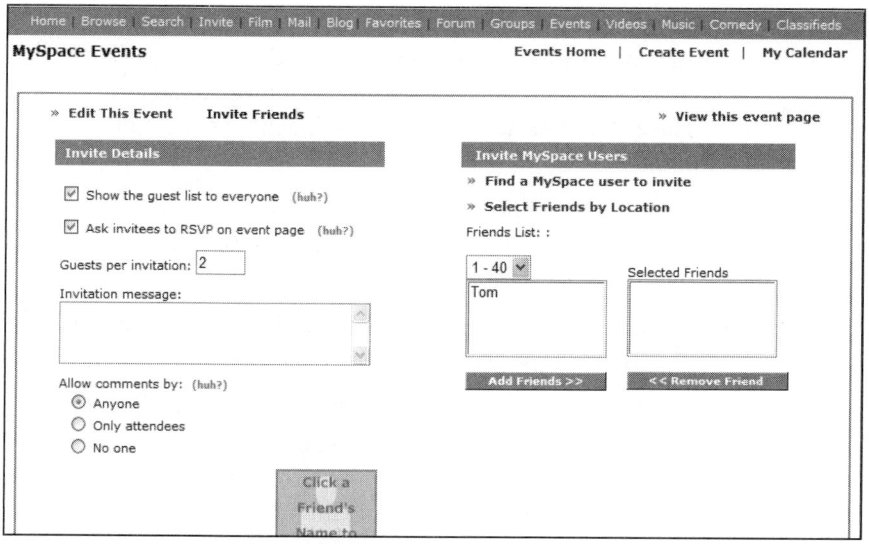

FIGURE 13-23 The event page

1. On the MySpace home page, click the Add/Edit Photos link to the right of your profile photo. The Photos page appears, as shown in Figure 13-24.

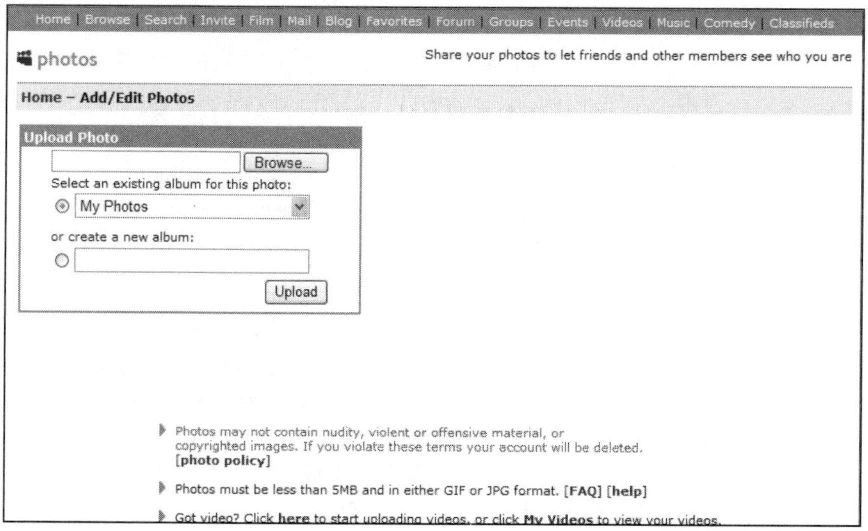

FIGURE 13-24 The Photos page

2. Read the photo policy by clicking the Photo Policy link so you are aware of what you can and cannot upload. Then create a new album by clicking the button to the left of the header "Or Create a New Album", and type the album name in the box.

3. In the Upload Photo area, click the Browse button to find your photo on your computer. The Choose File dialog box appears.

4. In the dialog box, navigate to the folder that contains the file you want to upload and then click the Open button. The up-loaded filename and path information appears in the file box.

5. Select the album to which you want to add the photo. The My Photos album is the default selection, but you can create a new album by clicking the radio button below the header "Or Create a New Album" and then type the new album name in the box.

6. Click the Upload button. MySpace uploads the photos.

7. Scroll down to the bottom of the screen. Under the Your Current Albums header you'll see that there is one photo and this notification appears under your album name, as shown in Figure 13-25.

8. If you want the photos to be viewed only by you, click the You button. If you want only your friends to see the photo, click Friends Only. The default selection is to let everyone see your photos.

9. View the photo by clicking the View button. The Mewsette album page appears with your photos, as shown in Figure 13-26.

   The text "Current default image" appears underneath the default photo—the one that appears on the profile page. Make another photo in your album the default photo by clicking the Set as Default button under the photo. If you change the default photo, it may take up to 24 hours for the new photo to appear to visitors.

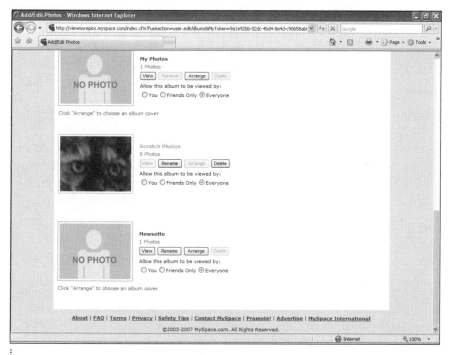

FIGURE 13-25 The number of photos appears under the Mewsette album head.

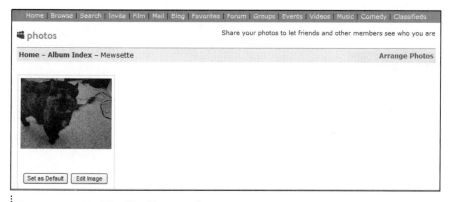

FIGURE 13-26 The My Photos album page

Now that you have opened your album page you can add a caption, move the photo to another album, or delete the photo. Here's how:

1. Click the Edit Image button under the image you want to edit. The Edit Image page appears, as shown in Figure 13-27.

2. Add a photo caption by typing the caption in the Caption box and then click the Save button.

3. To move your photo to another album, select the new album from the Move To drop-down list, in which you see "Choose an Album," or create a new album by typing in a new photo album name in the box provided and clicking the Move button.

4. To delete the photo from your album, simply click the Delete button that appears below the photo.

Chapter 4 has more information about editing and arranging your photos as well as creating a slideshow of your photos to make your visitors jealous that they weren't at your event.

FIGURE 13-27 The Edit Image page

Chapter 14

Using MySpace Classified Advertising and More

MySpace is not only a good way to make friends and learn more about what's going on in your local community, but it's also a way to sell your stuff to interested buyers as well as hunt for any type of job you're looking for (such as a contract job with a technology company in your area). You can also use MySpace in tandem with Craigslist and other networking sites to broaden your reach to meet your short-term goal like getting a job or selling that stash of old comic books that you have in your attic.

MySpace isn't the only social networking site available on the web. The success of MySpace has brought an explosion of social networking sites, and later in this chapter I'll list 49 more places where you can do social networking online.

USE MYSPACE CLASSIFIEDS

If you're looking to sell or buy something, a great place to start is the MySpace Classifieds pages. Access MySpace Classifieds by clicking the Classifieds link in the main menu bar. The Classifieds page for the default city, Los Angeles, appears, as shown in Figure 14-1.

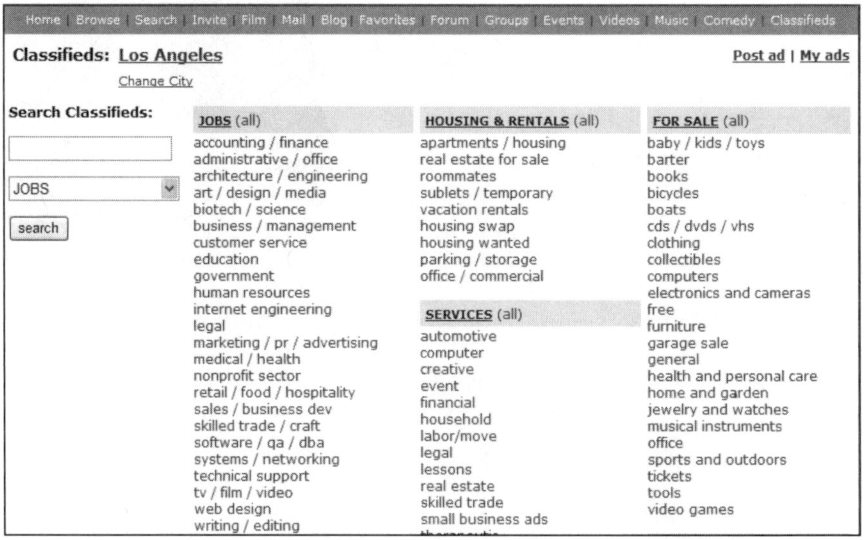

FIGURE 14-1 The Classifieds page

The Classified ads section places all the ad areas into 11 categories. I don't live in Los Angeles and I'm not looking for jobs in that area, either. I want to look for classifieds in the area I live in: the Sacramento area. Here's how to change the city and search for the items that interest you:

1. Click the Change City link at the top of the page. The Classifieds–Change City page appears, as shown in Figure 14-2.

2. Click the city that's closest to yours. I'm in the Sacramento area so I'll click Sacramento. The Classifieds: Sacramento page appears, as shown in Figure 14-3.

3. Now that I'm in the Classifieds page for Sacramento, I can click on any classifieds topic page I want. For example, I'll click the Electronics and Cameras link in the For Sale section to view cameras and other electronic equipment for sale, as shown in Figure 14-4.

The newest ad appears at the top of the page. You can search for items to buy by typing your keywords into the Keyword box (and/or

FIGURE 14-2 The Change City page

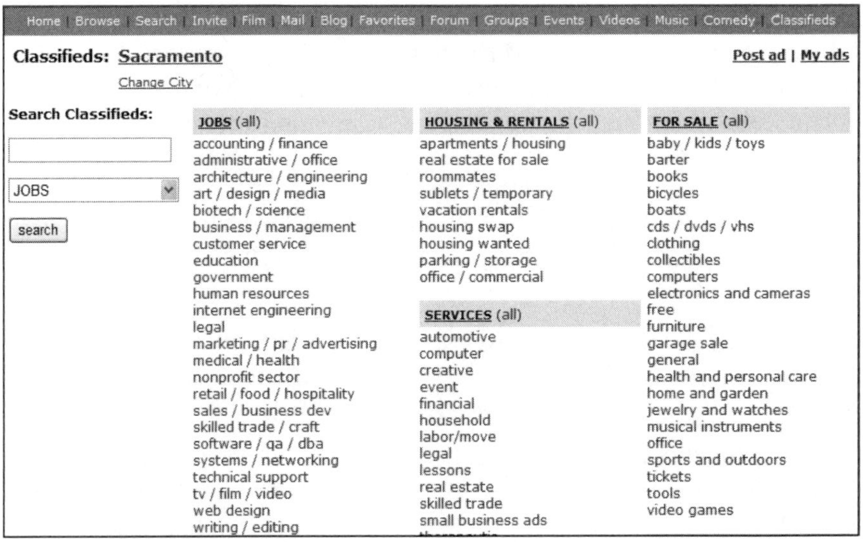

FIGURE 14-3 The Classifieds: Sacramento page

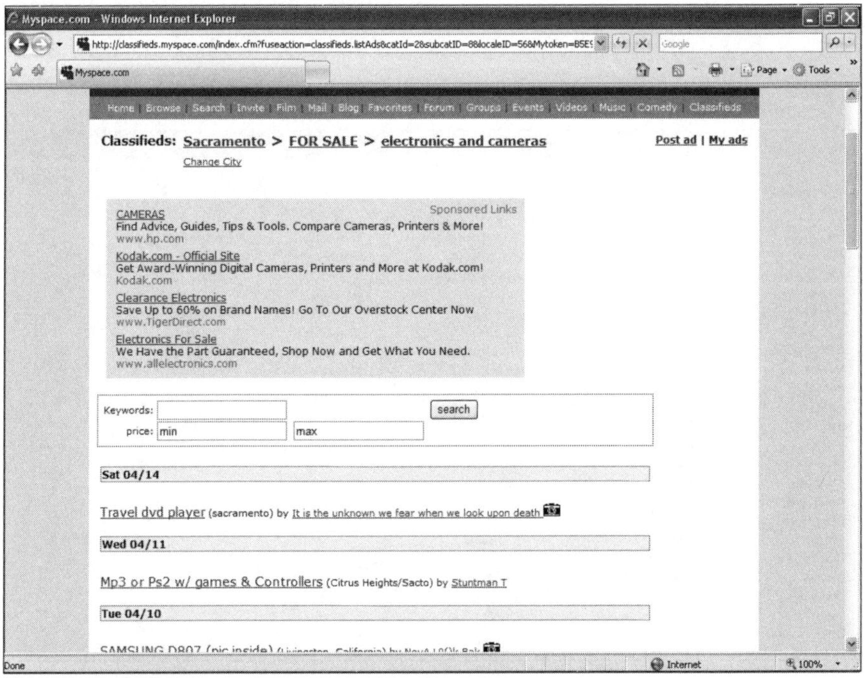

FIGURE 14-4 The Electronics and Cameras page

the minimum or maximum price of what you want to buy) and then clicking the Search button. MySpace will filter out the ads in the list to show you the ads that meet your criteria.

Scroll down the page to view older ads. If you want to view even older ads, you can click the Next link at the bottom of the page, as shown in Figure 14-5.

Post a New Ad

You can also post ads for other users to see by clicking the Post Ad link on any Classifieds page, as shown in Figure 14-6.

After you click the Post Ad link, the Posting On page appears, as shown in Figure 14-7.

Here's how to post a new ad on MySpace:

1. If you want to change the city in which you want the ad to appear, click the Change City link.

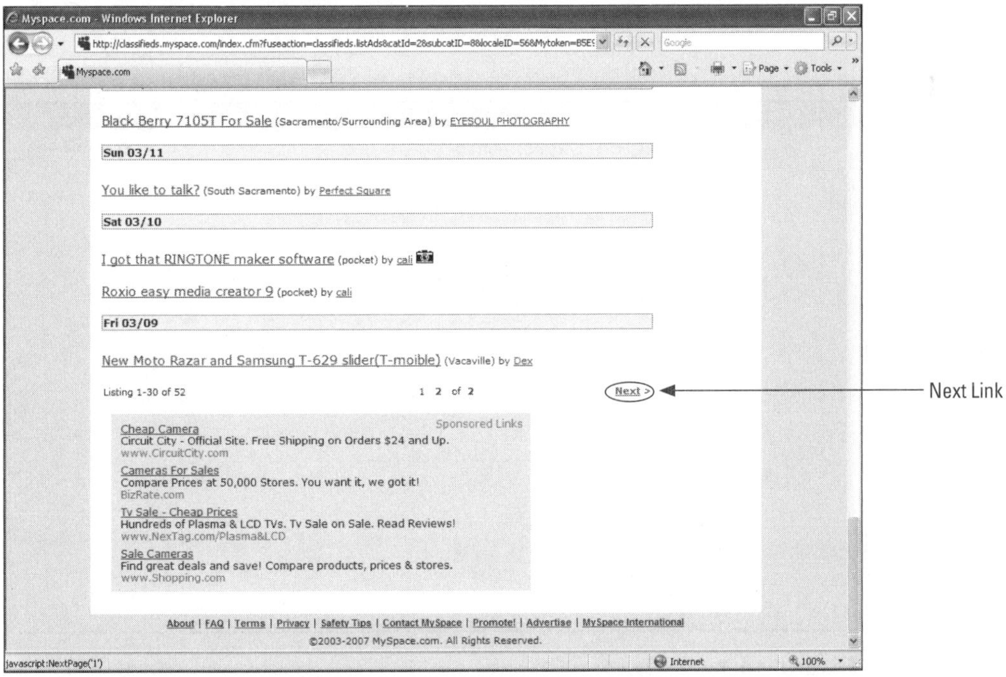

FIGURE 14-5 The Next link

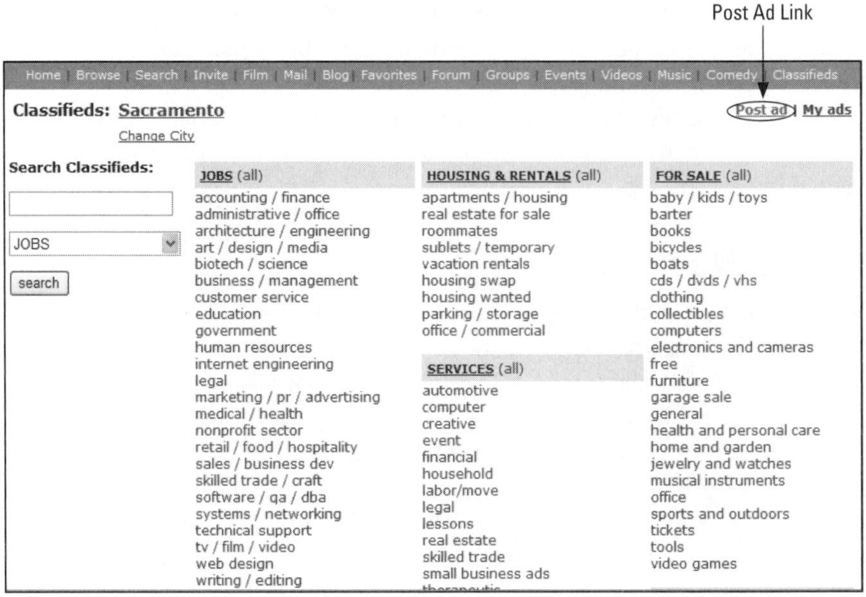

Post Ad Link

FIGURE 14-6 The Post Ad link

FIGURE 14-7 The Posting On page

2. Read the rules carefully because if you violate them, you could be called out by other MySpace users and your account could be deleted.

3. Select the classified category into which you want to place the ad in the Category list. Another list appears to the right so you can select the subcategory. In this example I'll select the For Sale category and the Electronics and Cameras subcategory, as shown in Figure 14-8.

4. Set the price range and type the neighborhood you're in.

5. Type the subject of the ad in the Subject box.

6. Type your message in the Message box. If you want to add an image to show what the product looks like, click the Img button. The Explorer User Prompt dialog box appears, as shown in Figure 14-9, so you can type the location where your image is located.

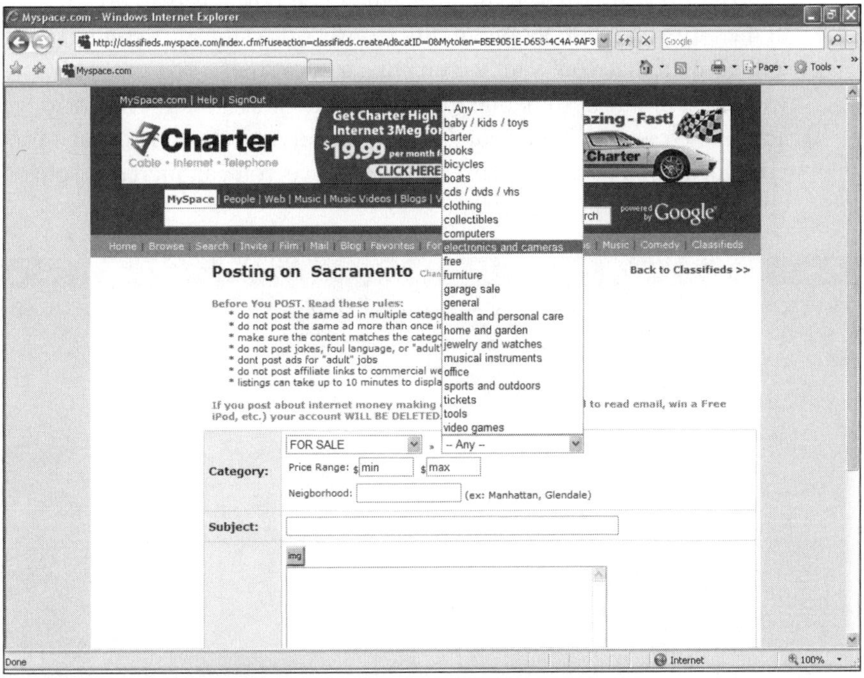

FIGURE 14-8 The Electronics and Cameras subcategory

FIGURE 14-9 The Explorer User Prompt dialog box

NOTE

The image must be located on another web server and you need to know the exact web address and the name of the image file, so be sure to have this information at the ready.

7. Click the Preview button. The Confirm Ad page appears, as shown in Figure 14-10.

8. Review the ad and then click the Post button to post the ad. If you want to edit the ad further, click the Edit button to return to the Posting On page.

An important tip to remember when you post ads is to do so in the city you want people to buy from. For example, if you have a large item that you want to sell (like a bookshelf), you probably want to sell that to someone locally instead of shipping it halfway across the country. So be sure to post the ad on a classifieds page for your local area (or the closest metro area) so you can increase your chances of selling your item.

FIGURE 14-10 The Confirm Ad page

JOB HUNTING AND NETWORKING

The MySpace Classifieds page not only contains categories for you to buy and sell stuff, but you can also do job hunting and networking on the Classifieds page.

Access Job Listings

Here's how to access job listings on MySpace:

1. Click the Classifieds link in the main menu bar. The Classifieds page appears, as shown in Figure 14-11.

2. Click on one of the subcategories under the Jobs category. For this example, I'll click the Marketing/Pr/Advertising link. The Marketing/Pr/Advertising ads page appears, as shown in Figure 14-12.

3. The newest ad appears at the top of the page underneath the Sponsored Links area. Scroll down the page to view the rest of the ads. If you want to view even older ads, you can click the Next button at the bottom of the page.

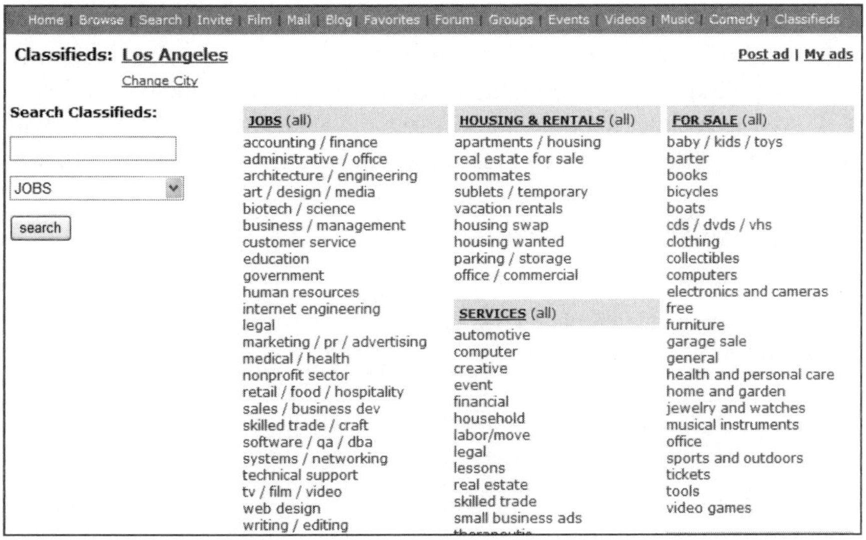

FIGURE 14-11 The Classifieds page

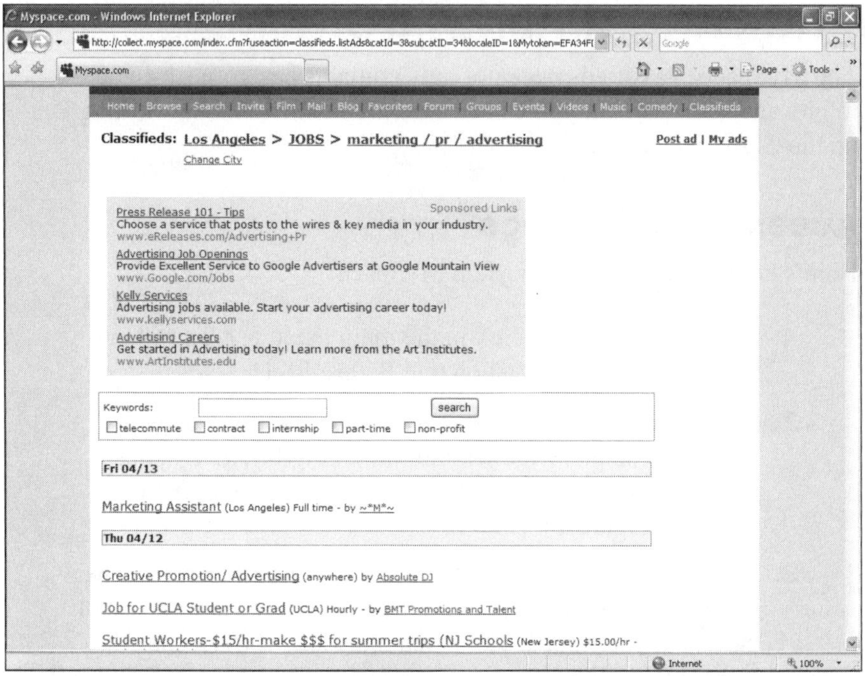

FIGURE 14-12 The Marketing/Pr/Advertising ads page

You can search for job postings by typing your keywords into the Keywords box, selecting the check boxes that match the type of job you're looking for, and then clicking the Search button. MySpace will filter out the ads in the list to show you the ads that meet your criteria.

Network Online

In addition to visiting business and career-related groups as you learned about in Chapter 11, you can also visit the career forum on MySpace so you can network online. Here's how you get there:

1. Click the Forum link in the main menu bar. The Forum Home page appears, as shown in Figure 14-13.

2. Click the Career Center link in the Forum Category table column. The Career Center category page appears, as shown in Figure 14-14.

FIGURE 14-13 The Forum Home page

3. Click the General subcategory name. The General page appears and displays the current messages with the forum rules message at the top.

Click a forum topic that contains the messages you want to read by clicking the topic name. If there isn't a topic that's of interest to you, you can start a new topic of your own by clicking the Post a Topic button. The Start New Topic page appears, as shown in Figure 14-15,

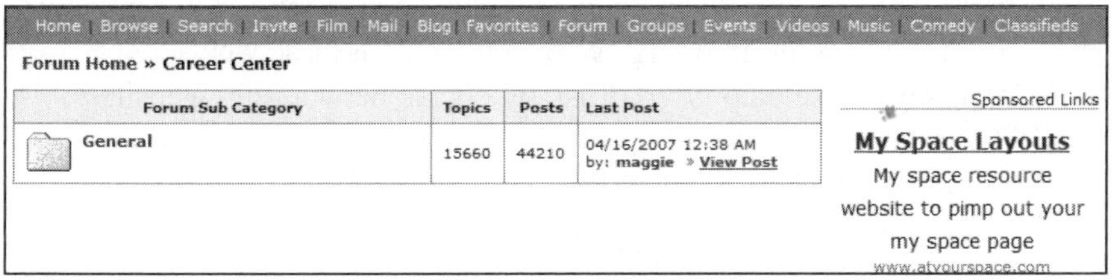

FIGURE 14-14 The Career Center category page

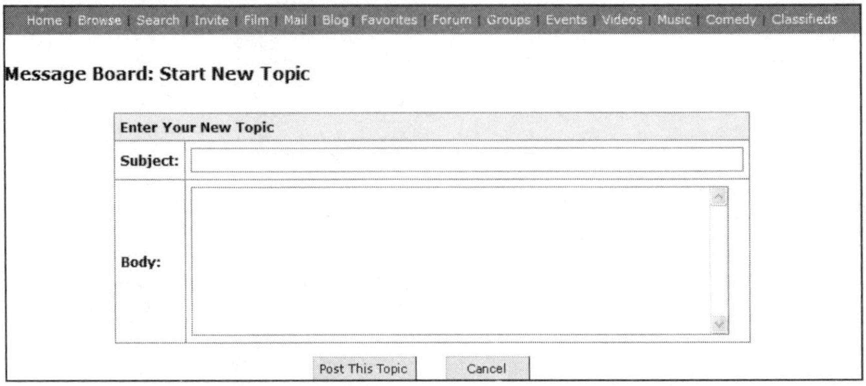

FIGURE 14-15 The Start New Topic page

so you can type a subject and the first message in the topic. Post the topic by clicking the Post This Topic button.

FORTY-NINE MORE PLACES FOR SOCIAL NETWORKING

There are plenty of social networking sites available on the web. Just type **social networking sites** into any search engine and you'll see plenty of hits. One of the first hits you'll see is a list of social networking sites on Wikipedia, the online user-maintained encyclopedia. Here is a list of 49 social networking sites open to everyone and the target audience for each site. This list is not complete, and though the Wikipedia list doesn't include Craigslist, I consider it to be a social networking site so I've included it as part of this list of 49. This list also doesn't include online dating sites. You can view the entire list (and find URL web addresses for these web sites) at http://en.wikipedia.org/wiki/List_of_social_networking_websites.

1. Advogato: Free software and open source developers

2. Bebo: Schools and colleges

3. BlackPlanet.com: African-Americans

4. Bolt: General

5. Broadcaster.com: Video sharing and webcam chat

6. CarDomain: Car enthusiasts

7. Care2: Green living and activism

8. Classmates.com: School, college, work, and the military

9. Craigslist: General

10. Dandelife: Collective narratives or "shared biographies"

11. Ecademy: Business

12. Facebook: College/high school students

13. Facebox: European young adults (14–24)

14. Flickr: Photo sharing

15. Fotki: Photo sharing

16. Friends: Reunited school, college, work, sport, and streets

17. Friendster: General

18. Frühstückstreff: General

19. FUPEI: General

20. Gazzag: General

21. Geni.com: Families, genealogy

22. Graduates.com: School, college, and work

23. Hi5: General

24. Last.fm: Music

25. LinkedIn: Business

26. MEETin: General

27. Meetup.com: General

28. MiGente.com: Latinos

29. MOG: Music

30. Multiply: "Real world" relationships

31. myYearbook: General

32. Passado: General

33. RateItAll: Consumer ratings and social networking

34. Reunion.com: Locating friends and family

35. Ringo.com: General

36. Ryze: Business

37. Sconex: American high schools

38. Stumbleupon: Websurfing

39. TakingITGlobal: Social action

40. The Student Center: Teens and colleges

41. Travellerspoint: Travel

42. Tribe.net: General

43. Vampire Freaks: Gothic industrial culture

44. WAYN: Travel and lifestyle

45. WebBiographies: Genealogy and biography

46. Xanga: Blogs and "metro" areas

47. XING: Business

48. Yelp: United States adults

49. Zaadz: Social consciousness

Chapter 15

Marketing Your Music on MySpace

By now, you know that MySpace is the Internet's latest (and greatest!) social networking site. "Social networking" on the Net, if you haven't come across the term yet, is the use of the web to allow informal social networks to connect across the globe. And instead of using the academic-sounding term "social networking site," it's obvious that MySpace has become a giant audition stage where millions of fans—perhaps fans for your music—lay waiting to be contacted.

WHY IS MYSPACE YOUR IDEAL MUSIC STAGE?

Well, you could argue that MySpace was built on rock 'n' roll from the start. Remember, MySpace was started by Tom Anderson and Chris DeWolfe, and Anderson was part of the independent rock band Swank. In 2003, when Anderson met DeWolfe, the vice president of the software company he was working for, the germ of the idea behind MySpace took off. In other words, music promotion has never been far from the minds of the creators, and it shows.

MySpace was meant right from the start as a place where bands can connect with their fans, and find new fans. Thanks to Anderson's roots in the Los Angeles music and club scenes, the site wasn't really the brainchild of Silicon Valley tech types or pinstriped New York venture capitalists. It was geared toward media and entertainment, not technology, commerce, or finance.

MySpace's earliest users included lots of models and musicians. As it happened, these artists embraced the use of blogs before many users on rival sites did—or at least they were the most influential of the user communities out there that did. And finally, the same attributes that had gotten MySpace into controversy before what gave the upstart site its appeal: The wide open, riotous self-expression that said "be yourself, we won't try to control what you do or post."

And the formula worked. Back in 2005, MySpace had generated more page views than Google, with a whopping 22 million members, and a growth rate of 2 million users a month. The next year, the number had jumped to an estimated 43 million, with 14 million unique visits per day. As of this publication, it still ranks in sheer numbers within striking distance of the giants like MSN.com, Yahoo!, and AOL as one of the major destinations on the web.

Best of all is the number of bands that have tapped into this creative wellspring. Ranging from established artists to newly formed garage bands, more than 600,000 bands are using MySpace. They use the site to upload songs and videos, announce shows, promote albums, and interact with fans.

Let's see how you can do the same.

> **NOTE** *Does "MySpace" mean "corporate bands"? Well, it depends on what you mean. MySpace is still wide open for independent artists, and there's no doubt that it's a great way to get exposure to your growing fan base. But yes, where there are large numbers of potential consumers to be found, there are corporate interests. For example: In 2006, media mogul Rupert Murdoch paid $580 million to acquire MySpace and its parent company, Intermix. In mid-2006, MySpace became the third most visited web domain (Google also grew by leaps and bounds to pass MySpace and become Number 1). As the result of the new corporate clout, MySpace has premiered new releases by several high-profile artists, including Madonna, Neil Diamond, and Nine Inch Nails.*

CREATING A BAND PROFILE

To create your band's profile, begin by creating an account on MySpace.com. But hold on a moment! If you're not careful, chances are you'll end up with a regular MySpace account. Why? Because the default account is a plain-Jane MySpace User account, not a MySpace Music account.

> **NOTE** *If you have already created a MySpace account for yourself, set up a new e-mail account for your band through one of the free services, like Yahoo or Hotmail, and use that e-mail when registering your band. Later in the chapter, I discuss a tool that can convert your regular account into a band account, which is another option for you.*

Make sure you do this the right way, and follow these steps:

1. Begin by navigating to www.myspace.com and click on Music in the navigation bar, as shown in Figure 15-1.

2. Next, click on Artist Signup in the top right of the screen, as shown in Figure 15-2.

Music Link

FIGURE 15-1 The main page, with the Music link highlighted

Artist Signup Link

FIGURE 15-2 The MySpace Music Page, with the Artist Signup link highlighted

3. You'll be taken to the Artist Signup page, as shown in Figure 15-3. Fill out the required fields. Note the warning that separates the fans from the musicians in using this particular page.

When filling this out, be sure to do the following:

■ Enter a valid e-mail address.

■ Enter your band's name.

■ Enter a password of your choice that you can remember easily but can't be readily cracked. (For example, don't make your band's name the password, or you're just asking to be hacked.)

■ Choose the best genre to describe your sound.

■ Enter your country and ZIP code.

4. Next, you'll need to verify your account by entering the text from the graphic in the box. Click the 'Sign Up' button.

5. You will be taken to a registration completion screen, as shown in Figure 15-4.

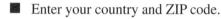

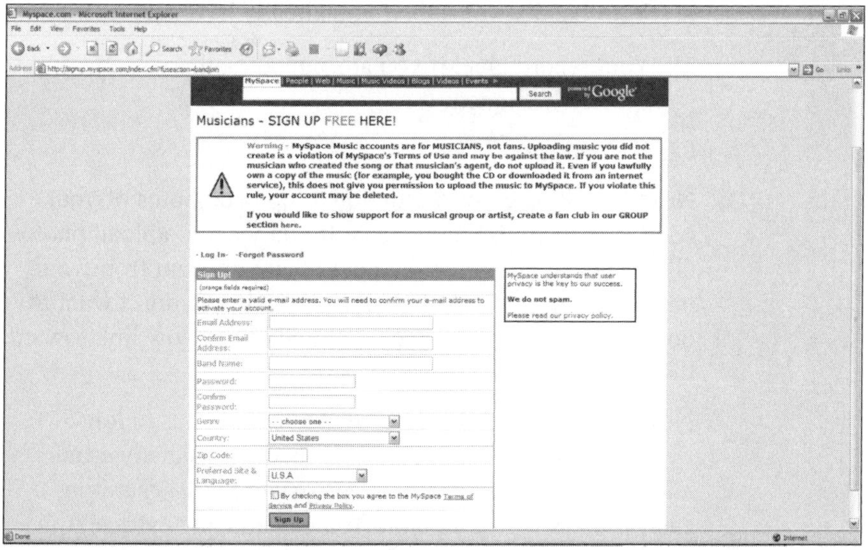

FIGURE 15-3 The Artist Signup page

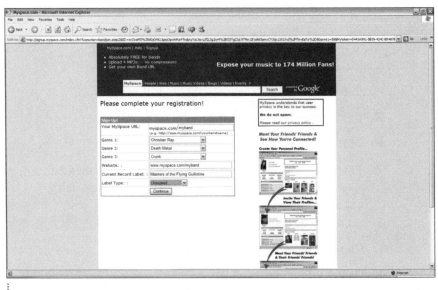

FIGURE 15-4 The completion page

Here you can enter

- Up to three subgenres your music falls under

- Your band's web site, if you already have one

- Your record label if you are signed—otherwise, just specify Unsigned

Click Continue.

6. Next, you'll be given the option to upload photos of your band, as shown in Figure 15-5. If you want to upload photos, click Choose File. Find the photo that you want from your hard drive, select it, and click Upload. If you don't want to do this right now, simply click the Skip for Now link toward the bottom.

7. Now you have the option to invite your friends to join MySpace. As shown in Figure 15-6, enter as many e-mail addresses as you like in the appropriate field, separating each address with a comma. You can add any extra text in the optional body section.

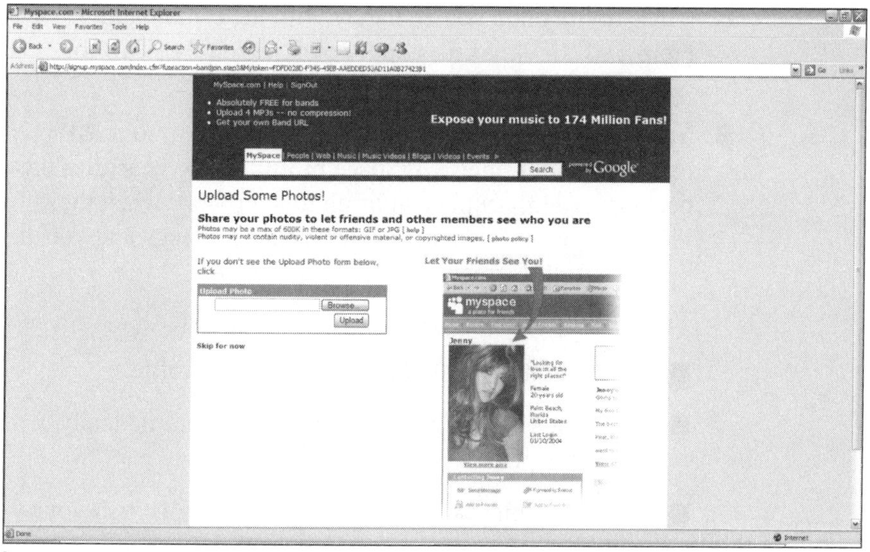

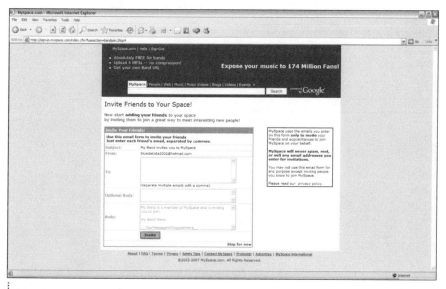

FIGURE 15-5 The option to add your band photos

FIGURE 15-6 The option to add to your fan list

8. Click Invite once you're happy with the e-mail and recipients, or skip this step by clicking on the Skip for Now link at the bottom.

9. You are next asked if you want to upload up to four MP3s onto your band's new MySpace profile. Once your files have been uploaded, people can listen to your work when they visit your page. To upload, select Manage Songs and you'll be taken to the screen shown in Figure 15-7.

   You have three independent options available:

   ■ Allow users to add your songs to their profile.

   ■ Have the first song on your page play automatically when people arrive on your page.

   ■ Have the songs randomly play when people visit your page.

10. In the top-right corner, click Add a Song to Your Profile, as in Figure 15-8. Be sure to fill out the required fields—the song name, the album it's on, the year of release, the record label if you have one, and lyrics if you like.

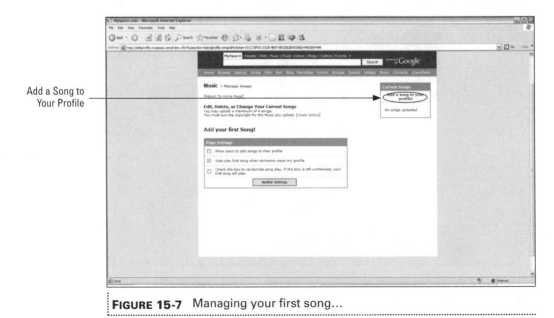

Add a Song to Your Profile

FIGURE 15-7 Managing your first song...

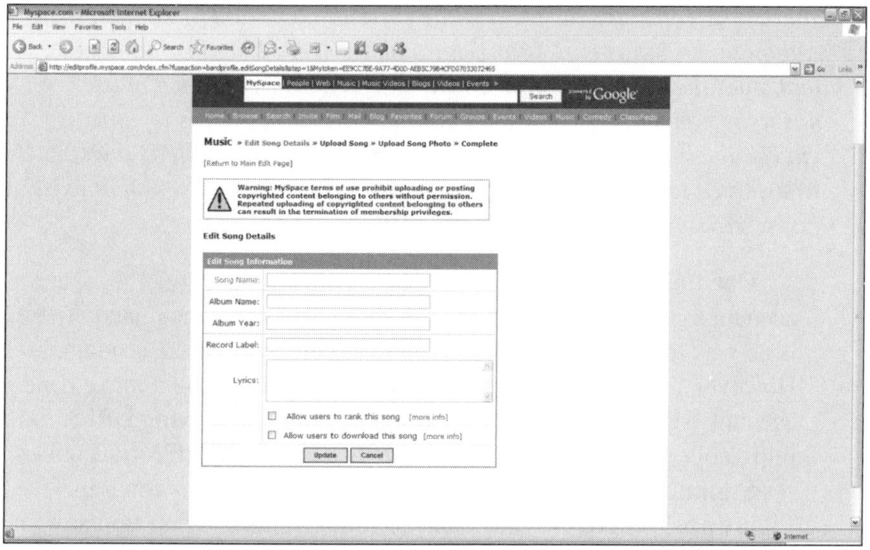

FIGURE 15-8 Required fields in the Edit Song Details screen

NOTE   *Be sure to decide whether you will allow users to rank the song—this is a good feedback mechanism for your work. Also, decide if you want to allow users to download the song. The tradeoff is whether you're worried more about royalties or getting your work out to the maximum number of people.*

11. Select Choose File and find the MP3 file on your computer's hard drive.

12. Click Upload. Typically, it takes a couple of minutes—sometime several minutes during high Internet traffic hours—for the song to upload, even on a cable modem or DSL.

13. Once the song has uploaded, you'll be given the option of uploading a photo to accompany your song. Go to Choose File, select a file from your hard drive, and click Upload.

When the upload is finished, MySpace will inform you that your song has been uploaded to one of the main MySpace servers.

NOTE *Your song won't appear for a while—usually a period of 24 hours. Although the Internet is known for making everything instant access, that's not the case with songs. That's because all uploaded music has to be converted to MySpace's streaming format. This is done via relatively sophisticated software, and the resulting file is then transferred to one of MySpace's specially dedicated servers that exist just to stream your music over an interested fan's speakers.*

One final question is whether one can convert a regular MySpace account to a band account, and vice versa. The answer is mixed: There is no way to convert a band account to a regular MySpace account. However, there may be a way to convert a regular account into a band account. MySpace offers a conversion tool at the following URL: http://collect.myspace.com/index.cfm?fuseaction=BandProfile.convert

Sign in to MySpace and then visit this URL. As shown in Figure 15-9, there are many of the same fields as what you saw in the directions earlier in this chapter.

Fill out the fields on each of the tabs to complete the conversion. However, there is one caveat. As of this publication, this tool offered by MySpace has proven to work only sporadically. Therefore, the best advice would be to avoid the problem altogether and simply create a new band account from scratch.

FIGURE 15-9 The Edit Band Bio screen

Chapter 16

Working the Net for Your Music Group

According to Websearch.com, as of the start of 2007, MySpace.com is second only to Yahoo.com in generating overall web traffic. Its closest competitor as a social networking site is Facebook.com, at No. 10. MySpace has, in the parlance of the Silicon Valley techies, the most "eyeballs"—and it also has "bounce" and "stick."

This means that while other web sites might have more visitors in total, MySpace has the most active network traffic at any time. That is, visitors who come to MySpace tend to visit other pages (bounce) that might interest them and they tend to stay around longer (stick) to download content, videos, and music. For the company, this means a whole bunch of active eyes on the page, which means, in turn, that you get a business model that keeps the site free for users.

And, not coincidentally, you also get a site that blows all other places on the Internet out of the water when it comes to connecting musicians to new fans and helping them stay connected to old ones.

EXPANDING YOUR BAND'S INFORMATION

Once you set up your band's basic profile, you can enter all sorts of information about your band. To do this, do the following:

1. Log in and go to your profile's home page.

2. Click Edit Band Profile. As shown in Figure 16-1, the screen defaults to fields where you enter information about the band's details.

The fields on this screen's tabs are great for fleshing out your profile as well. The fields under each tab include Listing Info, Manage Songs, Band Details, Basic Info, and Upcoming Shows. Let's look at each of these in turn and how they affect your band's marketing information.

Basic Information

As seen in Figure 16-2, the Basic Info tab is exactly what it sounds like. Insert your band's name and where your band is from (country, city, ZIP code, and so on).

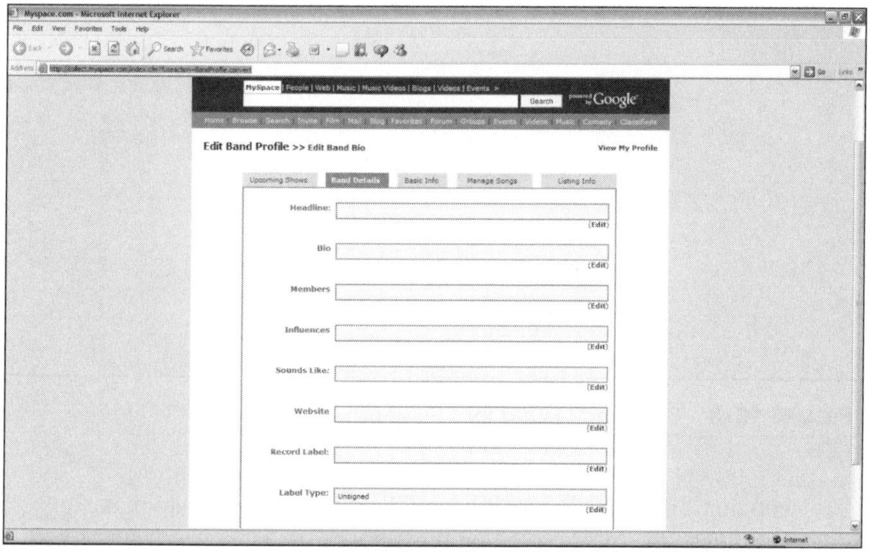

FIGURE 16-1 The Edit Band Profile screen

Band Listing Info

Your band's Listing Info tab allows you to define what your sound genre is, which helps users who are searching for music that is similar to yours find you. Because of this, be sure you select a few related genres for your band, as in Figure 16-3. This is also where you get to create the web address (URL) for your band. Do it carefully, as

FIGURE 16-2 The Band Profile Basic Info screen

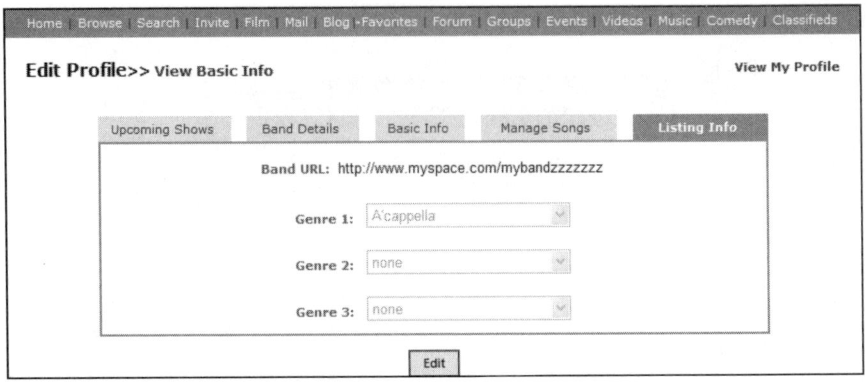

FIGURE 16-3 The Band Listing Info Screen

you don't want to change it later. Click the Edit button to make any changes to the information on this screen.

NOTE *The genres you choose will ultimately decide where MySpace decides to place your music among the thousands of other bands. So if you're not sure what genre your music falls into (maybe you're that experimental avant-garde sort of group that is blending in Scottish bagpipe with the theremin), search for the band that you feel sounds the most like yours, and follow what genre(s) they have chosen.*

Managing Songs

The Manage Songs tab is where you get to list your songs for your visitors to listen to. Basically, MySpace sets up your songs in its own format and then streams them over the web. (In case you're curious, *streaming* means to feed pieces of the song through the Internet at a constant pace or "stream" of data so that the user can hear it without having to wait for the whole thing to arrive. Not surprisingly, if you've set up your band's profile using the directions in Chapter 15, the descriptions will sound very familiar. As shown in Figure 16-4, you have three independent options available:

■ **Allow users to add your songs to their profile** This is useful if you want to encourage the spread of your music over the Internet as quickly as possible. Doing so would also cut into your royalties, so it's probably best to do this only to a certain point, or when you are still starting out.

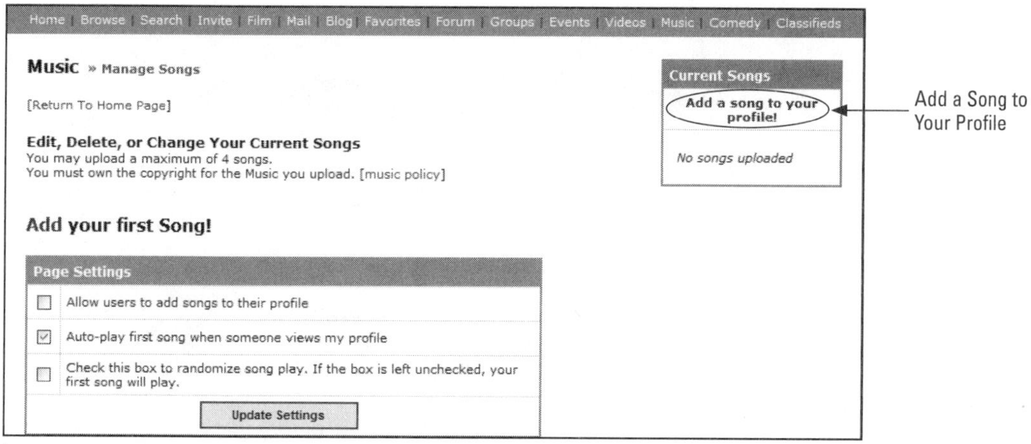

FIGURE 16-4 The Manage Songs screen

- **Have the first song on your page play automatically when people arrive on your page**   A good and popular choice, though if you get a lot of repeat visits, people may be annoyed by hearing the same thing over and over again.

- **Have the order of songs played randomized when people visit your page**   An excellent choice, though it presupposes that you already have a body of work put together. (Having only two or three songs available to randomize from isn't much of a choice.)

Once you've made your choices from the three options, take a look at the top-right corner of the page. Click Add a Song to Your Profile. Be sure to fill out the required fields, as shown in Figure 16-5, then select Choose File. Browse to find the MP3 file on your desktop or hard drive, and then click Upload. Once the song has uploaded, you'll be given the option of uploading a photo to accompany your song. Go to Choose File, select a file from your hard drive, and click Upload.

Typically, it can take anywhere from a couple of minutes to an entire day for MySpace to process the upload, particularly during high Internet traffic hours. This is true regardless of the connection you are using—there is no apparent speed advantage that's been observed,

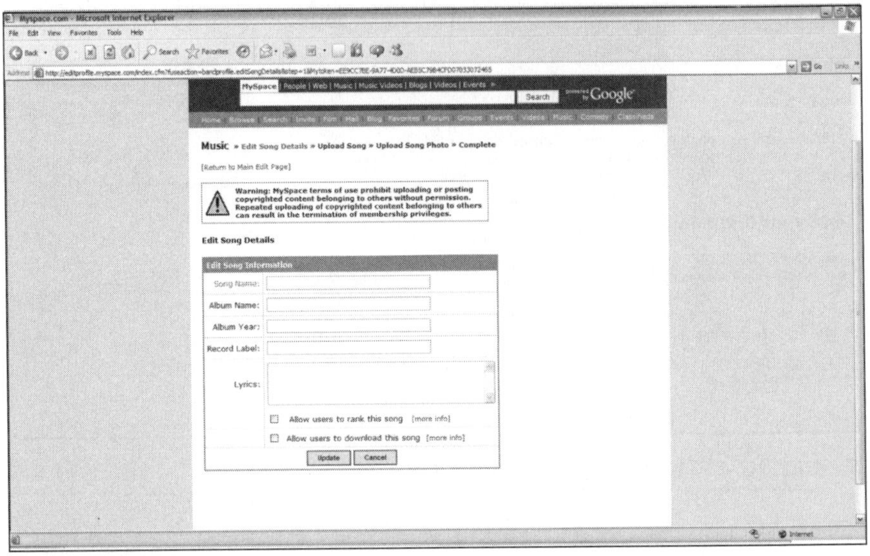

FIGURE 16-5   Required fields in the Edit Song Details screen

even if you're using a cable modem or DSL. When the upload is finished, MySpace will inform you that your song has been uploaded to one of the main MySpace servers.

Band Details

The Band Details page is perhaps one of the most important parts of creating a good profile page for your band. That's because, as shown in Figure 16-6, you get to define what your band's influences are and what you sound like in even more detail than in the Band Listing Info tab. Again, the more specific and popular terms you use, the more hits you'll get from people looking for specific kinds of bands and music.

Listing Your Upcoming Shows

The Upcoming Shows tab is probably the second most important tab when you're starting out as a band—second, that is, only to the Band Details tab. But it's certainly going to become the most important as you grow your work. And it'll be the one that you update the most often as well.

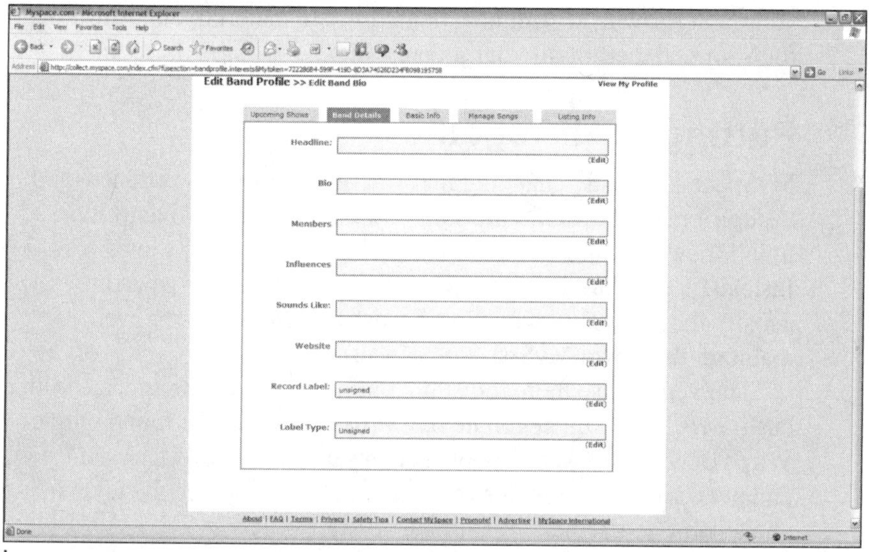

FIGURE 16-6 The Band Details screen

When you select the Upcoming Shows tab you'll see a screen similar to Figure 16-7. Filling out the fields is pretty self-explanatory. However, be sure to put in enough text in the Description box at the bottom. You need to make sure that your audience knows whether

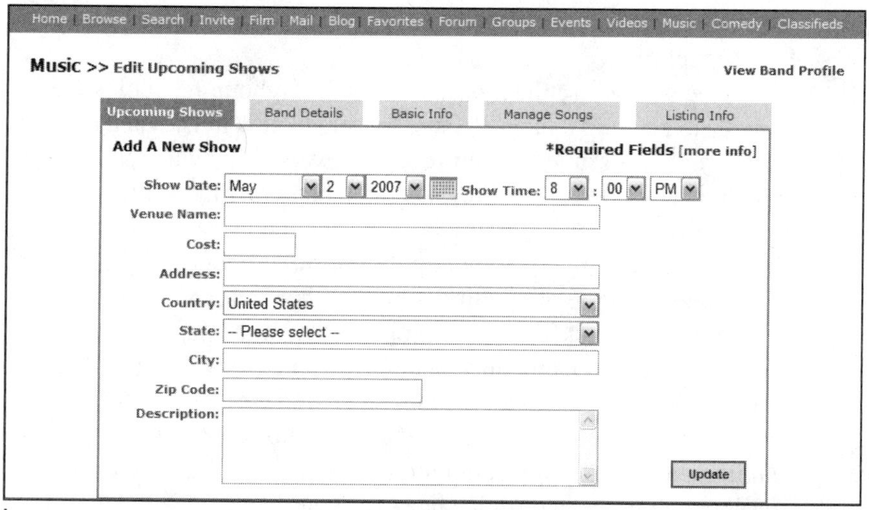

FIGURE 16-7 The Upcoming Shows screen

your next show is a 30-minute demo of new material, or a full-blown four-hour concert of all your greatest hits.

Putting It All Together

MySpace is already changing the way music business is done—and we don't mean how CDs are sold. For example, many bands have found they no longer need to mail press kits to line up shows. Instead, if there are local venues with an Internet-savvy person, usually these places contact local artists via MySpace, or even maintain their own MySpace presences.

The venues use them to list upcoming shows, communicate with customers, and even negotiate pay with bands they've found online. Why? Because the venue bookers can sample the band's music and even see the comments from the fan base to gauge the level of excitement generated.

But the real magic of using MySpace to boost your band's profile isn't just in posting music and a bare-bones listing. Rather, people visit your profile to get a personal connection to your band and your music that they can't find anywhere else. People enjoy the opportunity to visit a musician's site and listen to up to four songs, or read bios and blogs. It's a combination of feeling like one is in the "in club" with the all-access pass behind the stage, and the hunch that maybe the band you're following becomes the next hip-hop sensation, the next Nirvana—or who knows?—the next Led Zeppelin!

So, be sure to use the tips and tricks throughout the book so far in order to keep up a blog. Be sure to upload new music on a regular basis—and if possible let your repeat viewers know when the new content is going to arrive. Plus, keep the band members' bios current. And finally, it's worth keeping in mind that the latest trend (thanks to Google and YouTube) is to put up decent-quality video clips.

A great example of "putting it all together" with MySpace is to do more than just film a video and post it on the page. Instead, consider making an announcement on your next MySpace bulletin that you're going to shoot the video, and sign up volunteer extras for your next concert crowd scene. Those who get to participate in a real live music video are certain to tell their friends, and so on—and you'll get a double and triple "bang for your buck" when you post the video on the site.

NOTE

A word on astroturfing—simply, don't consider doing it. What is it? Well, given its ties to so many people, MySpace is a classic place to do grass-roots marketing. However, there are programs out there that mechanically allow you to find more people to invite, or to even "buy" friends to put into your profile. This isn't real grass-roots marketing, but fake—hence the term "astroturfing." While there's nothing illegal about doing this, we've intentionally left out recommendations or reviews of products that do these things. Why? Because without growing your audience in as organic a way as possible, you'll miss out on how much impact your work really has in the music marketplace. And we'd rather you stick to gathering an audience the old-fashioned way.

A COUPLE OF SUCCESS STORIES ON MYSPACE

The success that many fledgling artists have found on MySpace has led to a fear that it would be quickly spotted by corporate interests, corralled, and branded into a new version of Friendster or Amazon.com. At first, it appeared that the worst fear was about to come true when Rupert Murdoch and his News Corp. bought MySpace for $580 million in 2006. Speculation ran rampant as people worried that the site would change for the worse or that they'd be charged to use it.

In extreme cases, people began creating multiple duplicate accounts in case something were to happen to one of them. (MySpace will delete profiles when it gets reports of adult material being posted, copyrighted material being improperly used, or for other rule violations.) In essence, people were concerned that the once-free expression on MySpace would be curtailed. To the founders' credit, so far the site's creators have stayed in charge and nothing drastically different has changed the site.

Believe it or not, MySpace has already generated its own celebrities, such as electro-pop musician Jeffree Star. Star was a relatively unknown artist outside of California before MySpace, but now has one of the most-added profiles. Regardless of what you think of him or his music, consider that his page has been viewed more than 14 million times. That puts his page in the top 1 percent of

MySpace page profiles, and just 2 million shy of the views of the page for the much more conventionally famous Justin Timberlake.

To take a more modest example, consider the MySpace success of one of the local Southern California bands interviewed for this book, DROP 8. A hard rock/metal band with Nu-Metal and older rock and metal roots, DROP 8 began around 2003 and aggressively used MySpace to build its audience. The group's page is an excellent example of what you can do with a page to generate audience interest and keep in touch with fans. As seen at their URL of www.myspace .com/drop8 and in Figure 16-8, the group makes use of several of the features discussed throughout the book that make their page worth visiting and revisiting:

- An eye-catching page design with the band logo that's not too distracting or hard to read.

- Four songs that can be streamed to a user's speakers when they arrive at the page.

- Multiple band videos that can be downloaded or streamed.

- A long and interesting band history and profiles of the individual members.

- A detailed list of influences and styles, allowing them to be found in multiple searches.

- Band merchandise for sale.

- A well-maintained blog and Upcoming Shows list.

According to Mike Hurley, who plays rhythm guitar for the band, "We got onto MySpace around 2005, the same time we signed on with CSG Music." Since its arrival on MySpace, DROP 8 has seen its fan base grow to 36,000 views and almost 19,000 friends.

Some of the friends are definitely more than the type of drop-in user just browsing around for new bands. "We get a lot of 'when are you coming to play in my home town' types of questions," said Hurley. "The best thing though is all the networking with other bands. We ended up 'trading' live shows with a band in Vegas called Dim. They lined up a show for us in Las Vegas, we did the same thing here in L.A. for them."

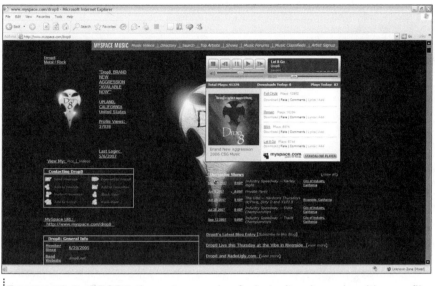

FIGURE 16-8   DROP 8: A great example of what a band can do with a profile page

Finally, Hurley confirmed that what many music marketers report on how MySpace is changing the industry is in fact true. For example, DROP 8 "doesn't mail out press kits trying to attract the attention of a promoter. Thanks to MySpace, we get a lot of promoters looking for us—by now, it's been easily into the dozens. And instead of mailing out press kits, we send them electronically."

Musically, we're definitely in a brave new world.

Part IV
Appendixes

Appendix A

HTML Commands from A to Z

The ultimate building blocks for your MySpace page are HTML commands. HTML stands for **H**yper **T**ext **M**arkup **L**anguage. Luckily, HTML is one of the easier programming languages to learn.

THE STRUCTURE OF HTML COMMANDS

Remember that HTML documents are made up of "tags." A tag is a command enclosed in angle brackets < and > (for example, <HTML>). The most basic tags are the starting and ending tags that tell when a given effect or command starts and stops within the document. For example:

Opening

<HTML>

Closing

</HTML>

Every HTML document will require the following tags:

- <HTML>
- <HEAD>
- <TITLE></TITLE>
- </HEAD>
- <BODY>
- </BODY>
- </HTML>

The <HTML> tag always begins the document. This tells the Internet browser that—absent a closing HTML tag—it is reading an HTML document as opposed to a text document. The <HEAD> tag is used for the general title of the page, or, in more complex formats, for the setup of frames and style sheets. <TITLE></TITLE> is the tag for the page's title itself. Use this tag by typing your title in between the opening and closing tags as shown in the following example:

<TITLE>This is my very own MySpace Page</TITLE>

Following your title opening and closing tags, don't forget to also add the ending </HEAD> tag. This separates the entire head/title area from the main body of your page you are building.

Not surprisingly, the <BODY> tag is where the bulk of your page will be, since it's where you'll put all your text, images, and links. Easily over 95% of everything you'd want to fit on your page will go between the starting and ending <BODY> tags. And of course, once you're done with the <BODY> tags, be sure to finish off the pair of the HTML tags you started with: the close tag </HTML>.

Sound very mechanical and uncreative? Not really—this is just the skeleton of the page, the basic format that has to be followed so that computers can make sense out of the text. The stuff you put between those tags—your own special content—can be as unique as you like.

DEFINING PARAMETERS INSIDE THE <BODY> TAGS

Although you'll be spending most of your time adding your own text, image, and links, you need to define some parameters inside the <BODY> tag. If you do not set them then they will default to black text, blue links, and white background.

- TEXT   This will determine the color of your text throughout your page.

- LINK   This will determine the color of your links throughout your page.

- VLINK   This will determine the color of your visited links throughout your page.

- ALINK   This will determine the color of your active links throughout your page.

- BGCOLOR   This will determine the color of your background throughout your page.

- BACKGROUND   This will determine the background image you load throughout your page.

For example, here's how you might select a color scheme for BGCOLOR:

```
<BODY TEXT="red" LINK="blue" VLINK="green" ALINK="black"
BGCOLOR="orange">
```

> **NOTE**
>
> *One of the reasons that HTML is so easy to learn is that if you see someone's page you like, you can view their source code and see exactly how they made it. In order to view the source code—that is, the individual HTML commands that make up the visual effect or placement you like—perform the following steps:*
> *1. Navigate to the page you like.*
> *2. Click on the View pull-down menu and select Source.*
> *3. A separate text window will appear, showing you the codes that are used to make up the page. Simply cut and paste these codes into your page and you'll have a duplicate of the original to edit and play with as you please.*

SOME BASIC HTML FORMATTING

The most basic formatting tags allow you to perform the same three most popular commands in most text editors: bolding, italicizing, and underlining. (Luckily, the creators of HTML simply named the commands after the first letter of the functions.) And again, the key is that all HTML commands use opening and closing tags.

For example, say you wanted to bold the words "brown fox jumped" in the sentence "The quick brown fox jumped over the lazy dog."

In HTML-speak, this would be written:

```
The quick <B>brown fox jumped</B> over the lazy dog.
```

On the screen, you wouldn't see the tags, but the sentence would appear as

The quick **brown fox jumped** over the lazy dog.

Changing the size of your text is similar to changing its appearance. HTML uses six different size font tags for headings, ranging from <H1> (huge) through <H6> (tiny). Again, simply enclose the text you want at a different size with the opening and closing tags.

AN ALPHABETICAL LISTING
OF THE MOST USEFUL TAGS

Tag	Description
`<!--...-->`	Defines a comment
`<!DOCTYPE>`	Defines the document type
`<a>`	Defines an anchor for a web link
`<abbr>`	Defines an abbreviation
`<acronym>`	Defines an acronym
`<address>`	Defines an address element
`<applet>`	Deprecated. Defines an applet
`<area>`	Defines an area inside an image map
`<b>`	Defines bold text
`<base>`	Defines a base URL for all the links in a page
`<basefont>`	Deprecated. Defines a base font
`<bdo>`	Defines the direction of text display
`<big>`	Defines big text
`<blockquote>`	Defines a long quotation
`<body>`	Defines the body element
` `	Inserts a single line break
`<button>`	Defines a push button
`<caption>`	Defines a table caption
`<cite>`	Defines a citation
`<code>`	Defines computer code text
`<col>`	Defines attributes for table columns
`<colgroup>`	Defines groups of table columns
`<dd>`	Defines a definition description
`<del>`	Defines deleted text
`<dir>`	Deprecated. Defines a directory list
`<div>`	Defines a section in a document
`<dfn>`	Defines a definition term
`<dl>`	Defines a definition list

Tag	Description
`<dt>`	Comes before each definition term
`<em>`	Defines emphasized text
`<fieldset>`	Defines a fieldset
`<font>`	Deprecated. Defines text font, size, and color
`<form>`	Defines a form
`<frame>`	Defines a subwindow (a frame)
`<frameset>`	Defines a set of frames
`<h1>` to `<h6>`	Defines header 1 to header 6
`<head>`	Defines information about the document
`<hr>`	Defines a horizontal line
`<html>`	Defines an HTML document
`<i>`	Defines italic text
`<iframe>`	Defines an inline subwindow (frame)
`<img>`	Defines an image
`<input>`	Defines an input field
`<ins>`	Defines inserted text
`<isindex>`	Deprecated. Defines a single-line input field
`<kbd>`	Defines keyboard text
`<label>`	Defines a label for a form control
`<legend>`	Defines a title in a fieldset
`<li>`	Defines a list item
`<link>`	Defines a resource reference
`<map>`	Defines an image map
`<menu>`	Deprecated. Defines a menu list
`<meta>`	Defines meta information
`<noframes>`	Defines a noframe section
`<noscript>`	Defines a noscript section
`<object>`	Defines an embedded object
`<ol>`	Defines an ordered (numbered) list
`<optgroup>`	Defines an option group

Tag	Description
`<option>`	Defines an option in a drop-down list
`<p>`	Defines a paragraph
`<param>`	Defines a parameter for an object
`<pre>`	Defines preformatted text
`<q>`	Defines a short quotation
`<s>`	Deprecated. Defines strikethrough text
`<samp>`	Defines sample computer code
`<script>`	Defines a script
`<select>`	Defines a selectable list
`<small>`	Defines small text
`<span>`	Defines a section in a document
`<strike>`	Deprecated. Defines strikethrough text
`<strong>`	Defines strong text (similar to bold)
`<style>`	Defines a style definition
`<sub>`	Defines subscripted text
`<sup>`	Defines superscripted text
`<table>`	Defines a table
`<tbody>`	Defines a table body
`<td>`	Defines a table cell
`<textarea>`	Defines a text area
`<tfoot>`	Defines a table footer
`<th>`	Defines a table header
`<thead>`	Defines a table header
`<title>`	Defines the document title
`<tr>`	Defines a table row
`<tt>`	Defines teletype text
`<u>`	Deprecated. Defines underlined text
`<ul>`	Defines an unordered list (bullet points)
`<var>`	Defines a variable
`<xmp>`	Deprecated. Defines preformatted text

ADDITIONAL HTML REFERENCES

- The best immediate reference: the Internet—simply navigate to a page that looks approximately like what you want to do, select View | Source, and see the code itself!

- Some of the best HTML and Cascading Style Sheets information: http://www.websitetips.com/html/

- Online courses—there are many. One of the better recommended is the Webmonkey HTML Tutorial http://www.webmonkey.com/

- W3C, the World Wide Web Consortium, has a free tutorial at http://www.w3.org/MarkUp/Guide/

- Are you a more visual person? A good HTML flash movie can be found at http://visualtutorials.com/

- There's even a free certification course plan at http://certification.about.com/cs/testin—or a paid one at http://www.hwg.org/

Of course, be sure to check out McGraw-Hill at http://www.mhprofessional.com to find books—the "dead tree" kind—on how to start in HTML. And remember, be patient as you learn the ins and outs of HTML. It's a simple language, but one with so many possibilities that it's easy to get lost in all the choices. Over time, you'll come to settle on a limited number of favorite colors and commands for your own unique niche on MySpace.

Appendix B

Color and Style Tables

COLOR TABLE

The following color names and their corresponding six-digit hexadecimal HTML codes are listed on the W3Schools web site. You can view this list and the actual colors on their site at http://www.w3schools.com/html/html_colornames.asp.

Color	Hexadecimal
AliceBlue	#F0F8FF
AntiqueWhite	#FAEBD7
Aqua	#00FFFF
Aquamarine	#7FFFD4
Azure	#F0FFFF
Beige	#F5F5DC
Bisque	#FFE4C4
Black	#000000
BlanchedAlmond	#FFEBCD
Blue	#0000FF
BlueViolet	#8A2BE2
Brown	#A52A2A
BurlyWood	#DEB887
CadetBlue	#5F9EA0
Chartreuse	#7FFF00
Chocolate	#D2691E
Coral	#FF7F50
CornflowerBlue	#6495ED
Cornsilk	#FFF8DC
Crimson	#DC143C
Cyan	#00FFFF
DarkBlue	#00008B
DarkCyan	#008B8B
DarkGoldenRod	#B8860B
DarkGray	#A9A9A9

Color	Hexadecimal
DarkGrey	#A9A9A9
DarkGreen	#006400
DarkKhaki	#BDB76B
DarkMagenta	#8B008B
DarkOliveGreen	#556B2F
Darkorange	#FF8C00
DarkOrchid	#9932CC
DarkRed	#8B0000
DarkSalmon	#E9967A
DarkSeaGreen	#8FBC8F
DarkSlateBlue	#483D8B
DarkSlateGray	#2F4F4F
DarkSlateGrey	#2F4F4F
DarkTurquoise	#00CED1
DarkViolet	#9400D3
DeepPink	#FF1493
DeepSkyBlue	#00BFFF
DimGray	#696969
DimGrey	#696969
DodgerBlue	#1E90FF
FireBrick	#B22222
FloralWhite	#FFFAF0
ForestGreen	#228B22
Fuchsia	#FF00FF
Gainsboro	#DCDCDC
GhostWhite	#F8F8FF
Gold	#FFD700
GoldenRod	#DAA520
Gray	#808080
Grey	#808080
Green	#008000

Color	Hexadecimal
GreenYellow	#ADFF2F
HoneyDew	#F0FFF0
HotPink	#FF69B4
IndianRed	#CD5C5C
Indigo	#4B0082
Ivory	#FFFFF0
Khaki	#F0E68C
Lavender	#E6E6FA
LavenderBlush	#FFF0F5
LawnGreen	#7CFC00
LemonChiffon	#FFFACD
LightBlue	#ADD8E6
LightCoral	#F08080
LightCyan	#E0FFFF
LightGoldenRodYellow	#FAFAD2
LightGray	#D3D3D3
LightGrey	#D3D3D3
LightGreen	#90EE90
LightPink	#FFB6C1
LightSalmon	#FFA07A
LightSeaGreen	#20B2AA
LightSkyBlue	#87CEFA
LightSlateGray	#778899
LightSlateGrey	#778899
LightSteelBlue	#B0C4DE
LightYellow	#FFFFE0
Lime	#00FF00
LimeGreen	#32CD32
Linen	#FAF0E6
Magenta	#FF00FF

Color	Hexadecimal
Maroon	#800000
MediumAquaMarine	#66CDAA
MediumBlue	#0000CD
MediumOrchid	#BA55D3
MediumPurple	#9370D8
MediumSeaGreen	#3CB371
MediumSlateBlue	#7B68EE
MediumSpringGreen	#00FA9A
MediumTurquoise	#48D1CC
MediumVioletRed	#C71585
MidnightBlue	#191970
MintCream	#F5FFFA
MistyRose	#FFE4E1
Moccasin	#FFE4B5
NavajoWhite	#FFDEAD
Navy	#000080
OldLace	#FDF5E6
Olive	#808000
OliveDrab	#6B8E23
Orange	#FFA500
OrangeRed	#FF4500
Orchid	#DA70D6
PaleGoldenRod	#EEE8AA
PaleGreen	#98FB98
PaleTurquoise	#AFEEEE
PaleVioletRed	#D87093
PapayaWhip	#FFEFD5
PeachPuff	#FFDAB9
Peru	#CD853F
Pink	#FFC0CB

Color	Hexadecimal
Plum	#DDA0DD
PowderBlue	#B0E0E6
Purple	#800080
Red	#FF0000
RosyBrown	#BC8F8F
RoyalBlue	#4169E1
SaddleBrown	#8B4513
Salmon	#FA8072
SandyBrown	#F4A460
SeaGreen	#2E8B57
SeaShell	#FFF5EE
Sienna	#A0522D
Silver	#C0C0C0
SkyBlue	#87CEEB
SlateBlue	#6A5ACD
SlateGray	#708090
SlateGrey	#708090
Snow	#FFFAFA
SpringGreen	#00FF7F
SteelBlue	#4682B4
Tan	#D2B48C
Teal	#008080
Thistle	#D8BFD8
Tomato	#FF6347
Turquoise	#40E0D0
Violet	#EE82EE
Wheat	#F5DEB3
White	#FFFFFF
WhiteSmoke	#F5F5F5
Yellow	#FFFF00
YellowGreen	#9ACD32

TABLE OF STYLES

HTML Dog has an excellent reference of CSS properties on its web site at http://www.htmldog.com/reference/cssproperties/. When you visit this web site you can click on the property to see the associated variables as well as a brief example, related properties, related tutorials, and working examples. Here is the list of categorized CSS properties from the HTML Dog site.

Text and Fonts

- font
- font-family
- font-size
- font-weight
- font-style
- font-variant
- line-height
- letter-spacing
- word-spacing
- text-align
- text-decoration
- text-indent
- text-transform
- vertical-align
- white-space

Colors and Backgrounds

- color
- background-color

- background
- background-image
- background-repeat
- background-position
- background-attachment

Dimensions, Padding, Margins, and Borders

- padding, padding-top, padding-right, padding-bottom, padding-left
- border, border-top, border-right, border-bottom, border-left
- border-style, border-top-style, border-right-style, border-bottom-style, border-left-style
- border-color, border-top-color, border-right-color, border-bottom-color, border-left-color
- border-width, border-top-width, border-right-width, border-bottom-width, border-left-width
- outline
- outline-style
- outline-color
- outline-width
- margin, margin-top, margin-right, margin-bottom, margin-left
- width

- height
- min-width
- max-width
- min-height
- max-height

Positioning and Display

- position
- top
- right
- bottom
- left
- clip
- overflow
- z-index
- float
- clear
- display
- visibility

Lists

- list-style
- list-style-type
- list-style-image
- list-style-position

Tables

- table-layout
- border-collapse
- border-spacing
- empty-cells
- caption-side

Generated Content

- content
- counter-increment
- counter-reset
- quotes

Paged Media

- page-break-before
- page-break-after
- page-break-inside
- orphans
- widows

Miscellaneous

- cursor
- direction
- unicode-bidi

Index